Shugo Chara!

3

PEACH-PIT

Translated by
Satsuki Yamashita

Adapted by
Nunzio DeFilippis and Christina Weir

Lettered by
North Market Street Graphics

KODANSHA
COMICS

A Kodansha Comics Trade Paperback Original.

Published in the United States by Kodansha Comics, an imprint of Kodansha USA Publishing, LLC., New York.

Publication rights for this English edition arranged through Kodansha Ltd., Tokyo.

First published in Japan in 2007 by Kodansha Ltd., Tokyo.

ISBN 978-1-61262-342-9

Original cover design by Akiko Omo.

Printed in Canada.

www.kodanshacomics.com

9 8 7 6 5 4 3

Translator: Satsuki Yamashita
Adapter: Nunzio DeFilippis and Christina Weir.
Lettering: North Market Street Graphics

Contents

Honorifics Explained

Throughout the Kodansha Comics books, you will find Japanese honorifics left intact in the translations. For those not familiar with how the Japanese use honorifics and, more important, how they differ from American honorifics, we present this brief overview.

Politeness has always been a critical facet of Japanese culture. Ever since the feudal era, when Japan was a highly stratified society, use of honorifics—which can be defined as polite speech that indicates relationship or status—has played an essential role in the Japanese language. When addressing someone in Japanese, an honorific usually takes the form of a suffix attached to one's name (example: "Asuna-san"), is used as a title at the end of one's name, or appears in place of the name itself (example: "Negi-sensei," or simply "Sensei!").

Honorifics can be expressions of respect or endearment. In the context of manga and anime, honorifics give insight into the nature of the relationship between characters. Many English translations leave out these important honorifics and therefore distort the feel of the original Japanese. Because Japanese honorifics contain nuances that English honorifics lack, it is our policy at Kodansha Comics not to translate them. Here, instead, is a guide to some of the honorifics you may encounter in Kodansha Comics books.

-san: This is the most common honorific and is equivalent to Mr., Miss, Ms., Mrs. It is the all-purpose honorific and can be used in any situation where politeness is required.

-sama: This is one level higher than "-san" and is used to confer great respect.

-dono: This comes from the word "tono," which means "lord." It is an even higher level than "-sama" and confers utmost respect.

-kun: This suffix is used at the end of boys' names to express familiarity or endearment. It is also sometimes used by men among friends, or when addressing someone younger or of a lower station.

-chan:	This is used to express endearment, mostly toward girls. It is also used for little boys, pets, and even among lovers. It gives a sense of childish cuteness.
Bozu:	This is an informal way to refer to a boy, similar to the English terms "kid" and "squirt."
Sempai/ Senpai:	This title suggests that the addressee is one's senior in a group or organization. It is most often used in a school setting, where underclassmen refer to their upperclassmen as "sempai." It can also be used in the workplace, such as when a newer employee addresses an employee who has seniority in the company.
Kohai:	This is the opposite of "sempai" and is used toward underclassmen in school or newcomers in the workplace. It connotes that the addressee is of a lower station.
Sensei:	Literally meaning "one who has come before," this title is used for teachers, doctors, or masters of any profession or art.
-[blank]:	This is usually forgotten in these lists, but it is perhaps the most significant difference between Japanese and English. The lack of honorific means that the speaker has permission to address the person in a very intimate way. Usually, only family, spouses, or very close friends have this kind of permission. Known as *yobisute*, it can be gratifying when someone who has earned the intimacy starts to call one by one's name without an honorific. But when that intimacy hasn't been earned, it can be very insulting.

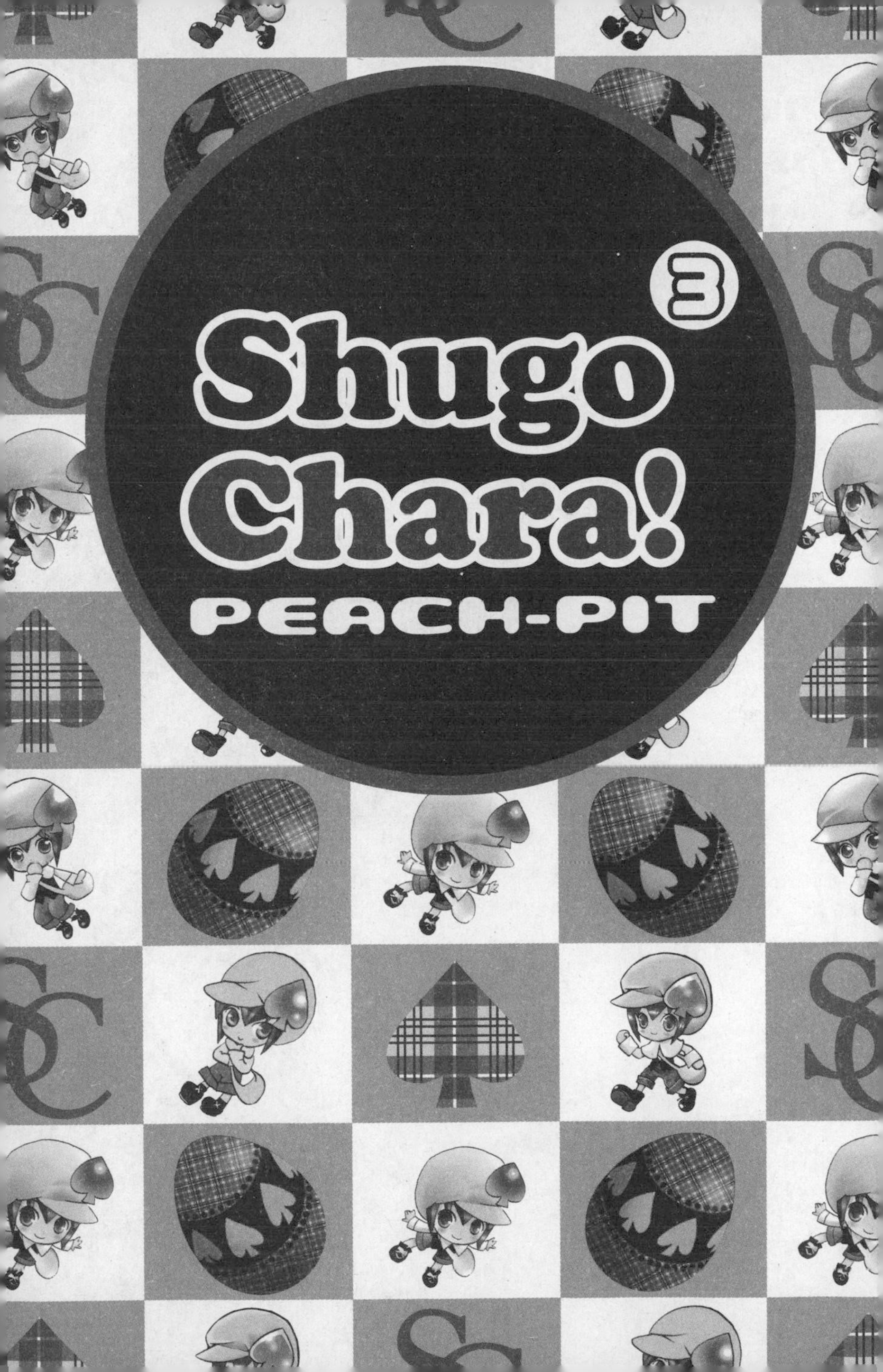
3
Shugo Chara!
PEACH-PIT

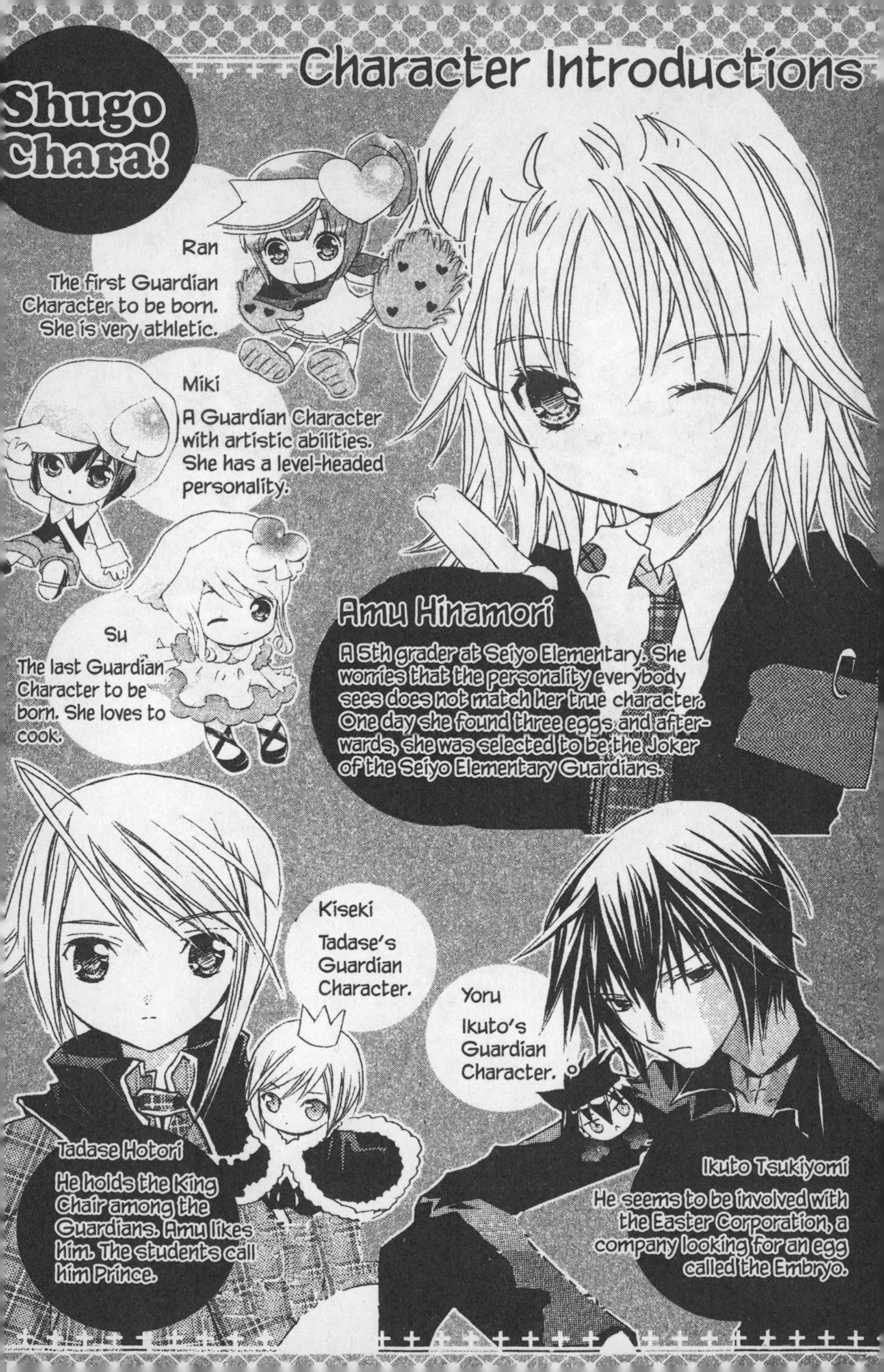
Character Introductions
Shugo Chara!
Ran
The first Guardian Character to be born. She is very athletic.
Miki
A Guardian Character with artistic abilities. She has a level-headed personality.
Su
The last Guardian Character to be born. She loves to cook.
Amu Hinamori
A 5th grader at Seiyo Elementary. She worries that the personality everybody sees does not match her true character. One day she found three eggs and afterwards, she was selected to be the Joker of the Seiyo Elementary Guardians.
Kiseki
Tadase's Guardian Character.
Yoru
Ikuto's Guardian Character.
Tadase Hotori
He holds the King Chair among the Guardians. Amu likes him. The students call him Prince.
Ikuto Tsukiyomi
He seems to be involved with the Easter Corporation, a company looking for an egg called the Embryo.

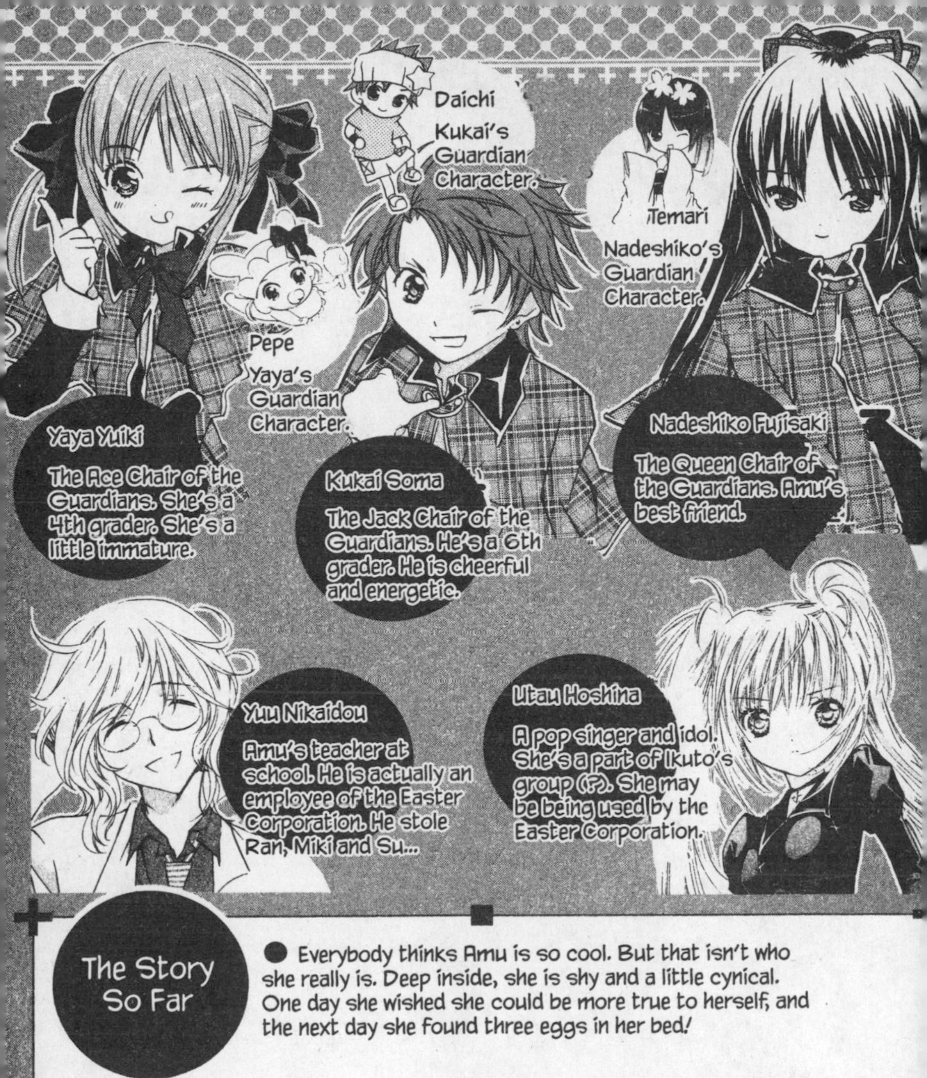
Temari
Nadeshiko's Guardian Character.
Nadeshiko Fujisaki
The Queen Chair of the Guardians. Amu's best friend.
Daichi
Kukai's Guardian Character.
Kukai Soma
The Jack Chair of the Guardians. He's a 6th grader. He is cheerful and energetic.
Pepe
Yaya's Guardian Character.
Yaya Yuiki
The Ace Chair of the Guardians. She's a 4th grader. She's a little immature.
Utau Hoshina
A pop singer and idol. She's a part of Ikuto's group (!?). She may be being used by the Easter Corporation.
Yuu Nikaidou
Amu's teacher at school. He is actually an employee of the Easter Corporation. He stole Ran, Miki and Su...

The Story So Far

● Everybody thinks Amu is so cool. But that isn't who she really is. Deep inside, she is shy and a little cynical. One day she wished she could be more true to herself, and the next day she found three eggs in her bed!

● Ran, Miki, and Su hatched from the eggs. They are Amu's "Guardian Characters." They say that they are Amu's "true selves," and when Amu Character Changes with them, she can become good at sports, art, or cooking! Soon after they hatched, Amu found herself recruited to become one of the Guardians of Seiyo Elementary.

● But Nikaidou-sensei is really an employee of the sinister Easter Corporation. They are searching for the Embryo, an egg known to grant any wish. He took away Ran, Miki, and Su!! What is Nikaidou-sensei really up to? And what is Amu going to do!?

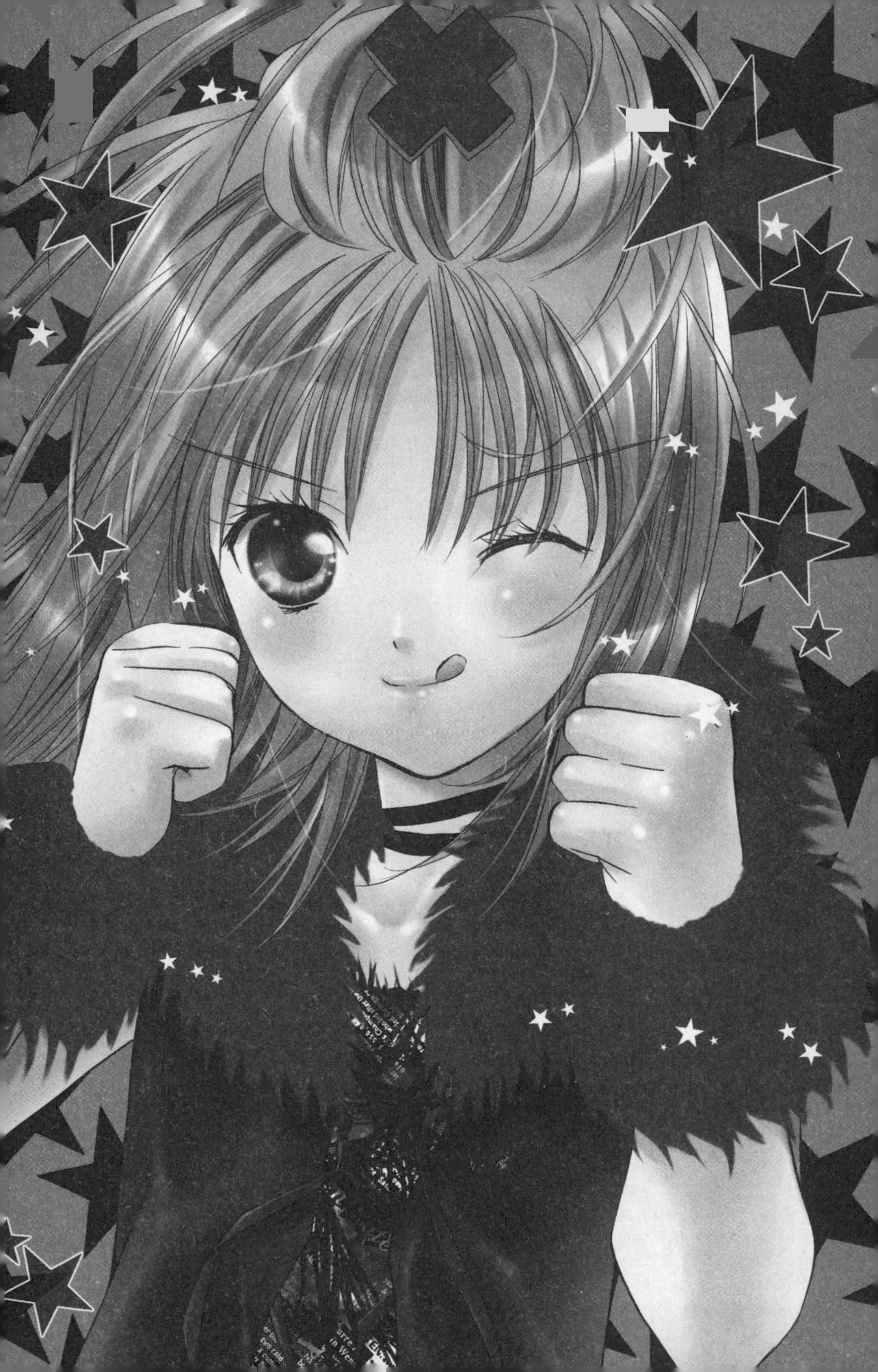

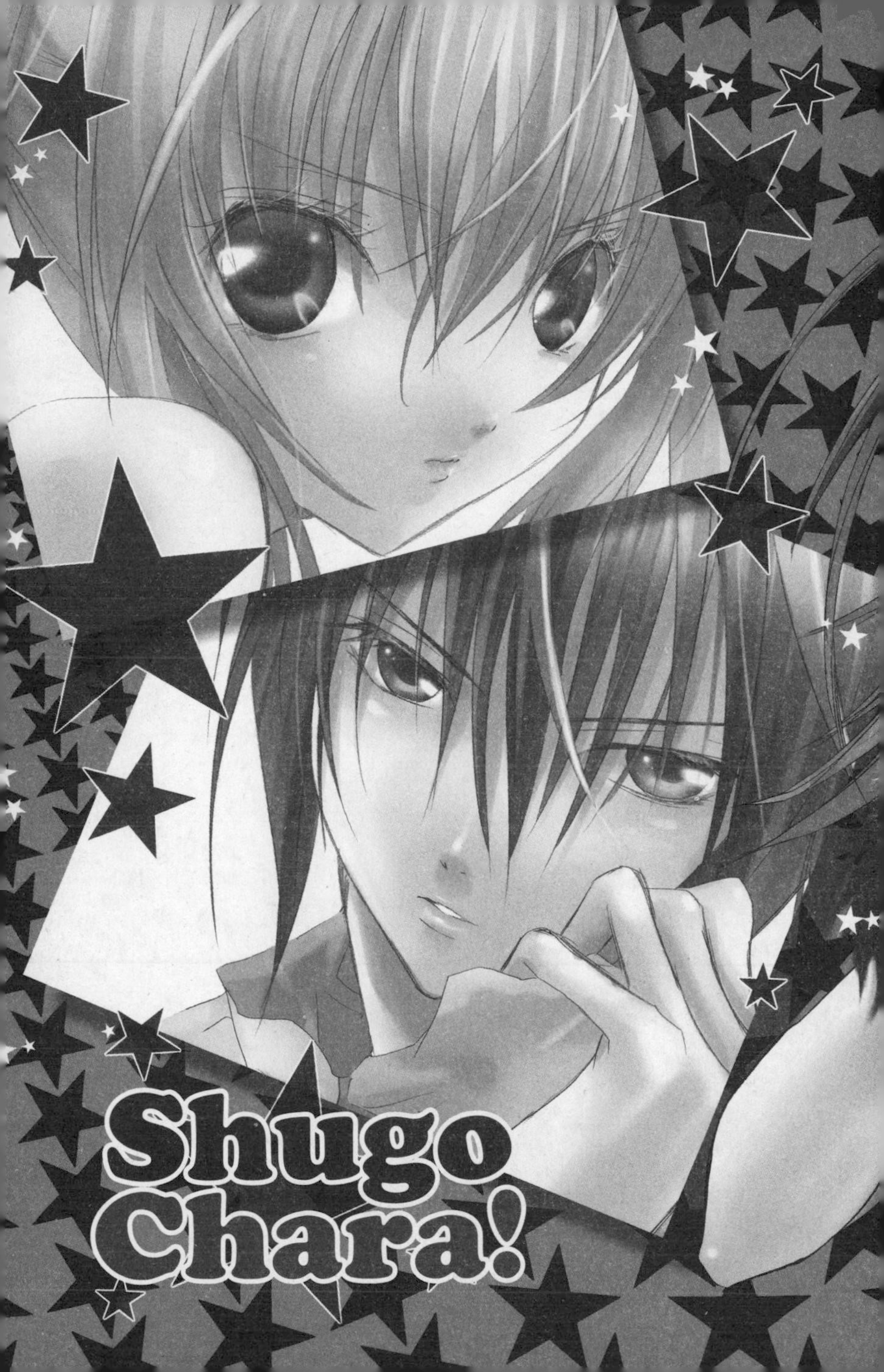
Shugo
Chara!

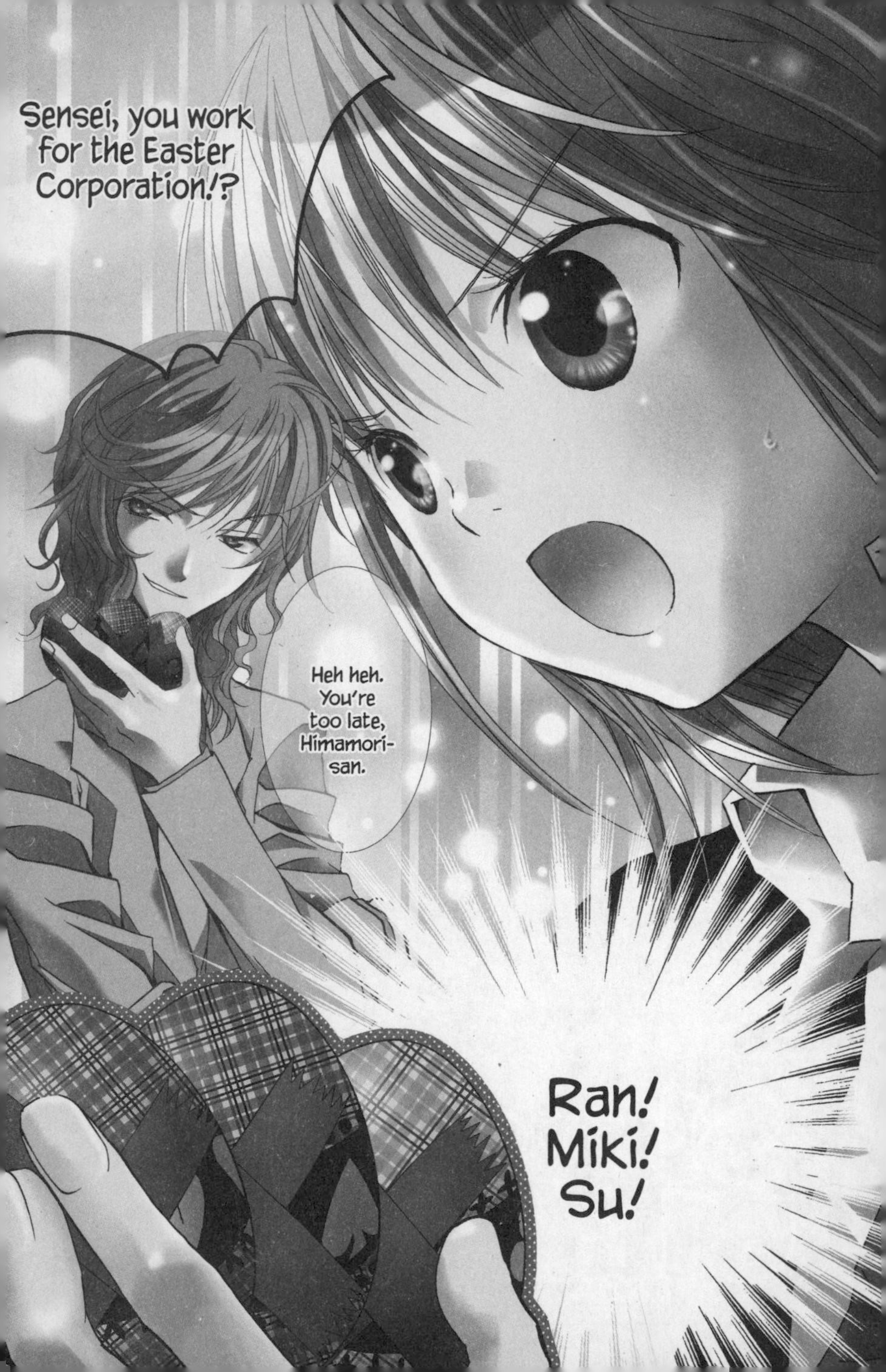
Sensei, you work for the Easter Corporation!?
Heh heh. You're too late, Himamori-san.
Ran! Miki! Su!

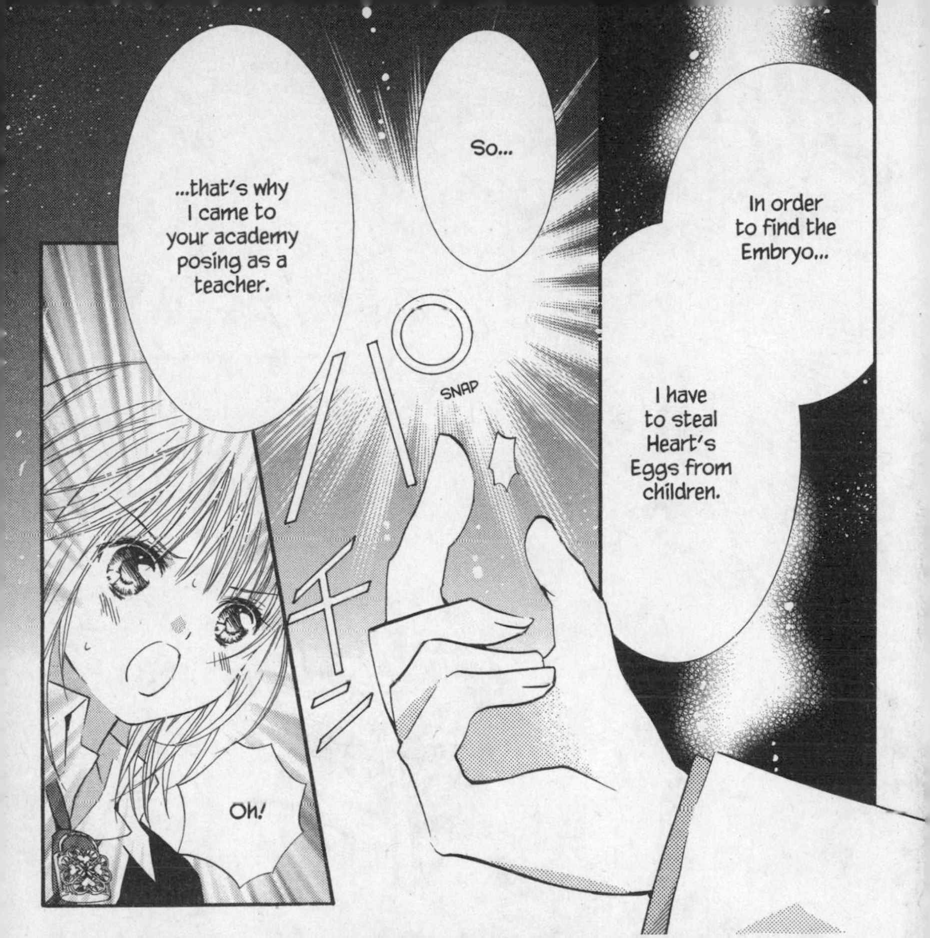
In order to find the Embryo...
I have to steal Heart's Eggs from children.
So...
...that's why I came to your academy posing as a teacher.
SNAP
Oh!

Hello, everyone ♡ Shugo Chara! is already on its third volume. This is Shibuko Ebara from PEACH-PIT! It's springtime already. I'm suffering from hay fever, but how is everyone else doing? I would like to move to Okinawa or Hokkaido! (They don't have pollen!)

Now we'll move on to the Q & A Corner ♡ In volume 3, we'll answer questions relating to us, PEACH-PIT. Everyone asks interesting questions...so let's go!

Q1: Do you like peaches?

A1: We do. We also like strawberries. And pears and tangerines and honeydew melon...

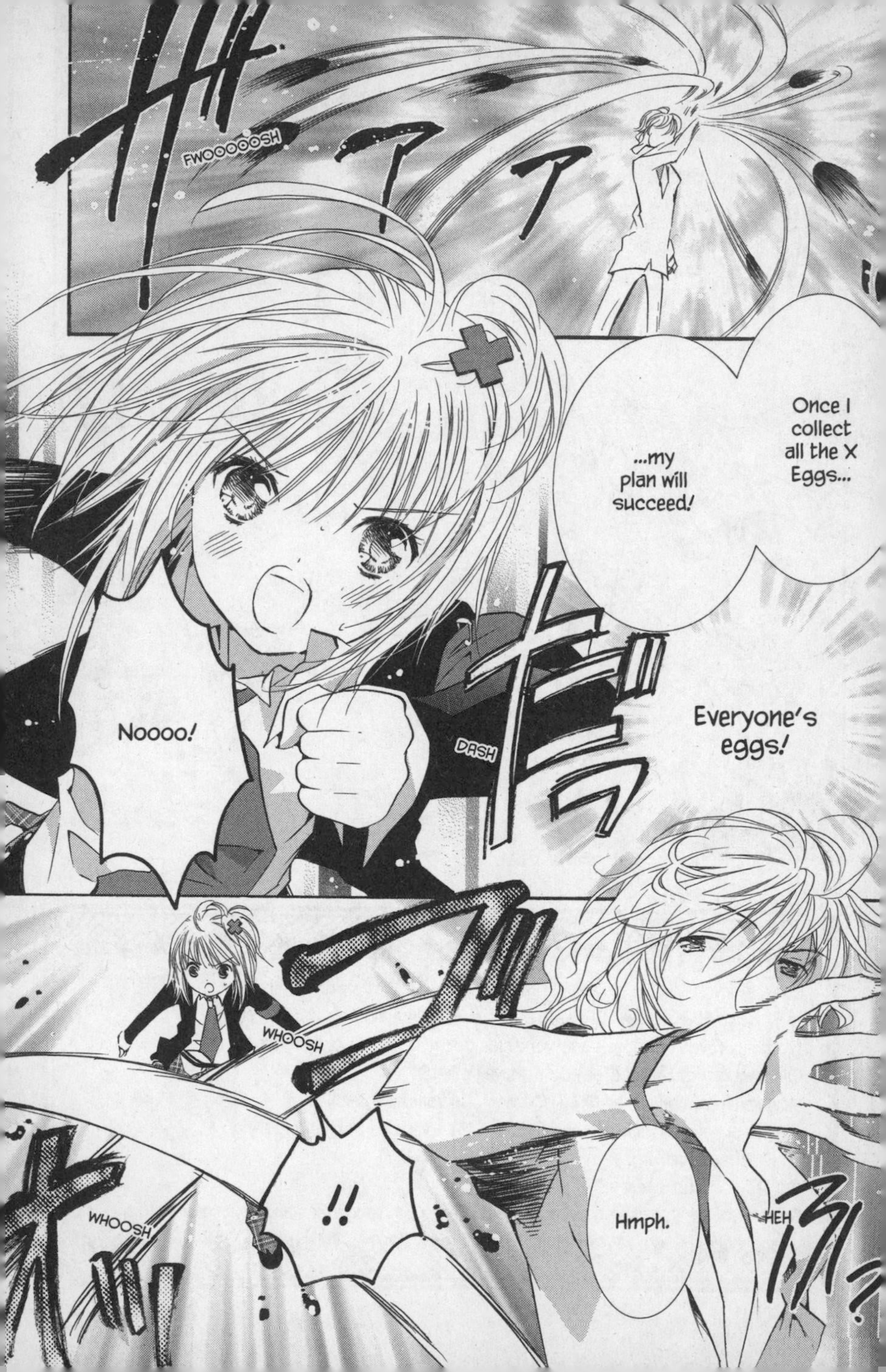
FWOOOOOSH
Once I collect all the X Eggs...
...my plan will succeed!
Everyone's eggs!
DASH
Noooo!
Hmph.
HEH
!!
WHOOSH
WHOOSH

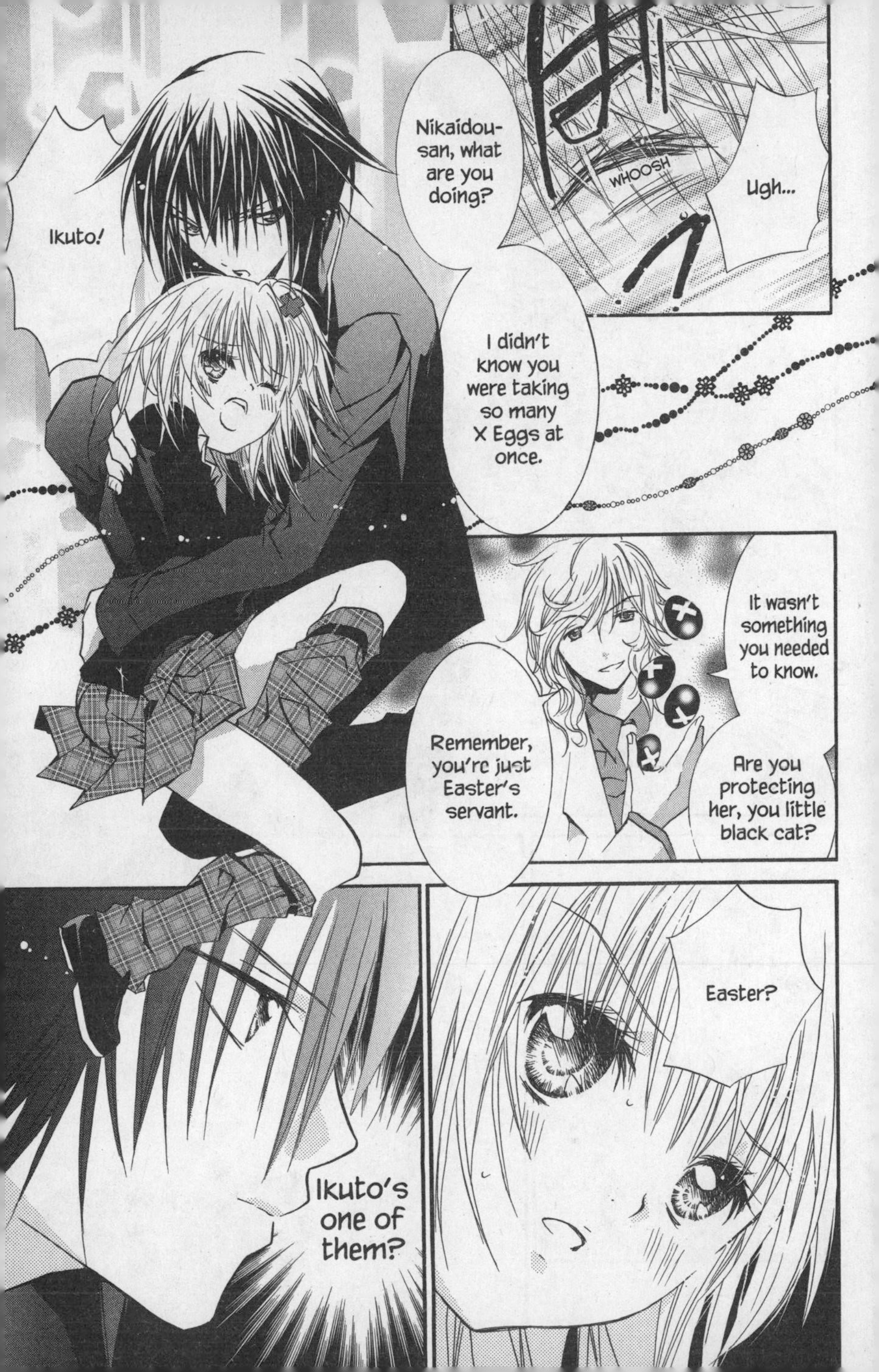

WHOOSH
Ugh...
Nikaidou-san, what are you doing?
I didn't know you were taking so many X Eggs at once.
It wasn't something you needed to know.
Are you protecting her, you little black cat?
Remember, you're just Easter's servant.
Ikuto!
Easter?
Ikuto's one of them?

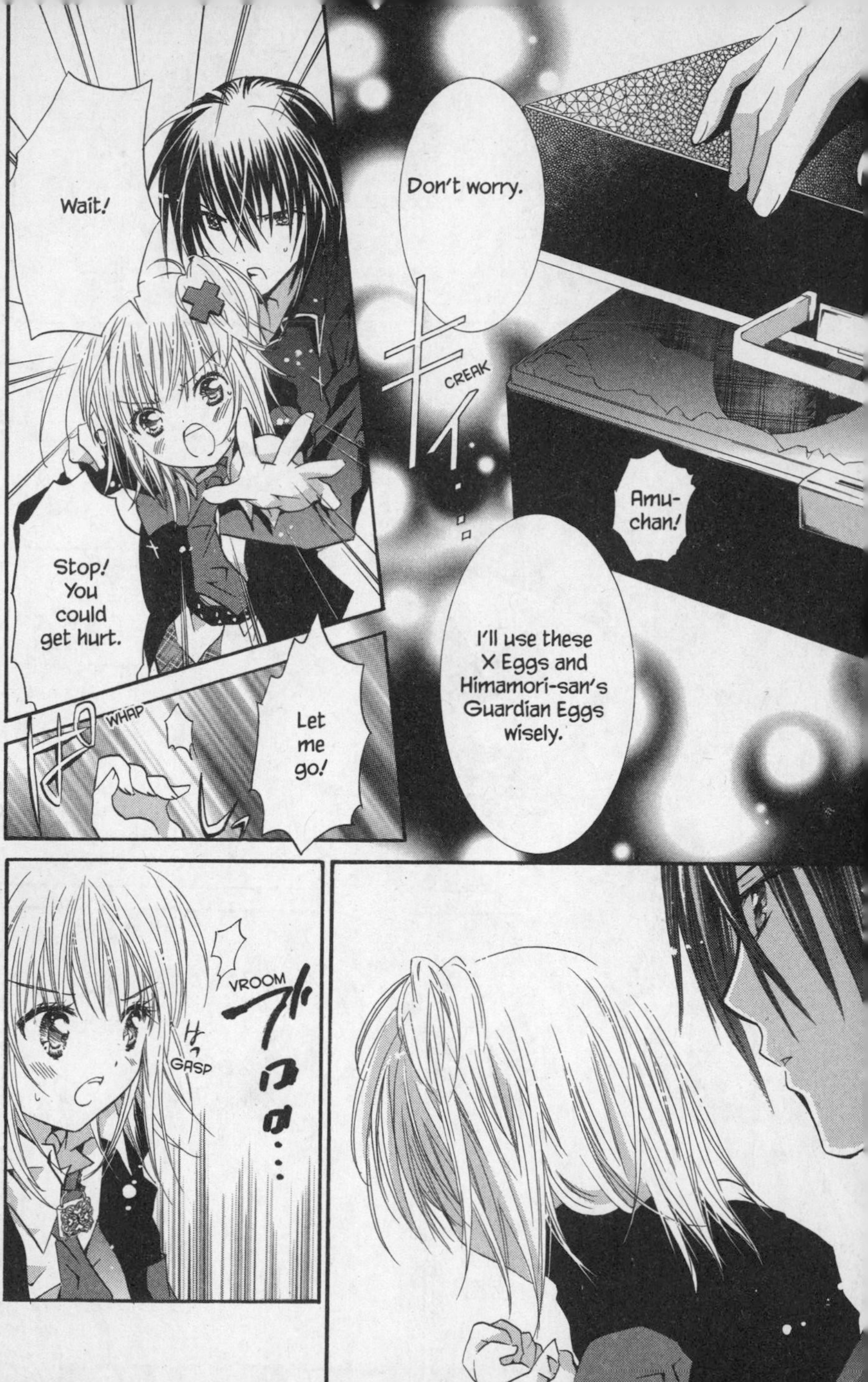
Don't worry.
CREAK
Amu-chan!
I'll use these X Eggs and Himamori-san's Guardian Eggs wisely.
Wait!
Stop! You could get hurt.
Let me go!
WHAP
VROOM
GASP

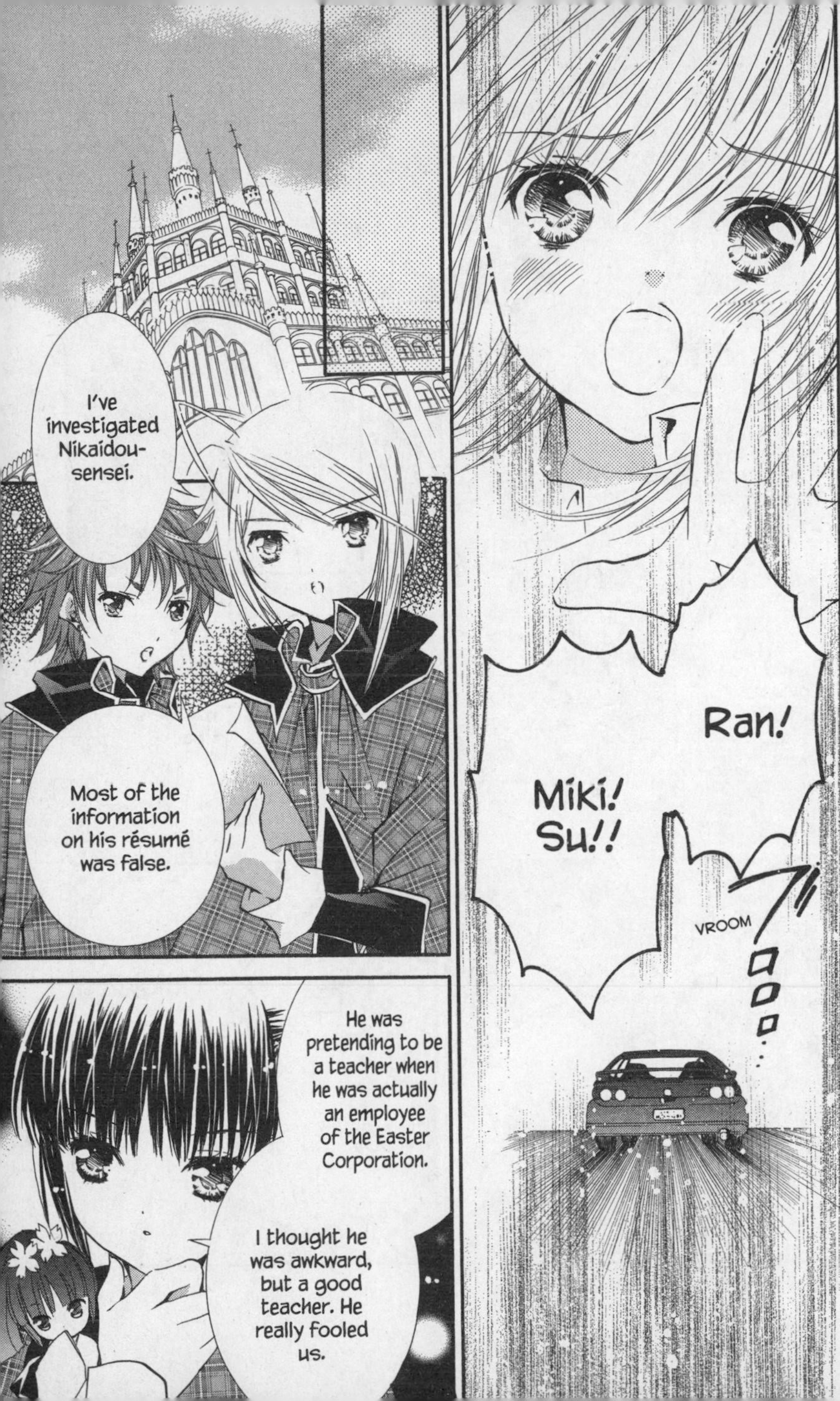
Ran! Miki! Su!!
VROOM
I've investigated Nikaidou-sensei.
Most of the information on his résumé was false.
He was pretending to be a teacher when he was actually an employee of the Easter Corporation.
I thought he was awkward, but a good teacher. He really fooled us.

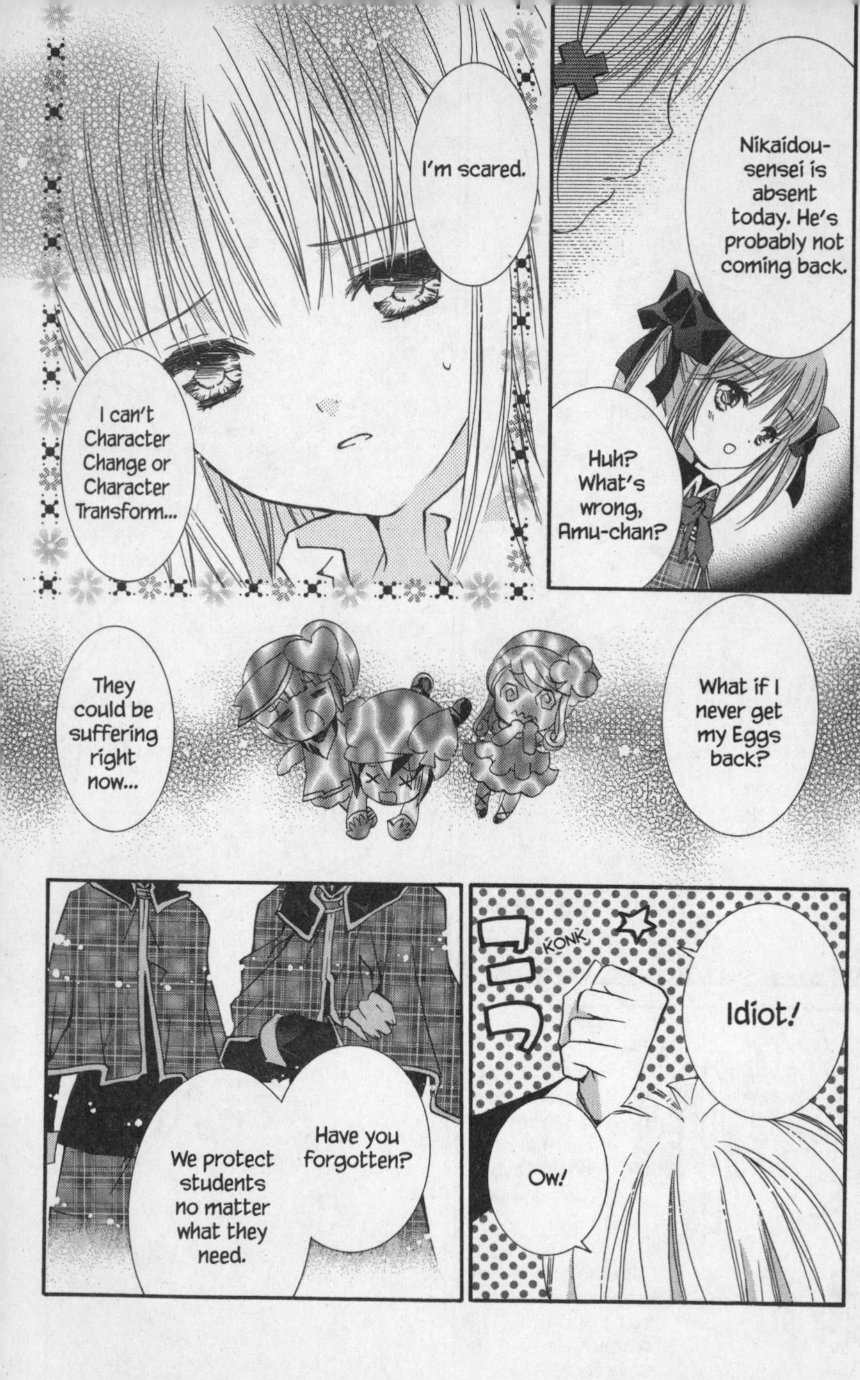

Nikaidou-sensei is absent today. He's probably not coming back.
Huh? What's wrong, Amu-chan?
I'm scared.
I can't Character Change or Character Transform...
What if I never get my Eggs back?
They could be suffering right now...
KONK
Idiot!
Ow!
Have you forgotten?
We protect students no matter what they need.

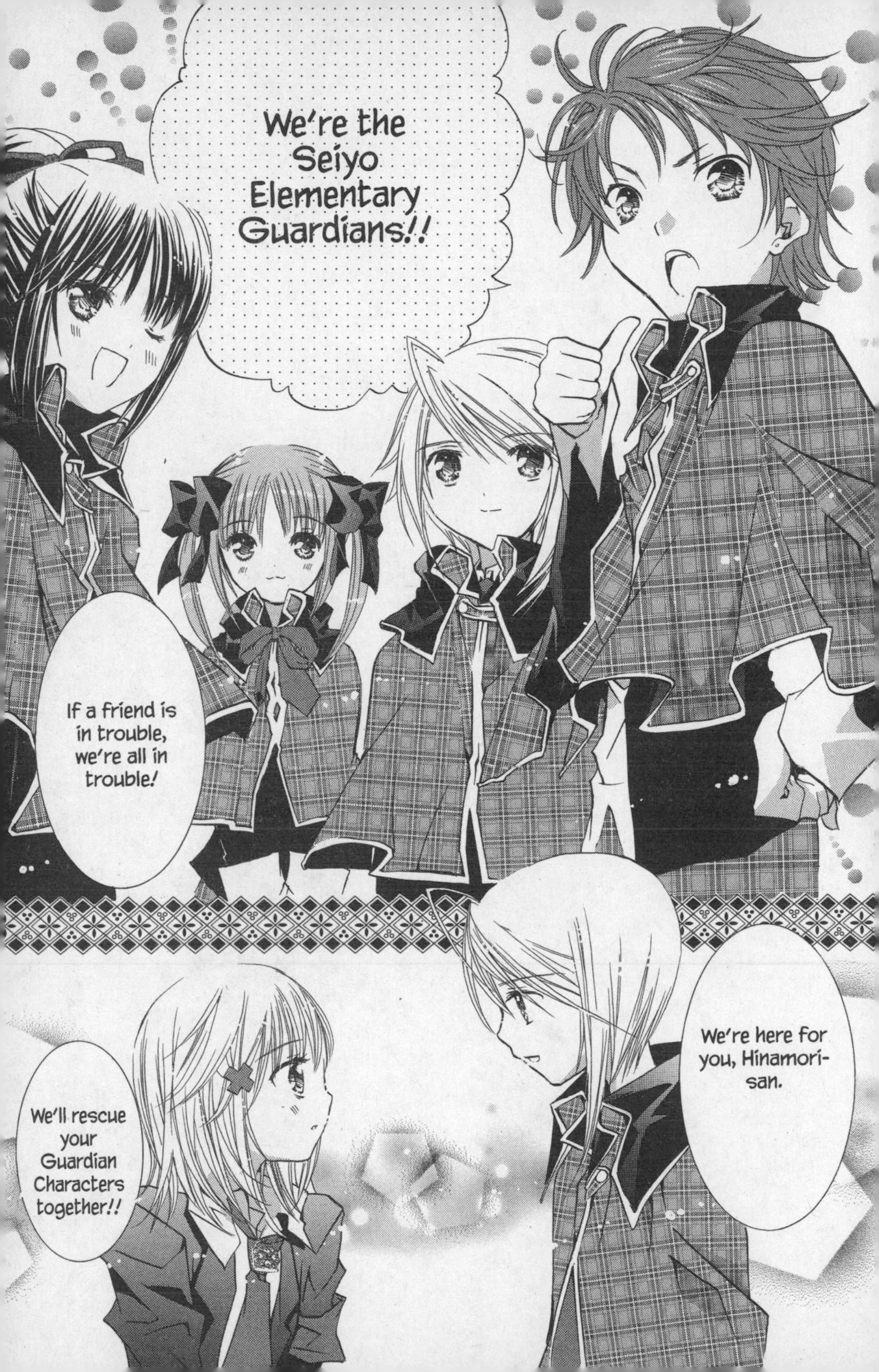
We're the Seiyo Elementary Guardians!!
If a friend is in trouble, we're all in trouble!
We're here for you, Hinamori-san.
We'll rescue your Guardian Characters together!!

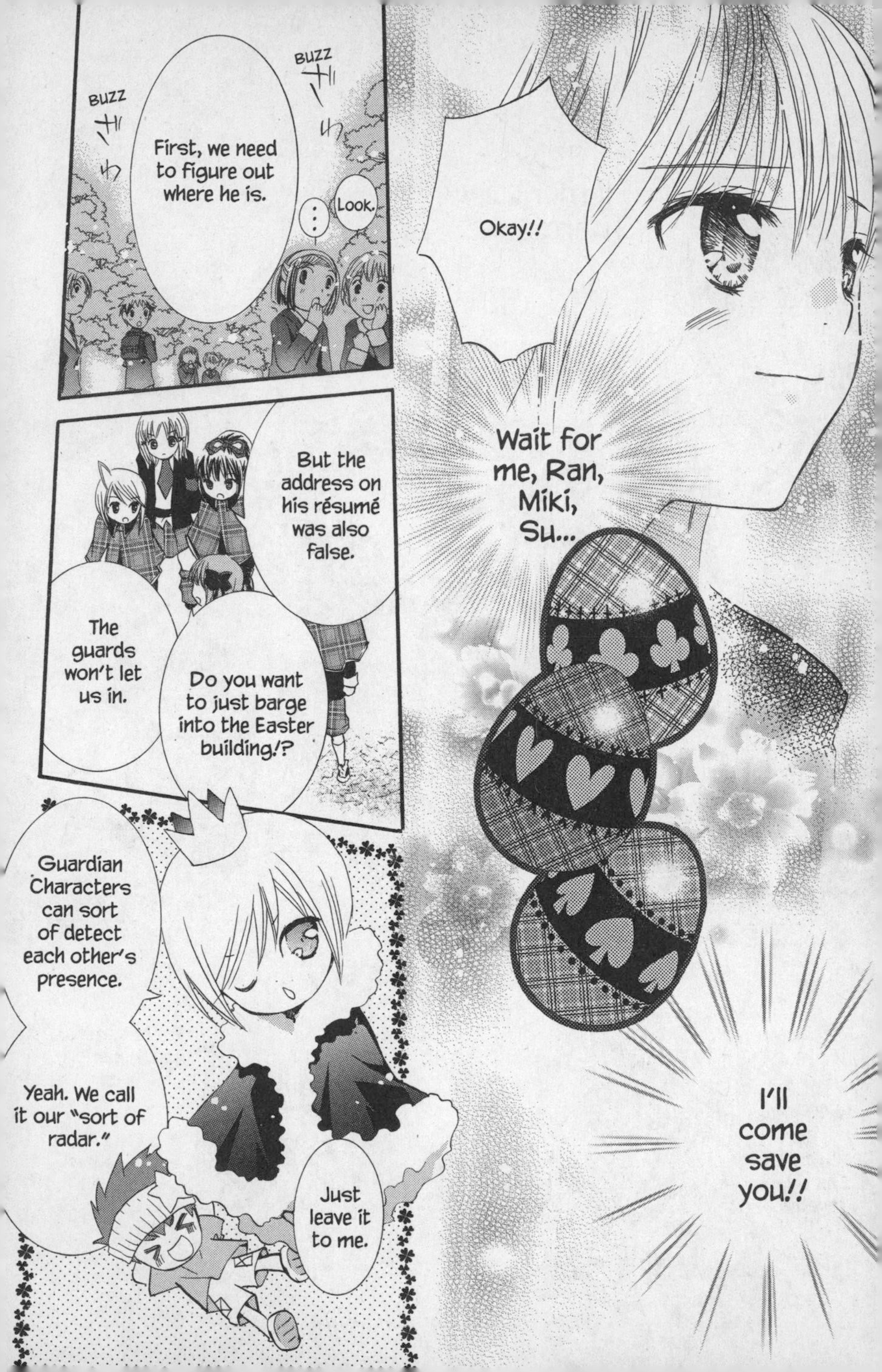
Okay!!
Wait for me, Ran, Miki, Su...
I'll come save you!!
BUZZ
Look.
...
First, we need to figure out where he is.
BUZZ
But the address on his résumé was also false.
Do you want to just barge into the Easter building!?
The guards won't let us in.
Guardian Characters can sort of detect each other's presence.
Yeah. We call it our "sort of radar."
Just leave it to me.

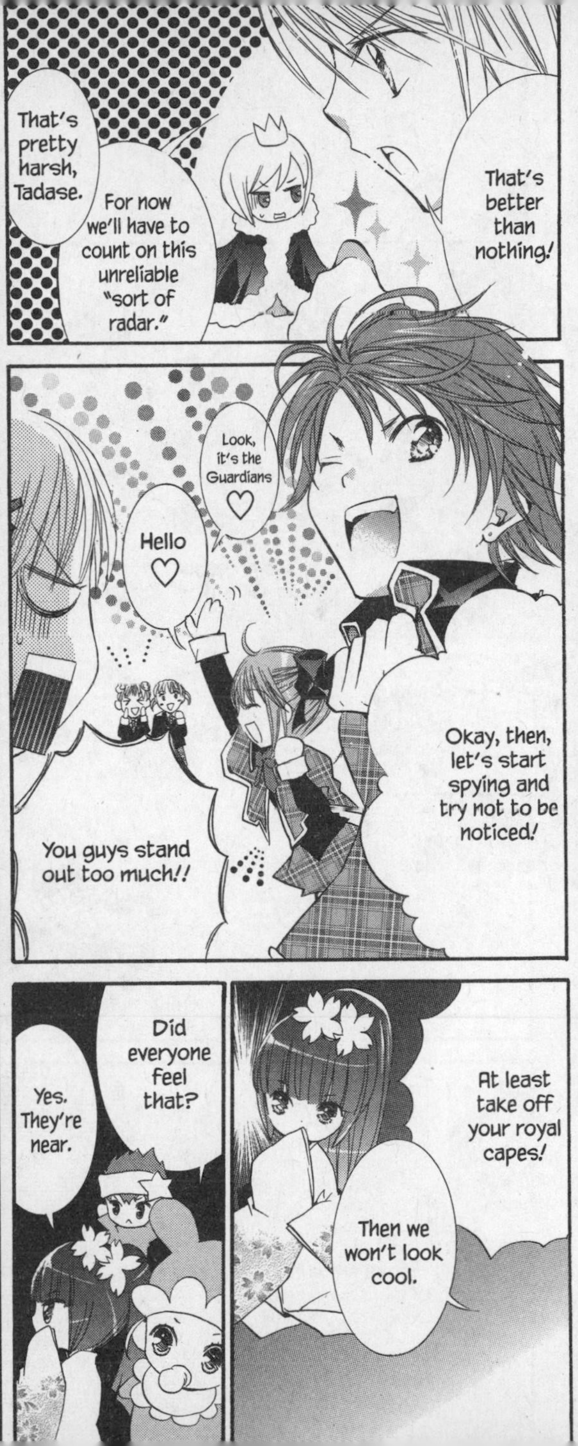
That's better than nothing!
That's pretty harsh, Tadase.
For now we'll have to count on this unreliable "sort of radar."
Okay, then, let's start spying and try not to be noticed!
Look, it's the Guardians ♡
Hello ♡
You guys stand out too much!!
At least take off your royal capes!
Then we won't look cool.
Did everyone feel that?
Yes. They're near.

character profile

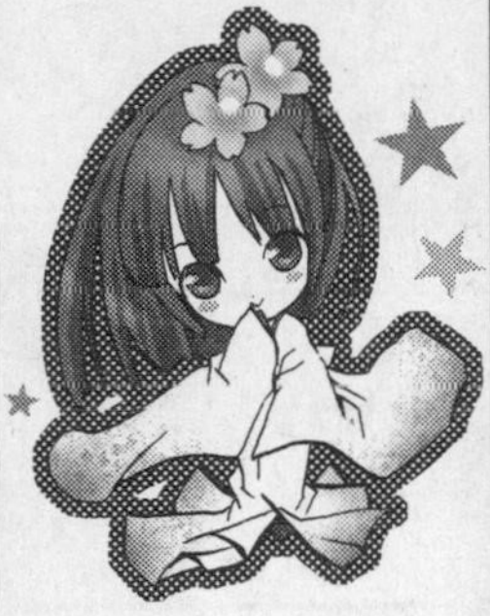

TEMARI

Guardian Character of: Nadeshiko
Special Skill: Naginata
Hates: Mud

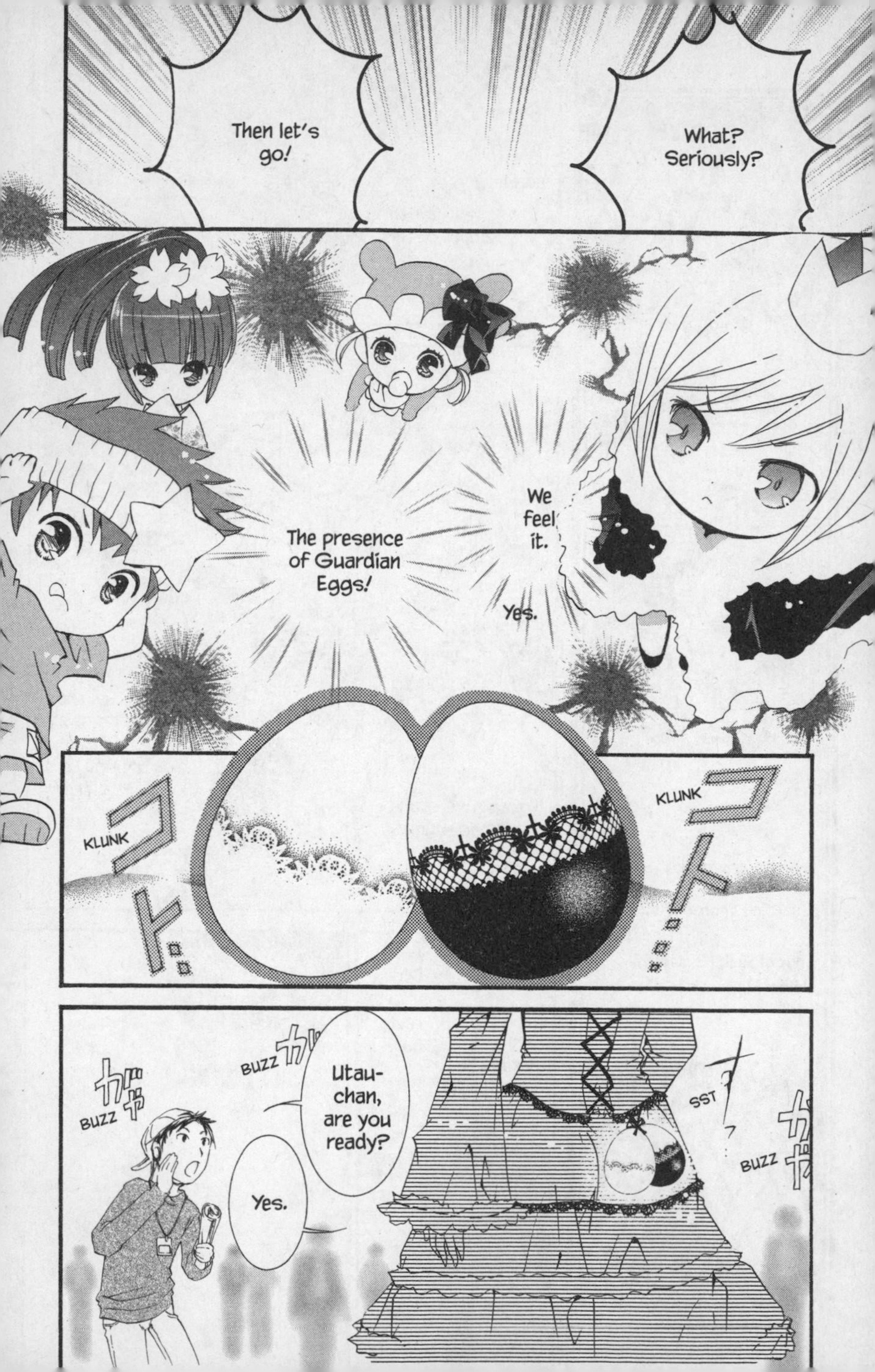
What? Seriously?
Then let's go!
We feel it.
The presence of Guardian Eggs!
Yes.
KLUNK
KLUNK
SST
BUZZ
BUZZ
Utau-chan, are you ready?
Yes.
BUZZ

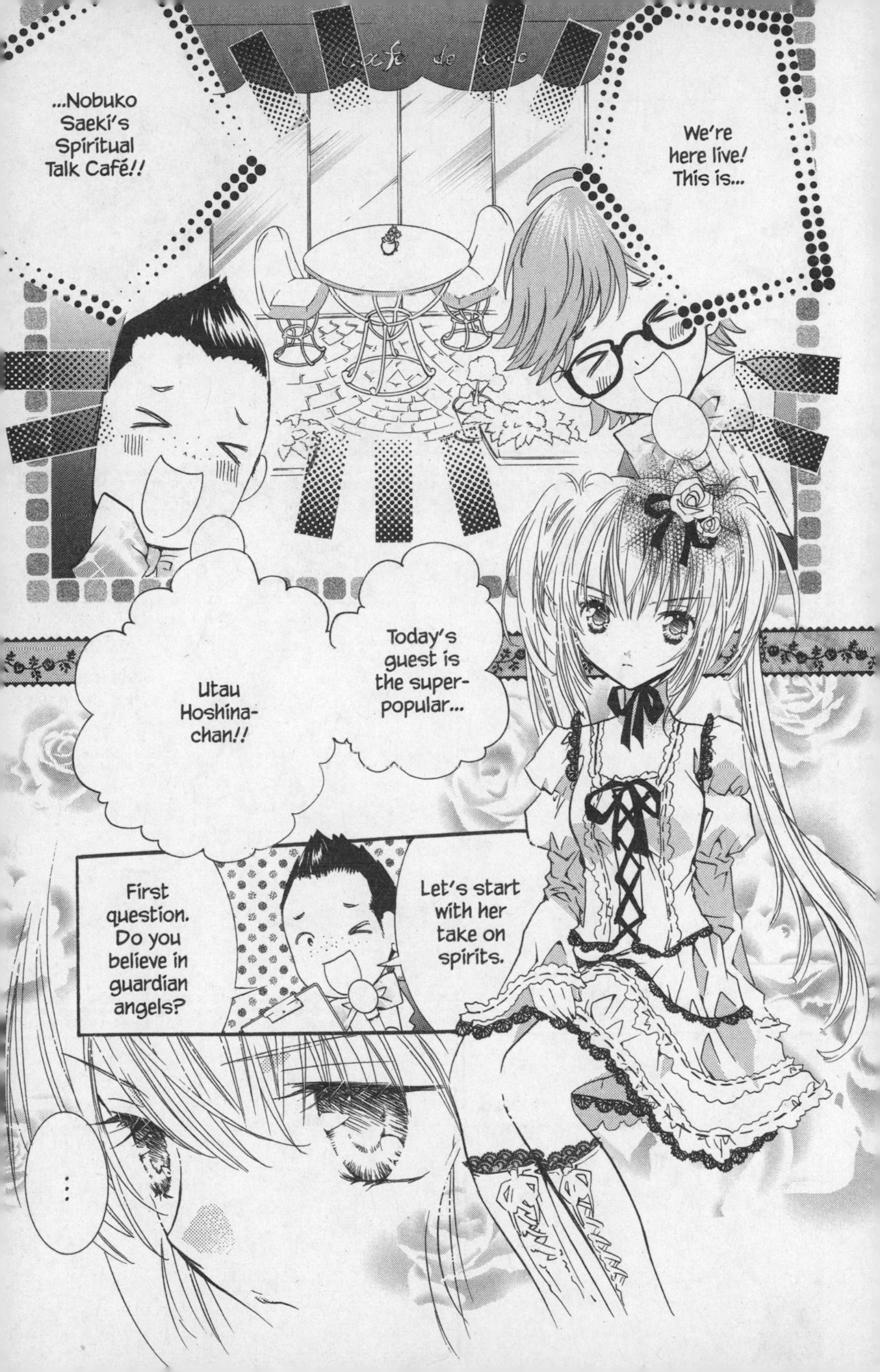
We're here live! This is...
...Nobuko Saeki's Spiritual Talk Café!!
Today's guest is the super-popular...
Utau Hoshina-chan!!
Let's start with her take on spirits.
First question. Do you believe in guardian angels?
...

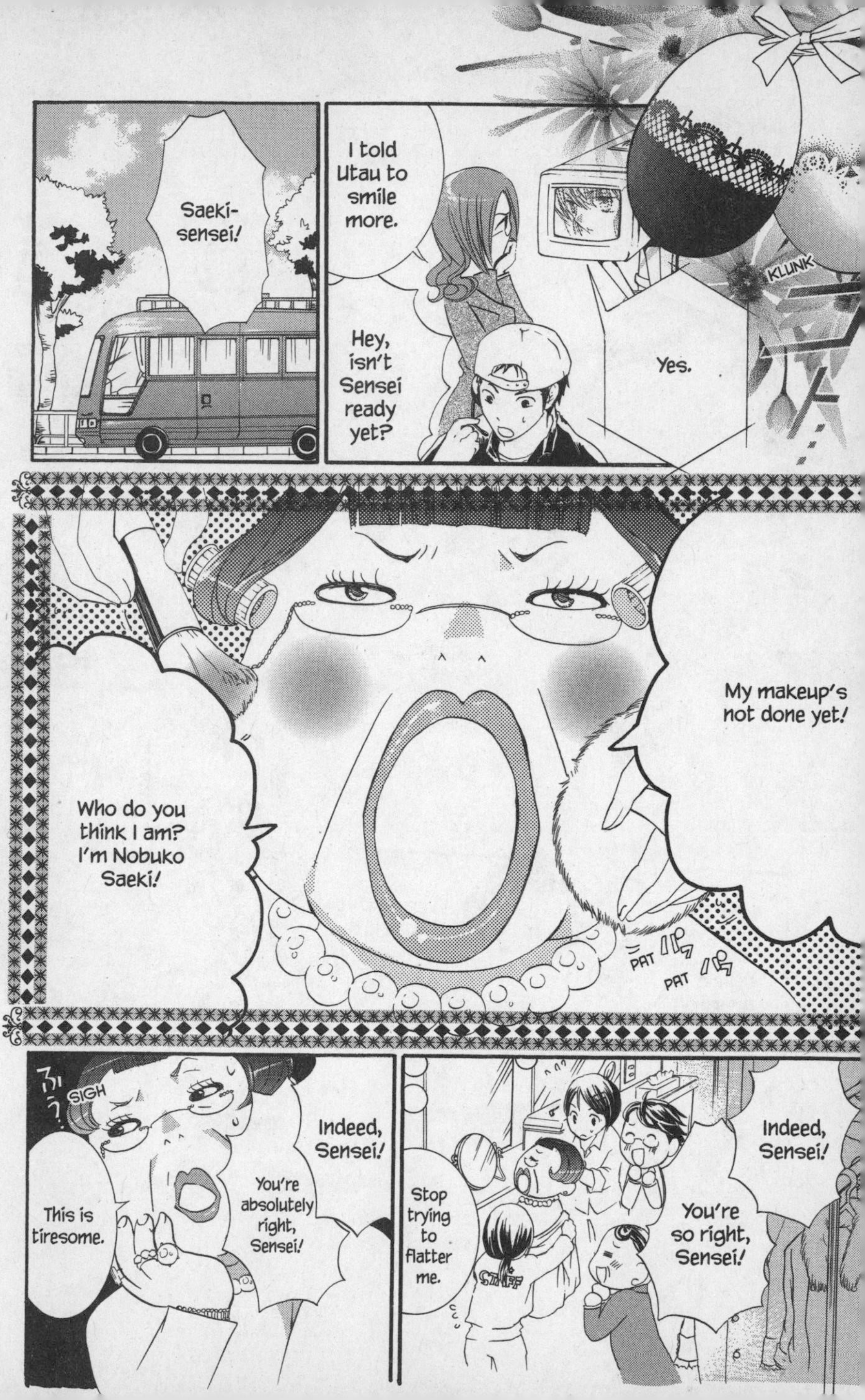
I told Utau to smile more.
KLUNK
Yes.
Hey, isn't Sensei ready yet?
Saeki-sensei!
My makeup's not done yet!
PAT PAT
Who do you think I am? I'm Nobuko Saeki!
Indeed, Sensei!
You're so right, Sensei!
Stop trying to flatter me.
SIGH
Indeed, Sensei!
You're absolutely right, Sensei!
This is tiresome.

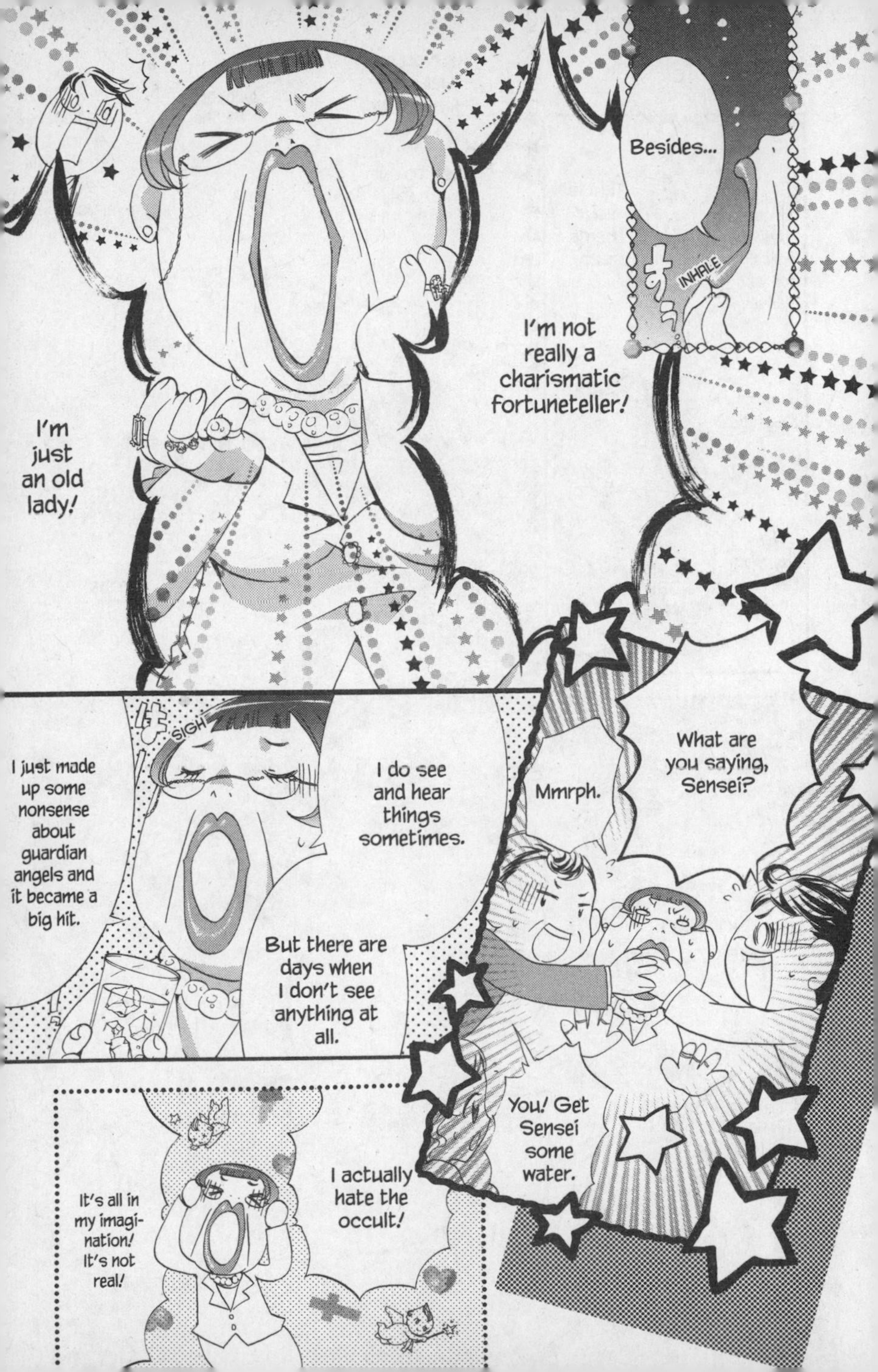
Besides...
INHALE
I'm not really a charismatic fortuneteller!
I'm just an old lady!
What are you saying, Sensei?
Mmrph.
You! Get Sensei some water.
SIGH
I do see and hear things sometimes.
I just made up some nonsense about guardian angels and it became a big hit.
But there are days when I don't see anything at all.
I actually hate the occult!
It's all in my imagination! It's not real!

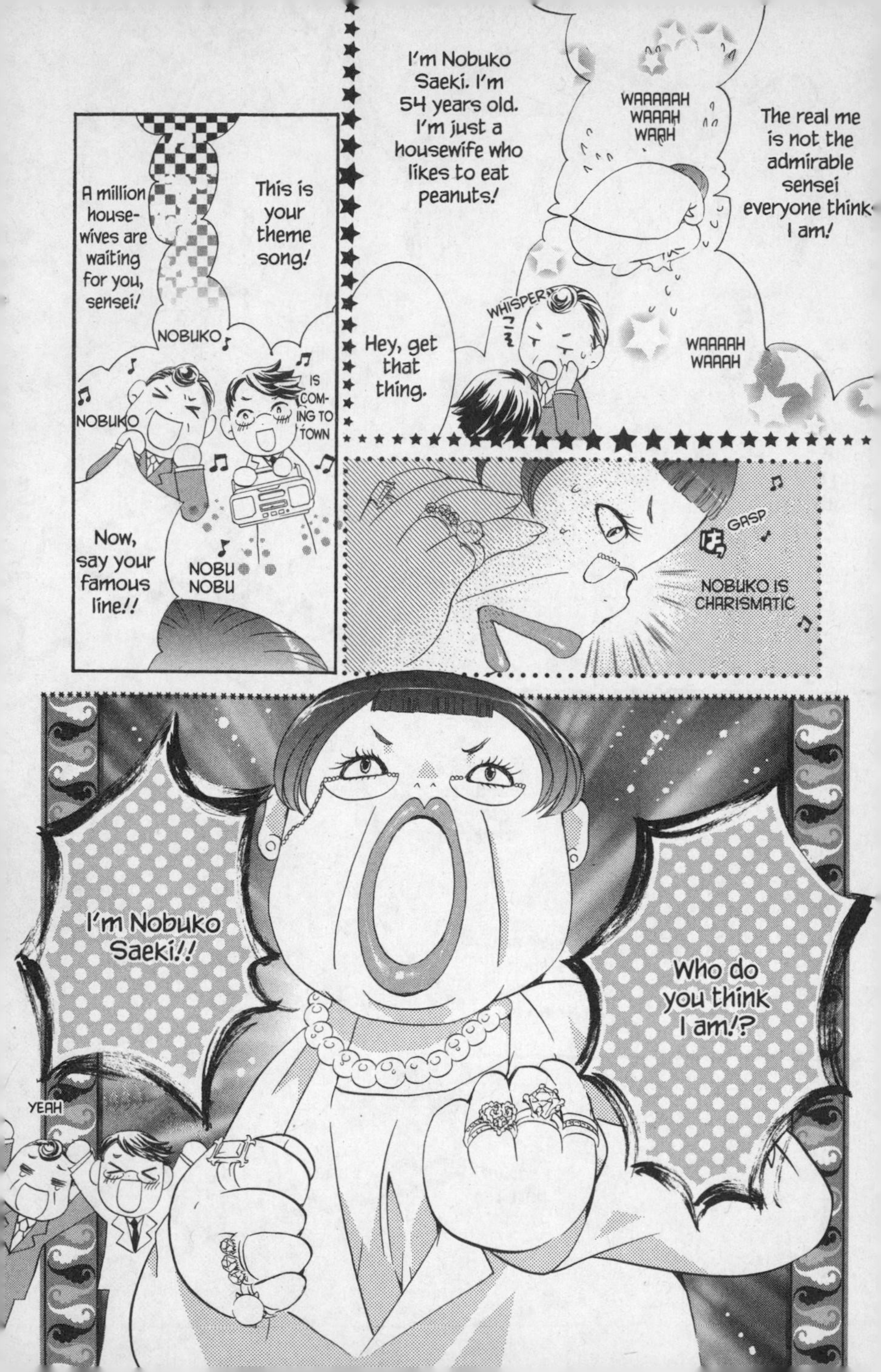

The real me is not the admirable sensei everyone think I am!
WAAAAAH WAAAH WAAH
I'm Nobuko Saeki. I'm 54 years old. I'm just a housewife who likes to eat peanuts!
WAAAAH WAAAH
WHISPER
Hey, get that thing.
GASP
NOBUKO IS CHARISMATIC
This is your theme song!
A million housewives are waiting for you, sensei!
NOBUKO
IS COMING TO TOWN
NOBUKO
Now, say your famous line!!
NOBU NOBU
Who do you think I am!?
I'm Nobuko Saeki!!
YEAH

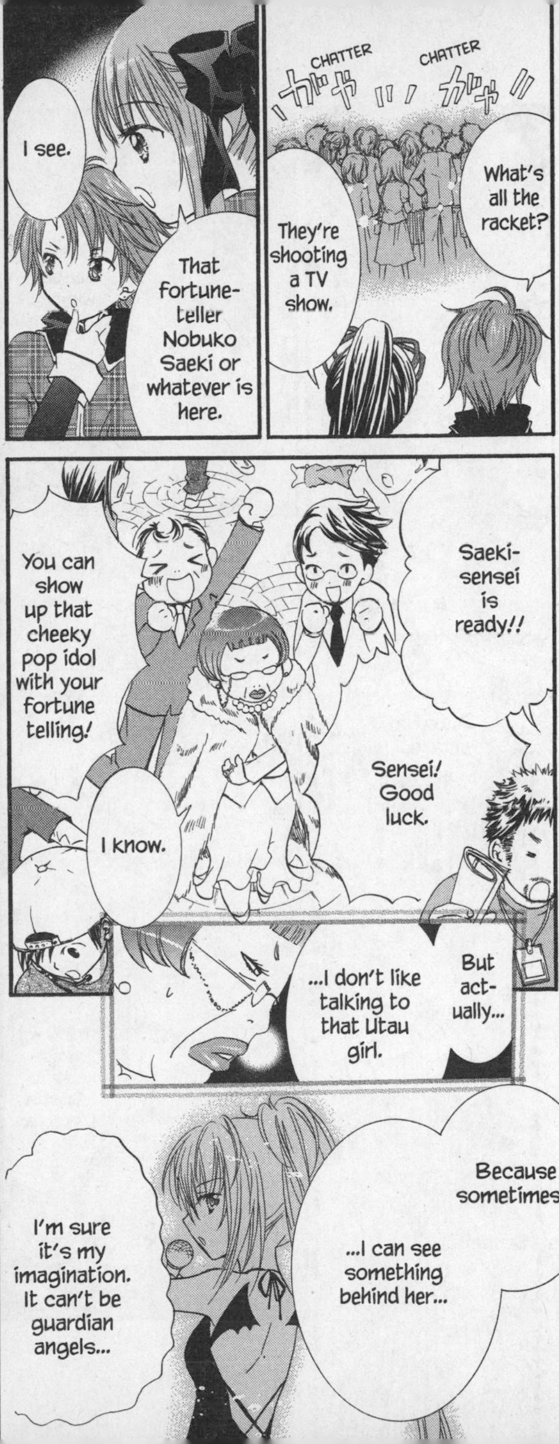
CHATTER
CHATTER
What's all the racket?
They're shooting a TV show.
That fortune-teller Nobuko Saeki or whatever is here.
I see.
Saeki-sensei is ready!!
You can show up that cheeky pop idol with your fortune telling!
Sensei! Good luck.
I know.
But actually...
...I don't like talking to that Utau girl.
Because sometimes...
...I can see something behind her...
I'm sure it's my imagination. It can't be guardian angels...

character profile

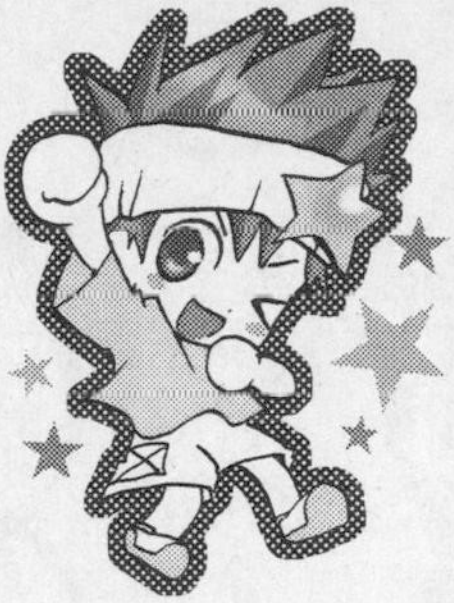

DAICHI

Guardian Character of: Kukai
Special Skill: Skateboarding
Hates: Sitting quietly

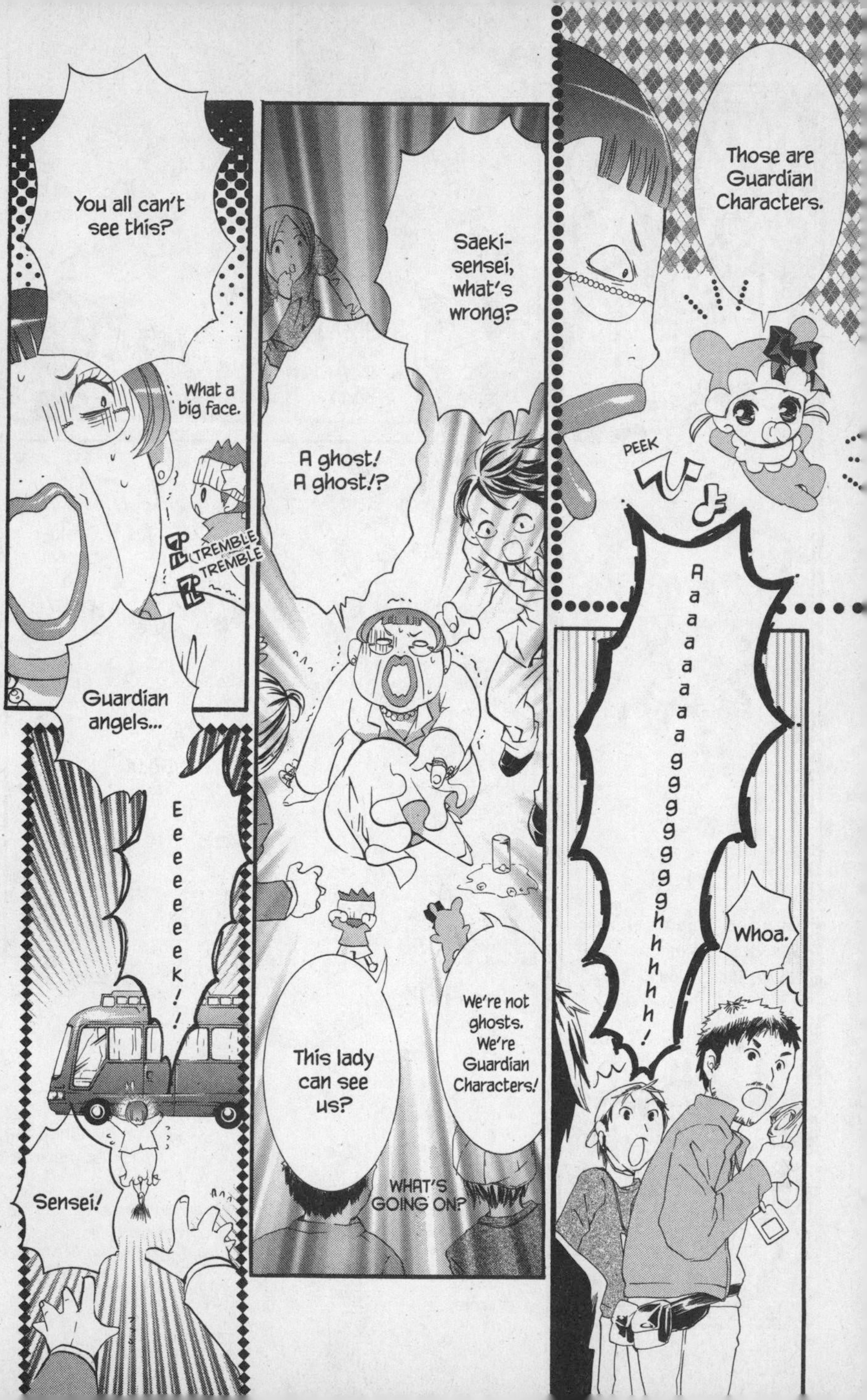
Those are Guardian Characters.
PEEK
Aaaaaaaggggggghhhhh!
Whoa.
Saeki-sensei, what's wrong?
A ghost! A ghost!?
We're not ghosts. We're Guardian Characters!
This lady can see us?
WHAT'S GOING ON?
You all can't see this?
What a big face.
TREMBLE TREMBLE
Guardian angels...
Eeeeeeeek!!
Sensei!

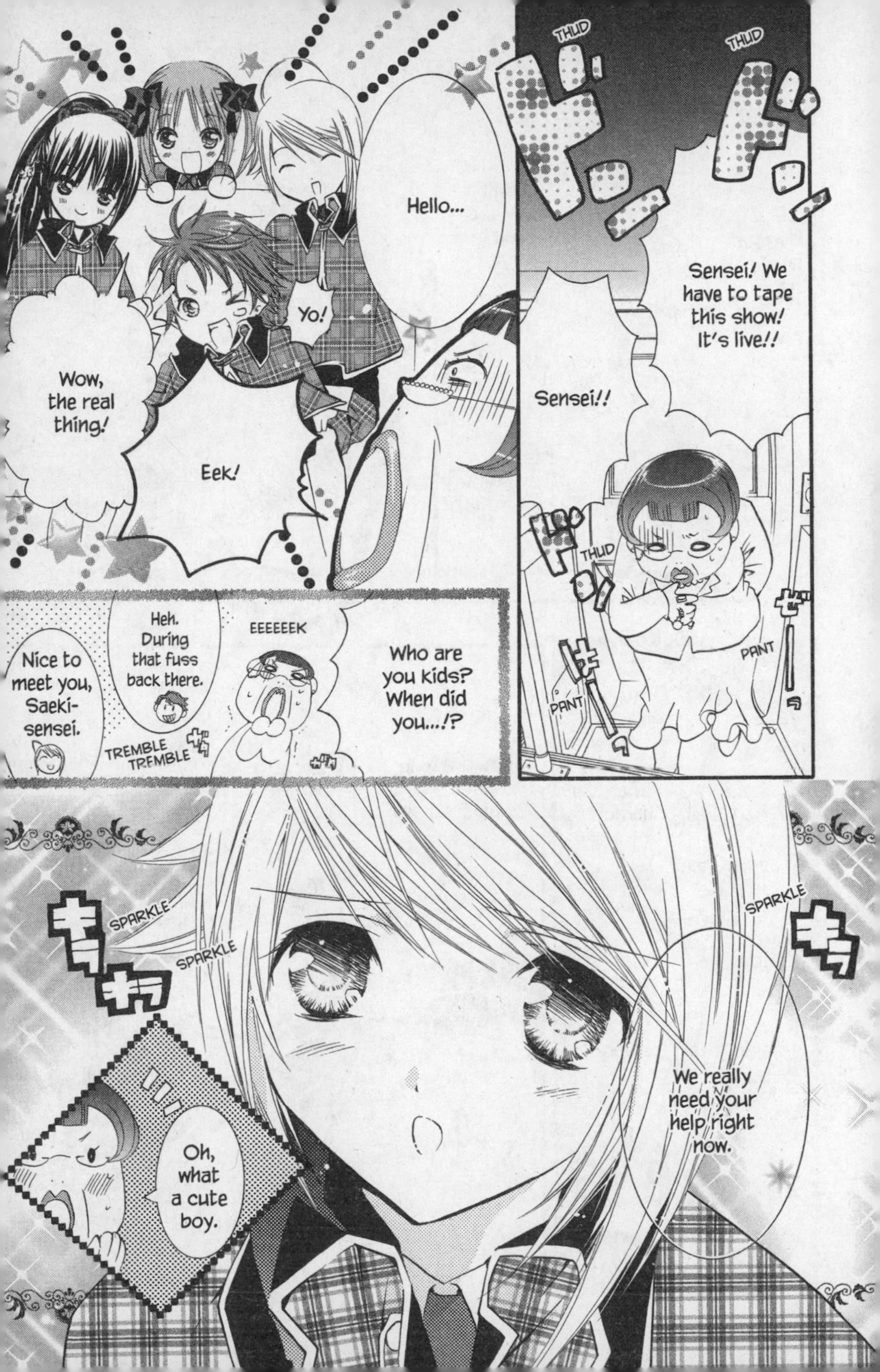
THUD
THUD
Sensei! We have to tape this show! It's live!!
Sensei!!
THUD
PANT
PANT
Hello...
Yo!
Wow, the real thing!
Eek!
Who are you kids? When did you...!?
EEEEEEK
Heh. During that fuss back there.
Nice to meet you, Saeki-sensei.
TREMBLE TREMBLE
SPARKLE
SPARKLE
SPARKLE
We really need your help right now.
Oh, what a cute boy.

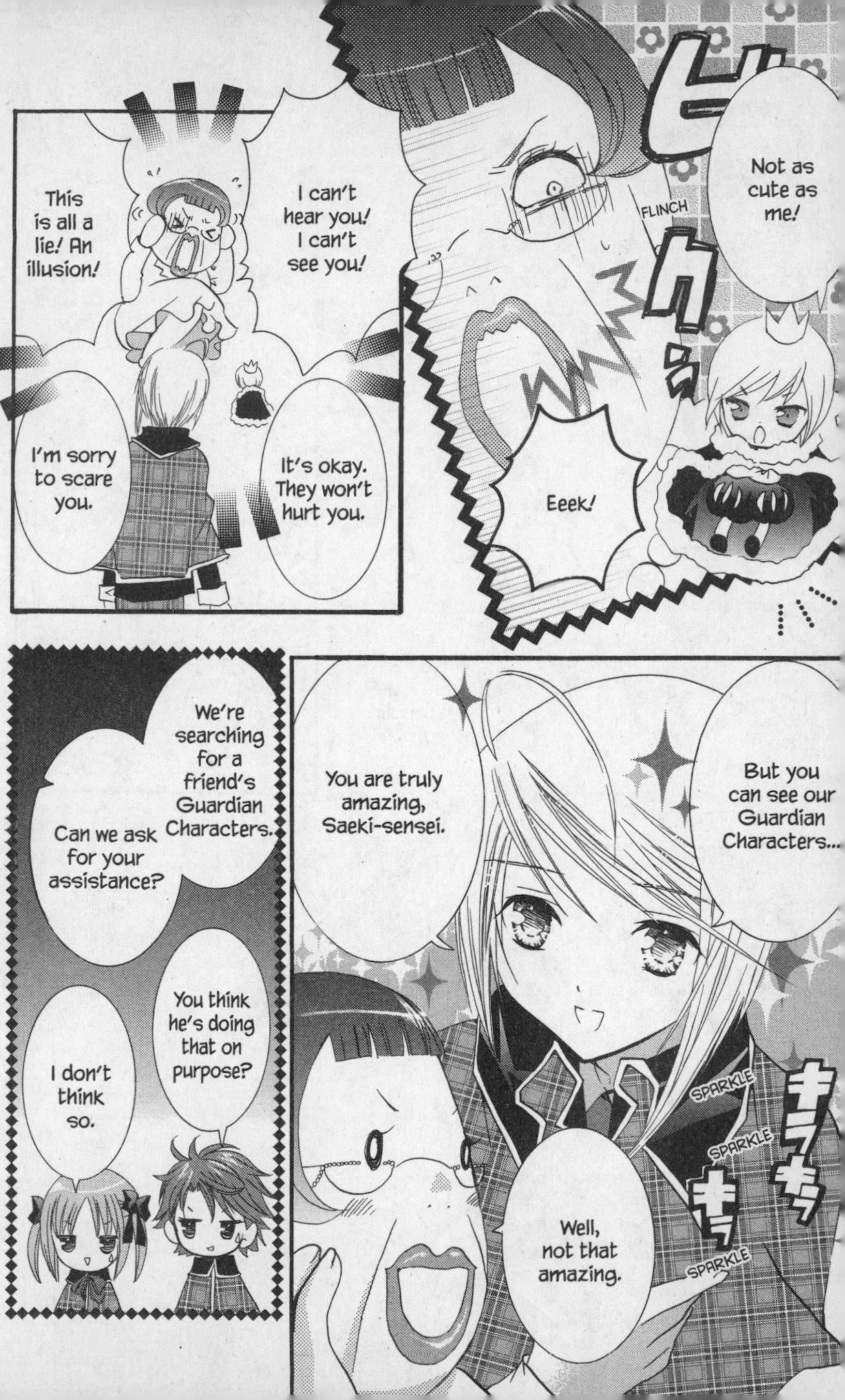
Not as cute as me!
FLINCH
Eeek!
I can't hear you! I can't see you!
This is all a lie! An illusion!
It's okay. They won't hurt you.
I'm sorry to scare you.
But you can see our Guardian Characters...
You are truly amazing, Saeki-sensei.
SPARKLE
SPARKLE
SPARKLE
Well, not that amazing.
We're searching for a friend's Guardian Characters.
Can we ask for your assistance?
You think he's doing that on purpose?
I don't think so.

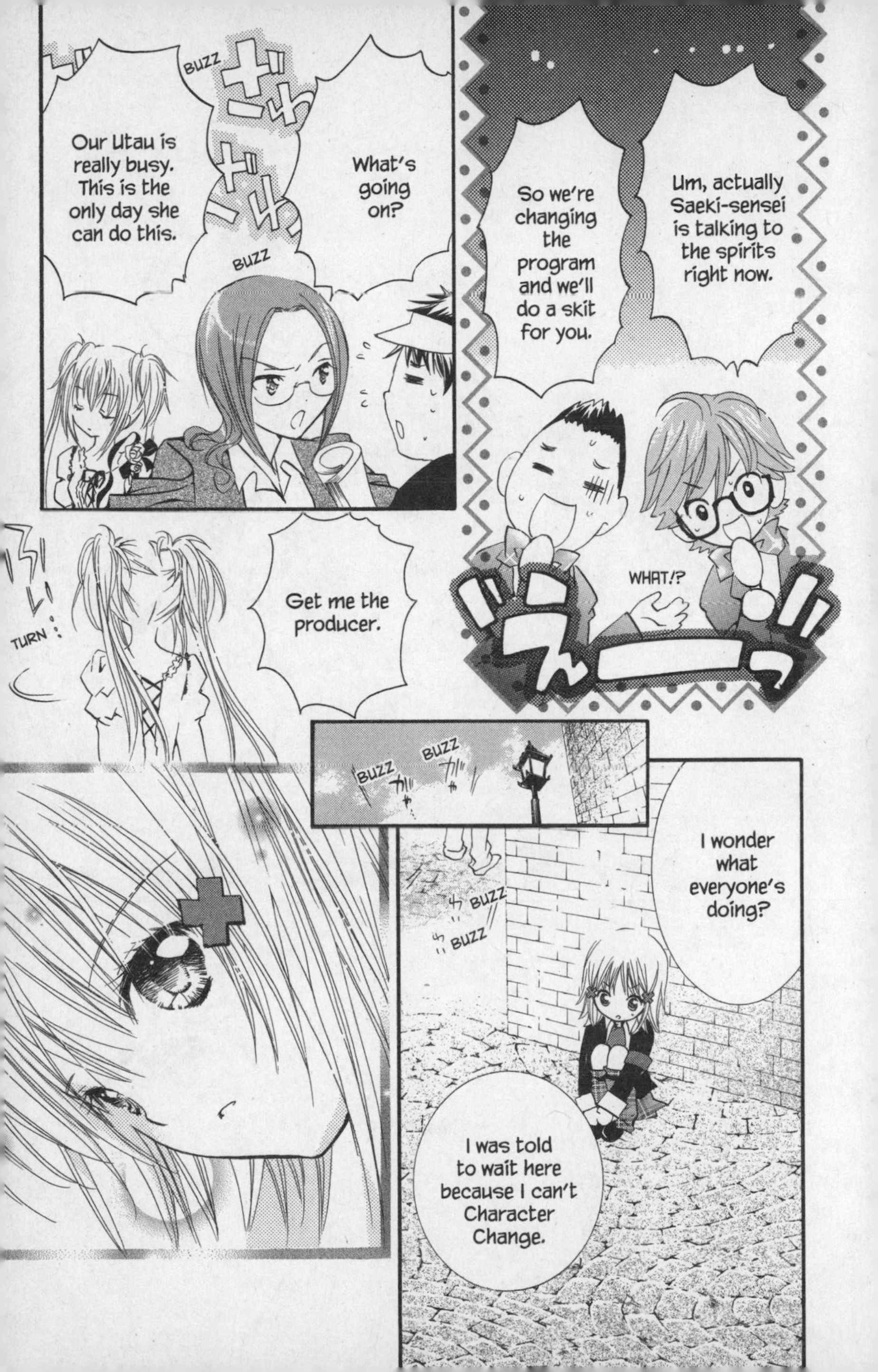
Um, actually Saeki-sensei is talking to the spirits right now.
So we're changing the program and we'll do a skit for you.
WHAT!?
BUZZ
What's going on?
Our Utau is really busy. This is the only day she can do this.
BUZZ
Get me the producer.
TURN
BUZZ
BUZZ
I wonder what everyone's doing?
BUZZ
BUZZ
I was told to wait here because I can't Character Change.

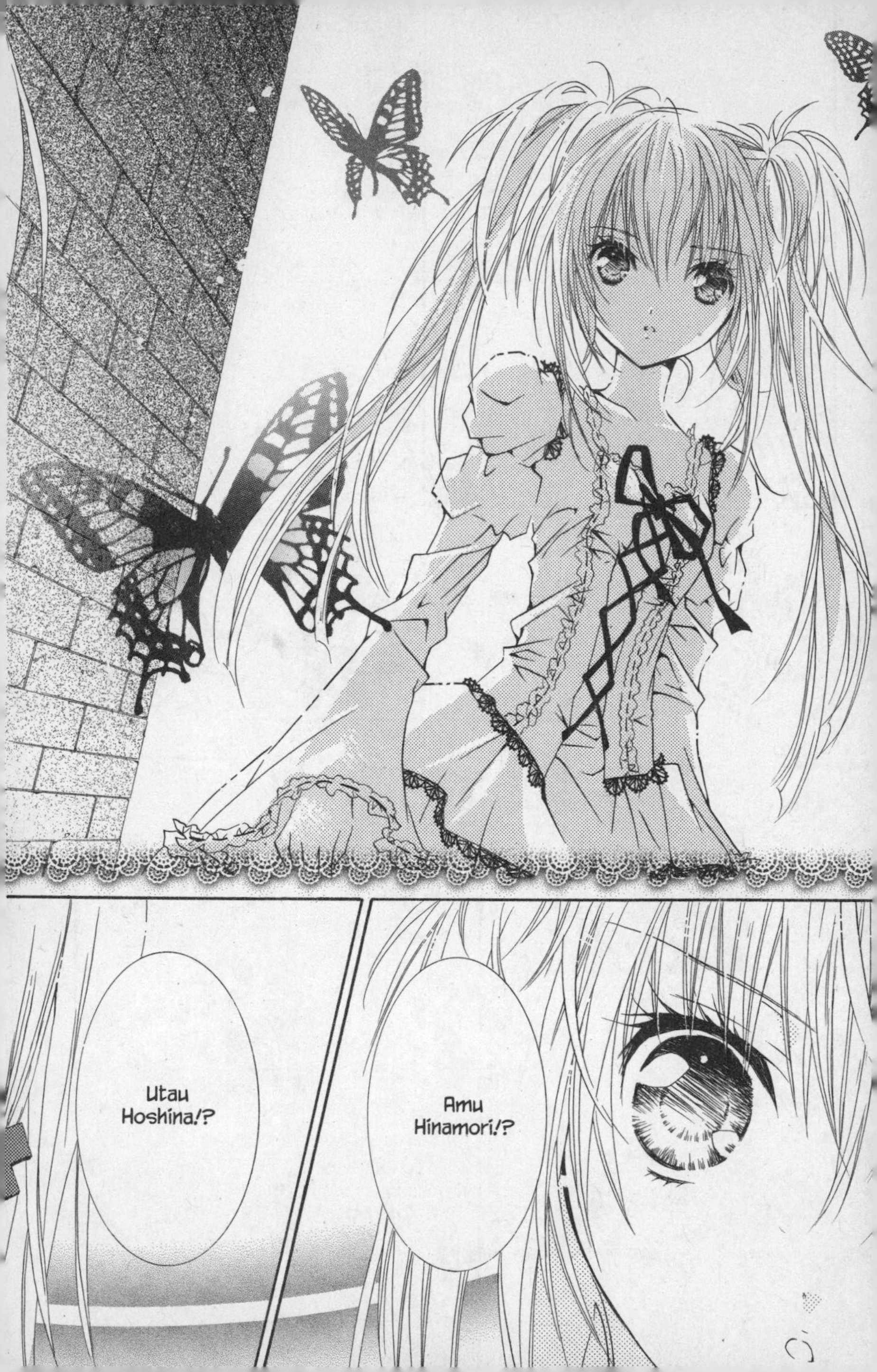
Amu Hinamori!?
Utau Hoshina!?

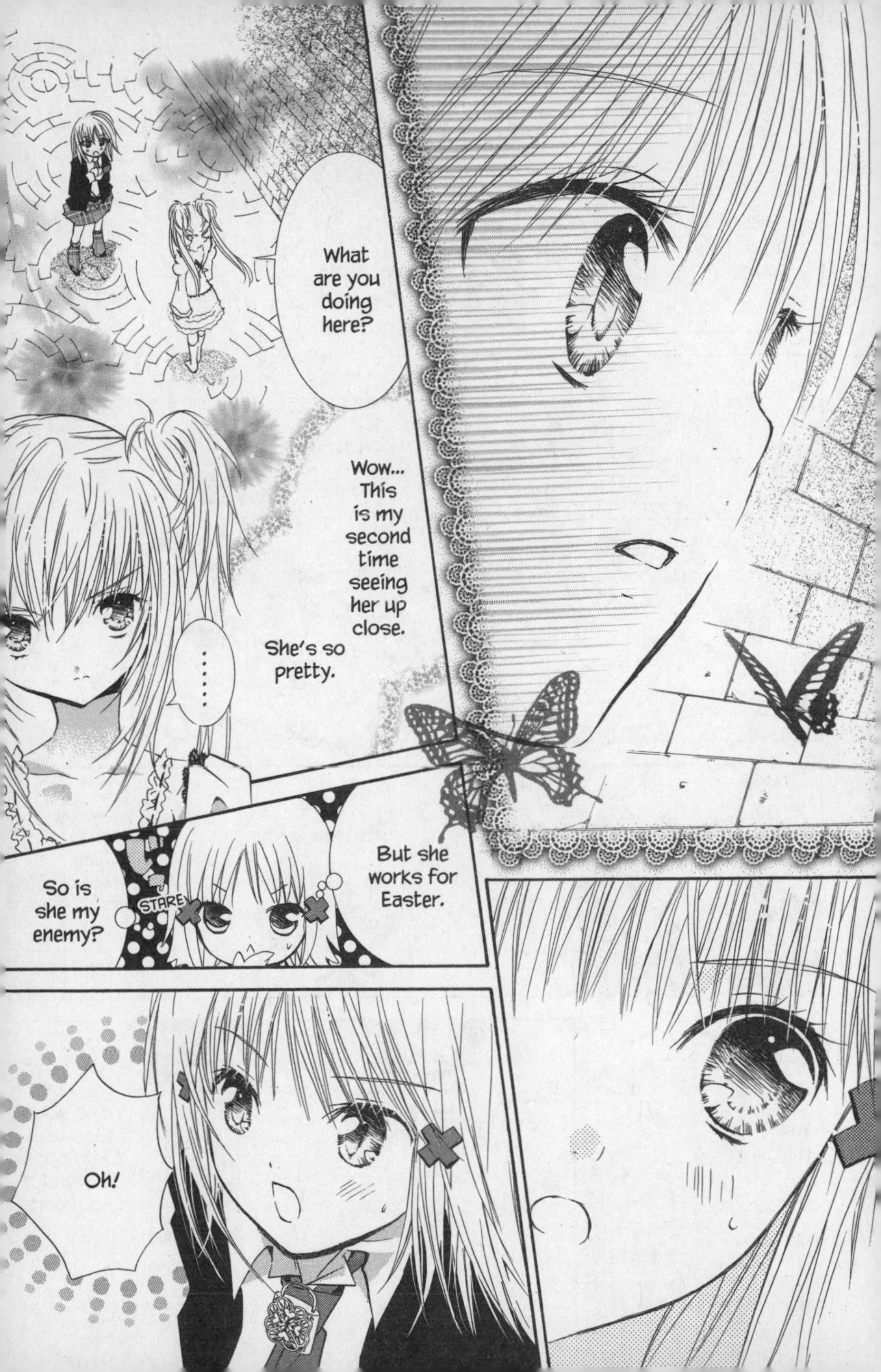
What are you doing here?
Wow... This is my second time seeing her up close.
She's so pretty.
......
But she works for Easter.
STARE
So is she my enemy?
Oh!

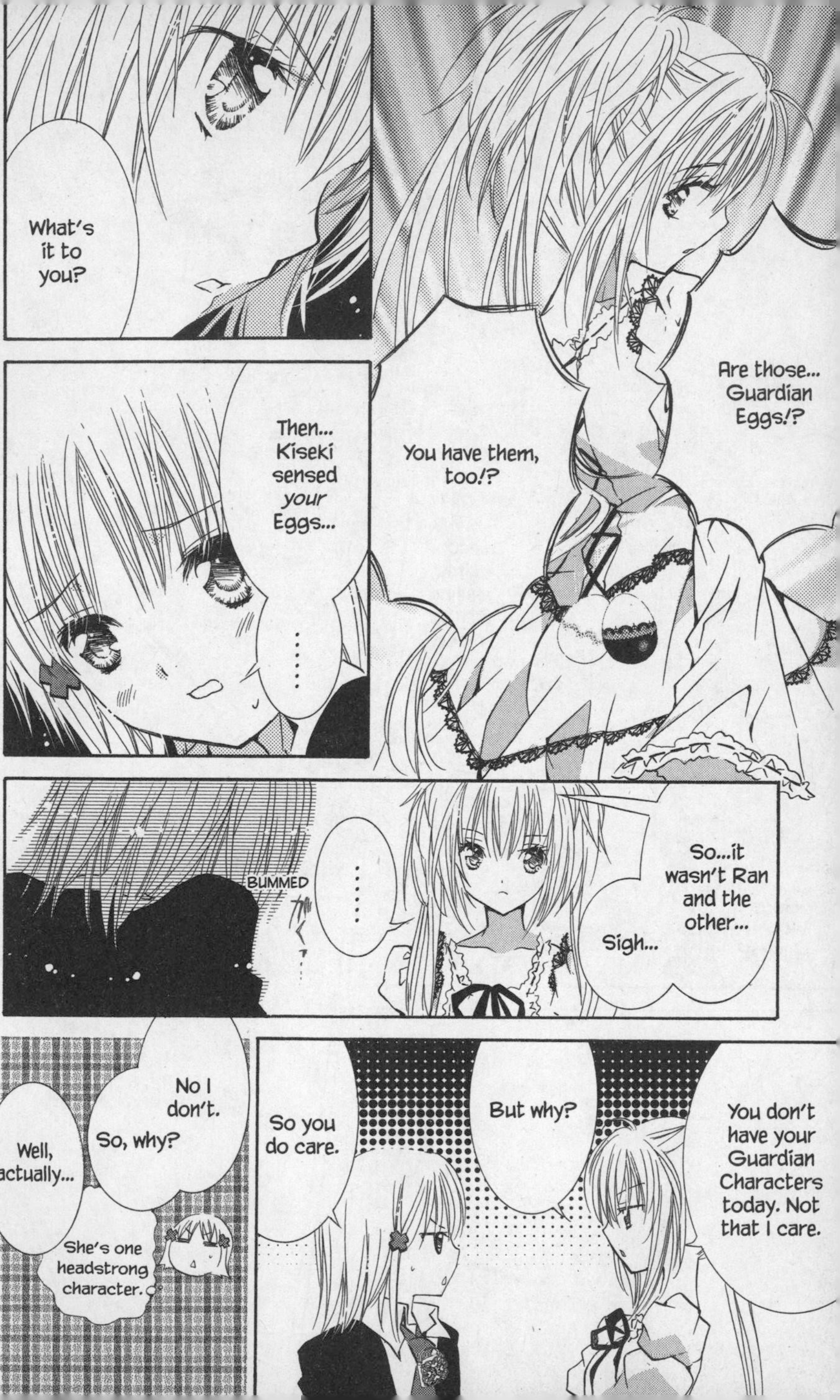
Are those... Guardian Eggs!?
You have them, too!?
What's it to you?
Then... Kiseki sensed *your* Eggs...
......
So...it wasn't Ran and the other...
Sigh...
......
BUMMED
You don't have your Guardian Characters today. Not that I care.
But why?
So you do care.
No I don't.
So, why?
Well, actually...
She's one headstrong character.

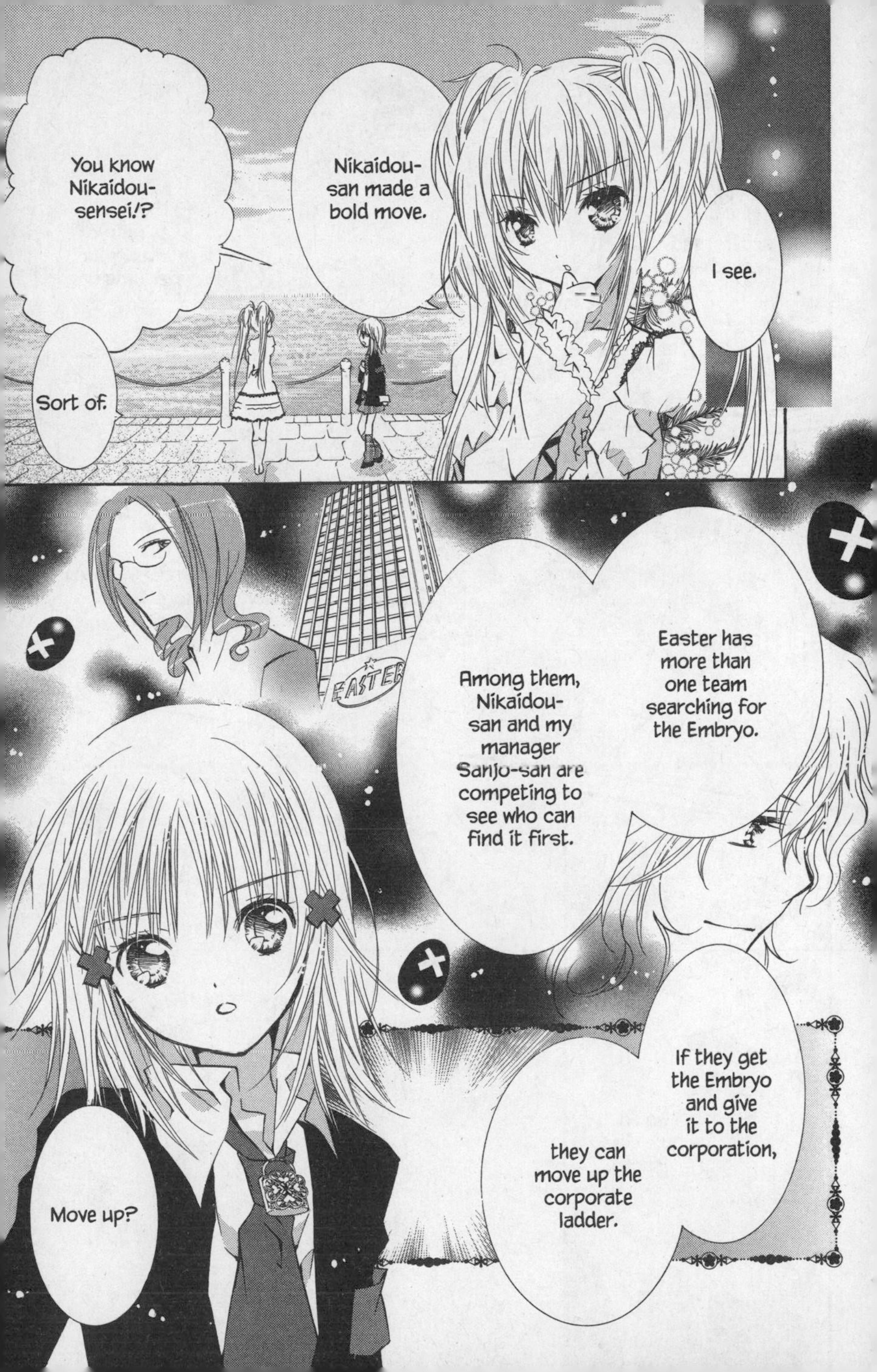
I see.
Nikaidou-san made a bold move.
You know Nikaidou-sensei!?
Sort of.
Easter has more than one team searching for the Embryo.
Among them, Nikaidou-san and my manager Sanjo-san are competing to see who can find it first.
EASTER
If they get the Embryo and give it to the corporation,
they can move up the corporate ladder.
Move up?

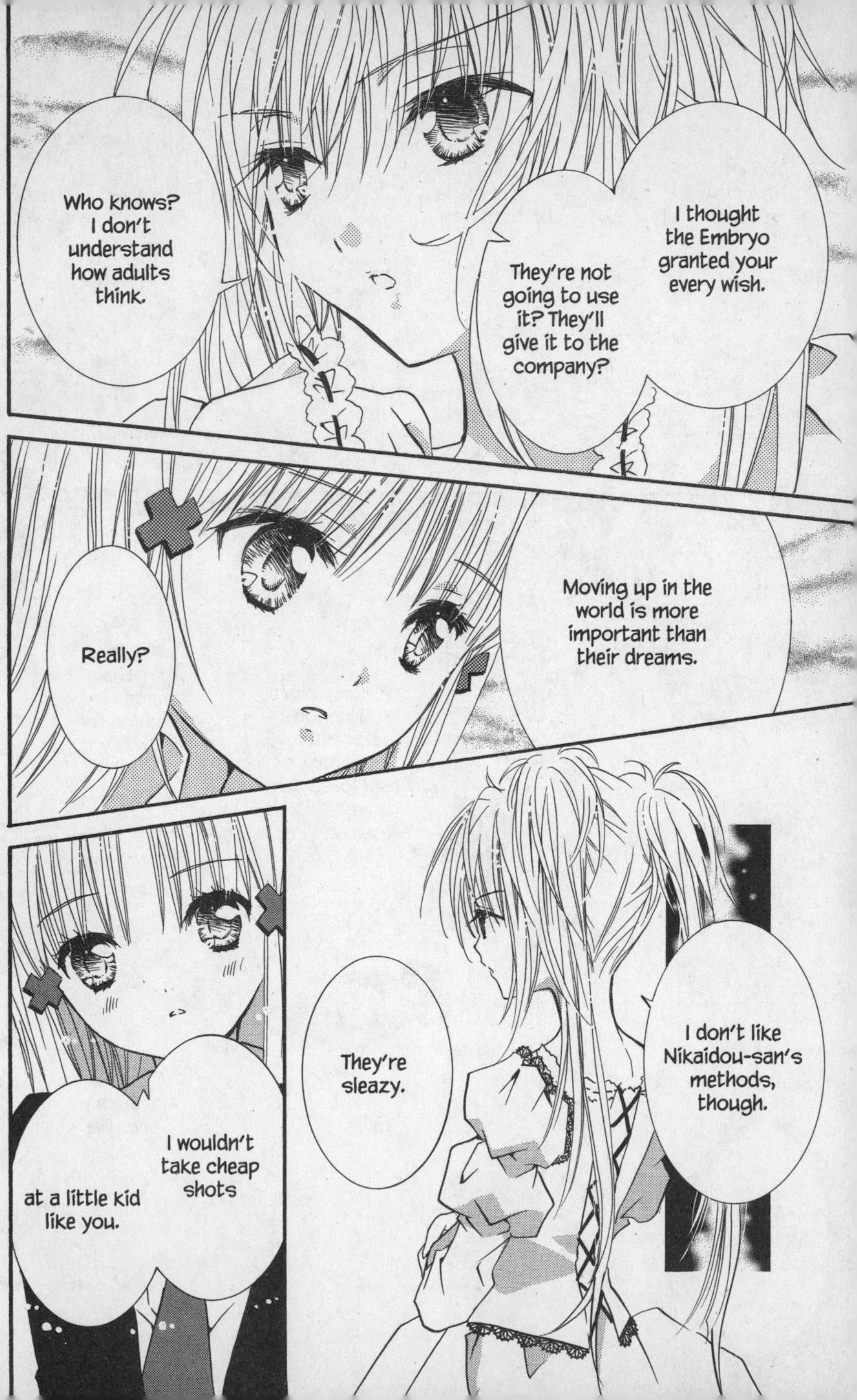
I thought the Embryo granted your every wish.
They're not going to use it? They'll give it to the company?
Who knows? I don't understand how adults think.
Moving up in the world is more important than their dreams.
Really?
I don't like Nikaidou-san's methods, though.
They're sleazy.
I wouldn't take cheap shots
at a little kid like you.

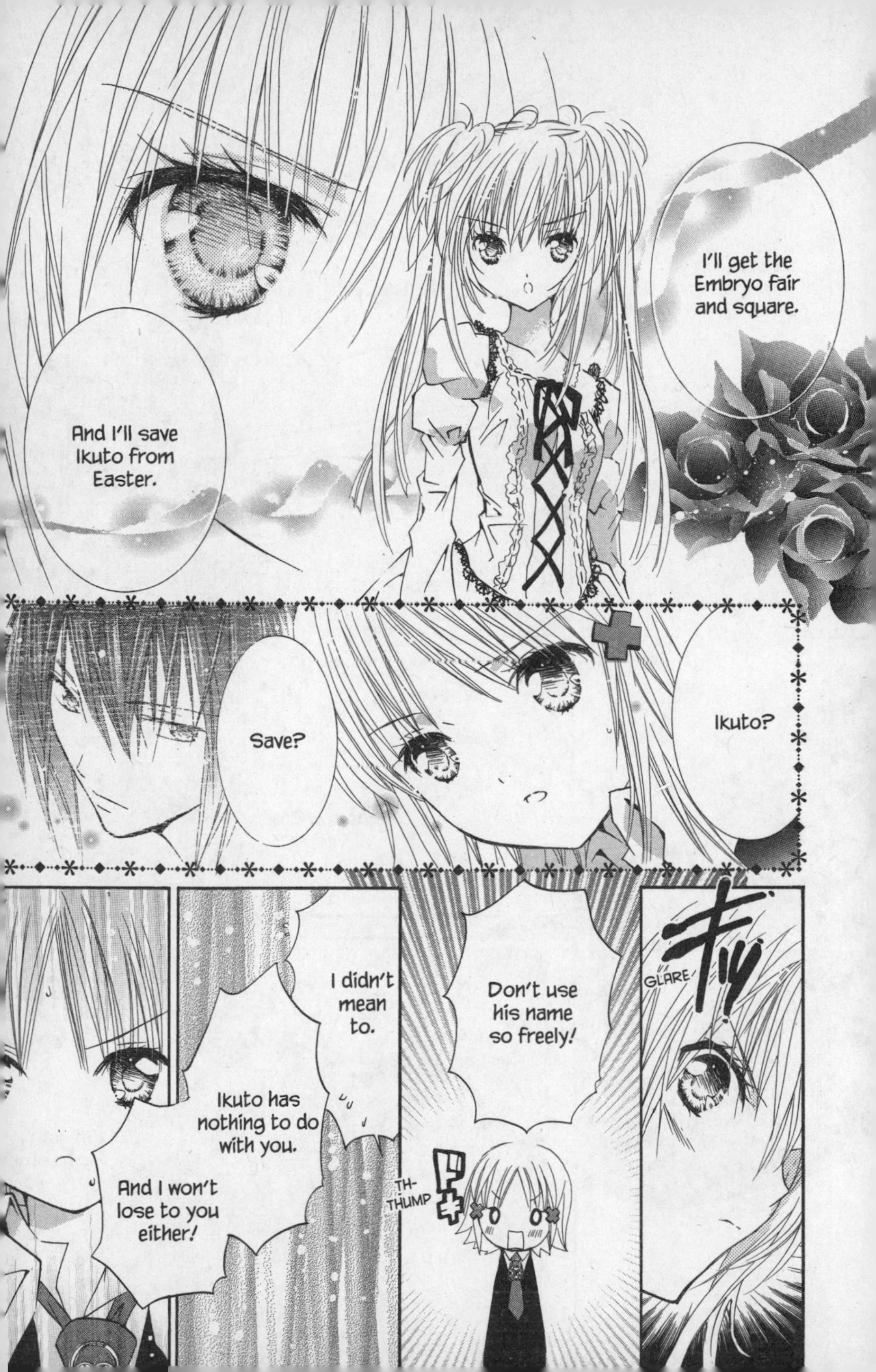
I'll get the Embryo fair and square.
And I'll save Ikuto from Easter.
Ikuto?
Save?
GLARE
Don't use his name so freely!
TH-THUMP
I didn't mean to.
Ikuto has nothing to do with you.
And I won't lose to you either!

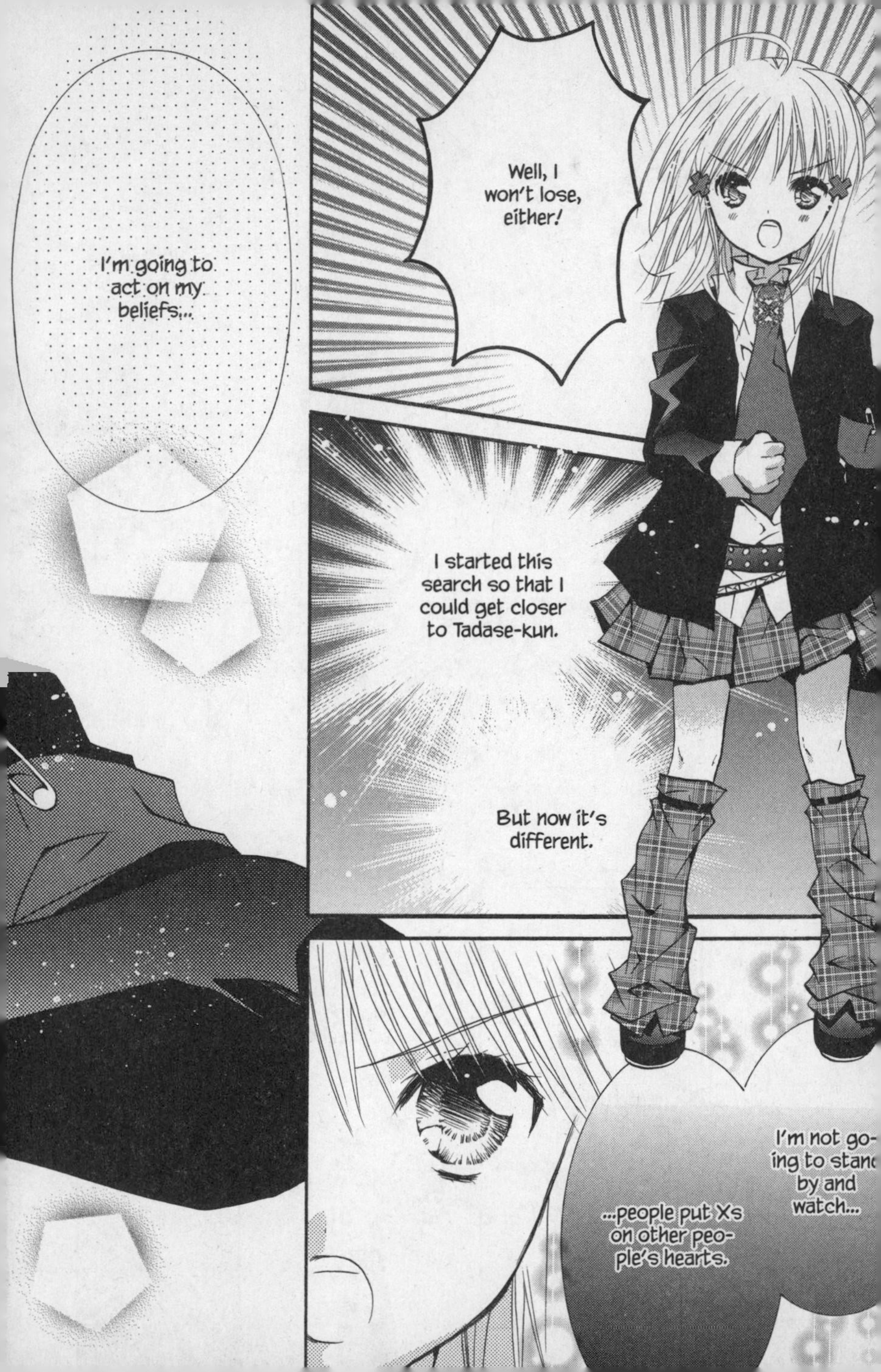
Well, I won't lose, either!
I started this search so that I could get closer to Tadase-kun.
But now it's different.
I'm not going to stand by and watch...
...people put Xs on other people's hearts.
I'm going to act on my beliefs...

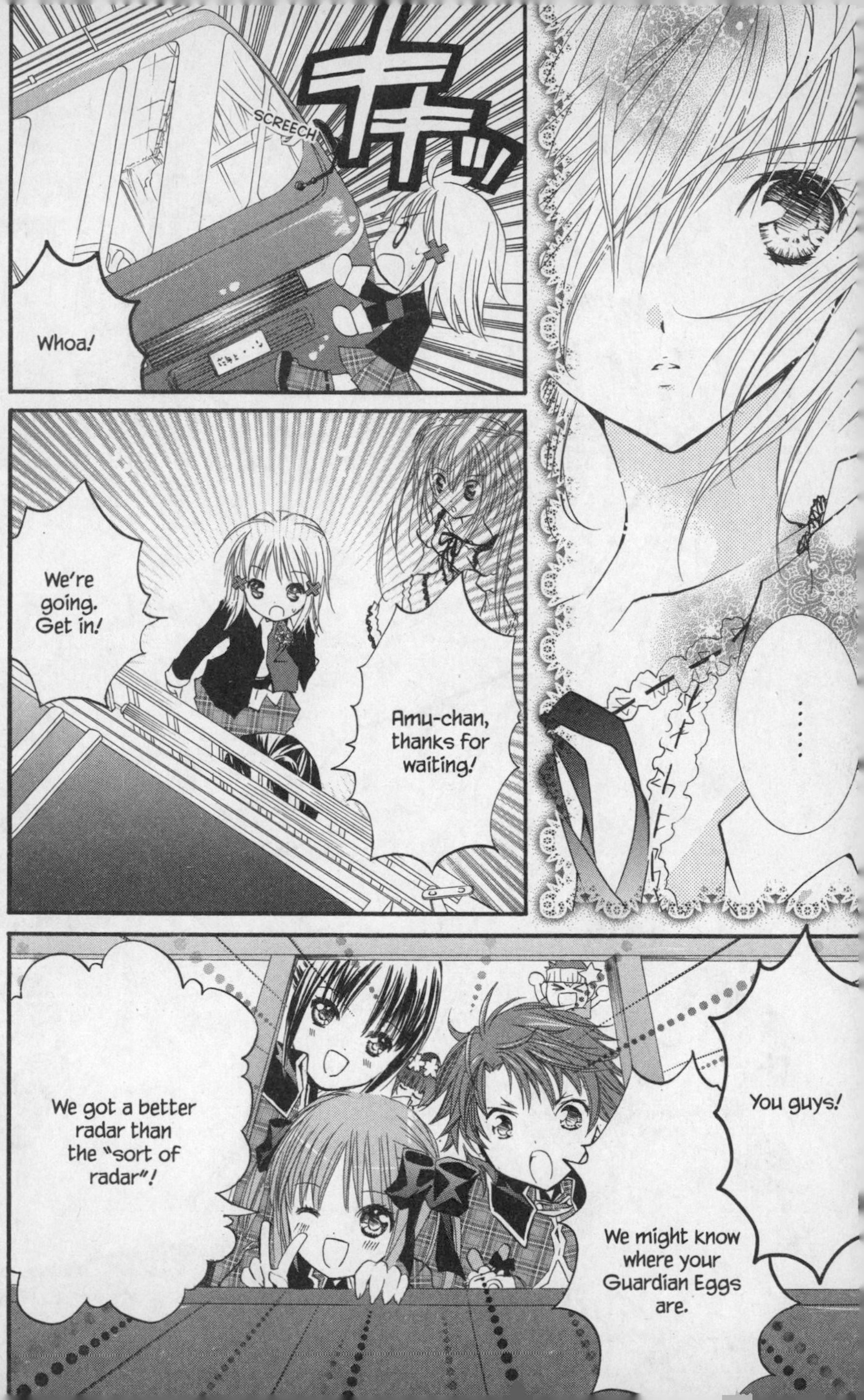
......
SCREECH!
キキッ
Whoa!
Amu-chan, thanks for waiting!
We're going. Get in!
You guys!
We might know where your Guardian Eggs are.
We got a better radar than the "sort of radar"!

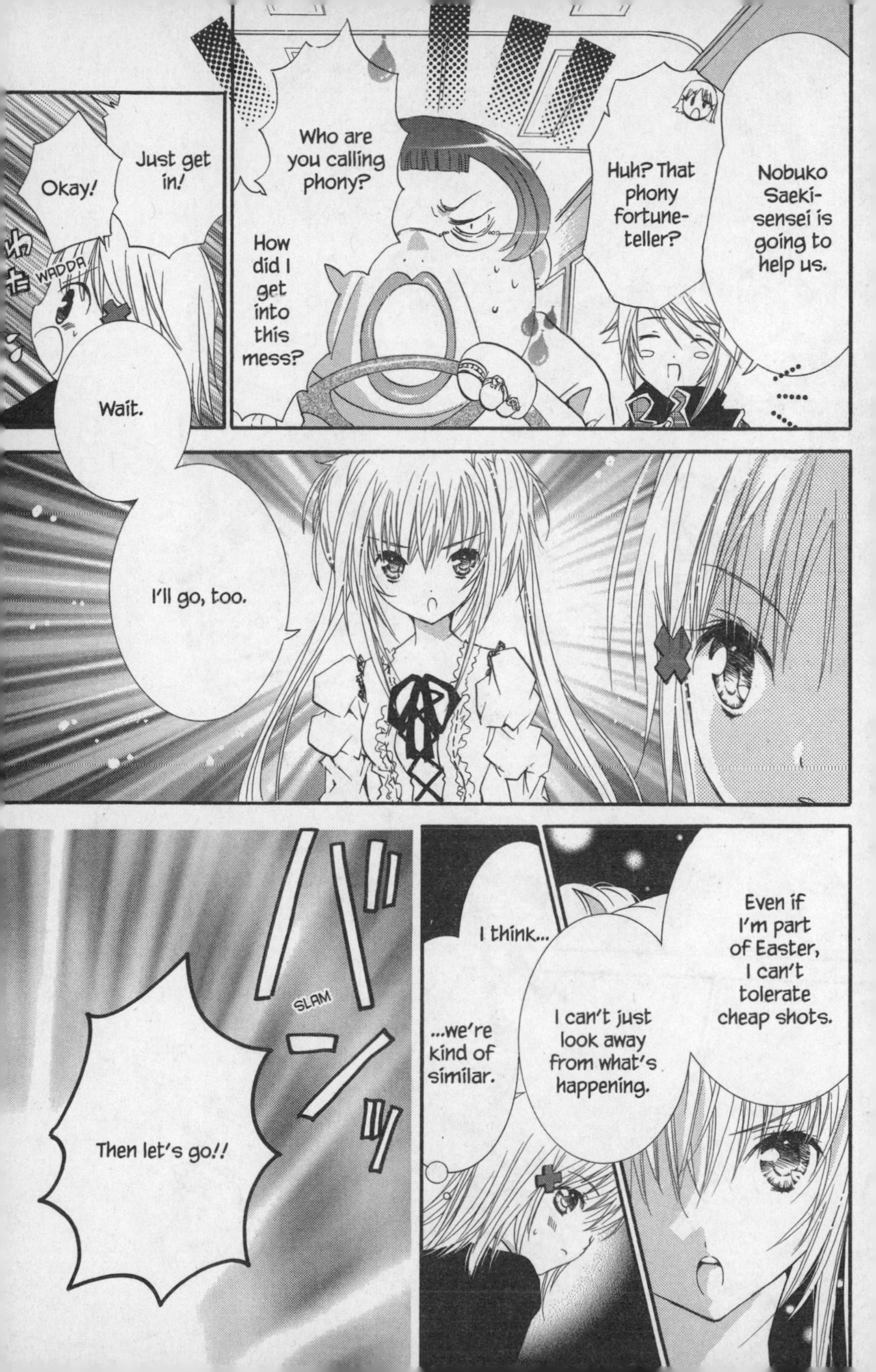
Nobuko Saeki-sensei is going to help us.
Huh? That phony fortune-teller?
......
Who are you calling phony?
How did I get into this mess?
Just get in!
Okay!
WADDA
Wait.
I'll go, too.
Even if I'm part of Easter, I can't tolerate cheap shots.
I can't just look away from what's happening.
I think...
...we're kind of similar.
SLAM
Then let's go!!

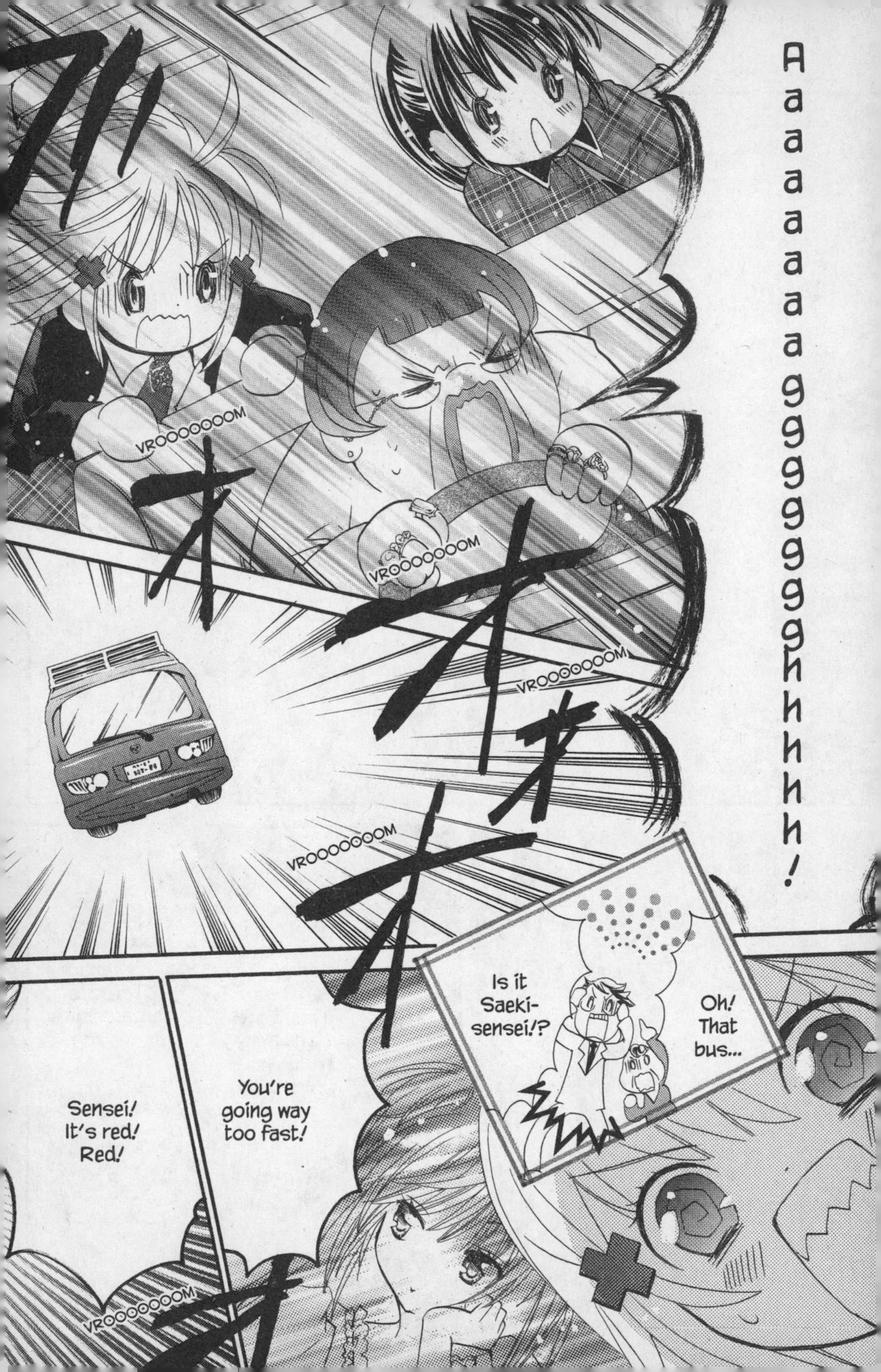
Aaaaaaagggggghhhhh!
VROOOOOOOM
VROOOOOOOM
VROOOOOOOM
VROOOOOOOM
Oh! That bus...
Is it Saeki-sensei!?
You're going way too fast!
Sensei! It's red! Red!
VROOOOOOOM

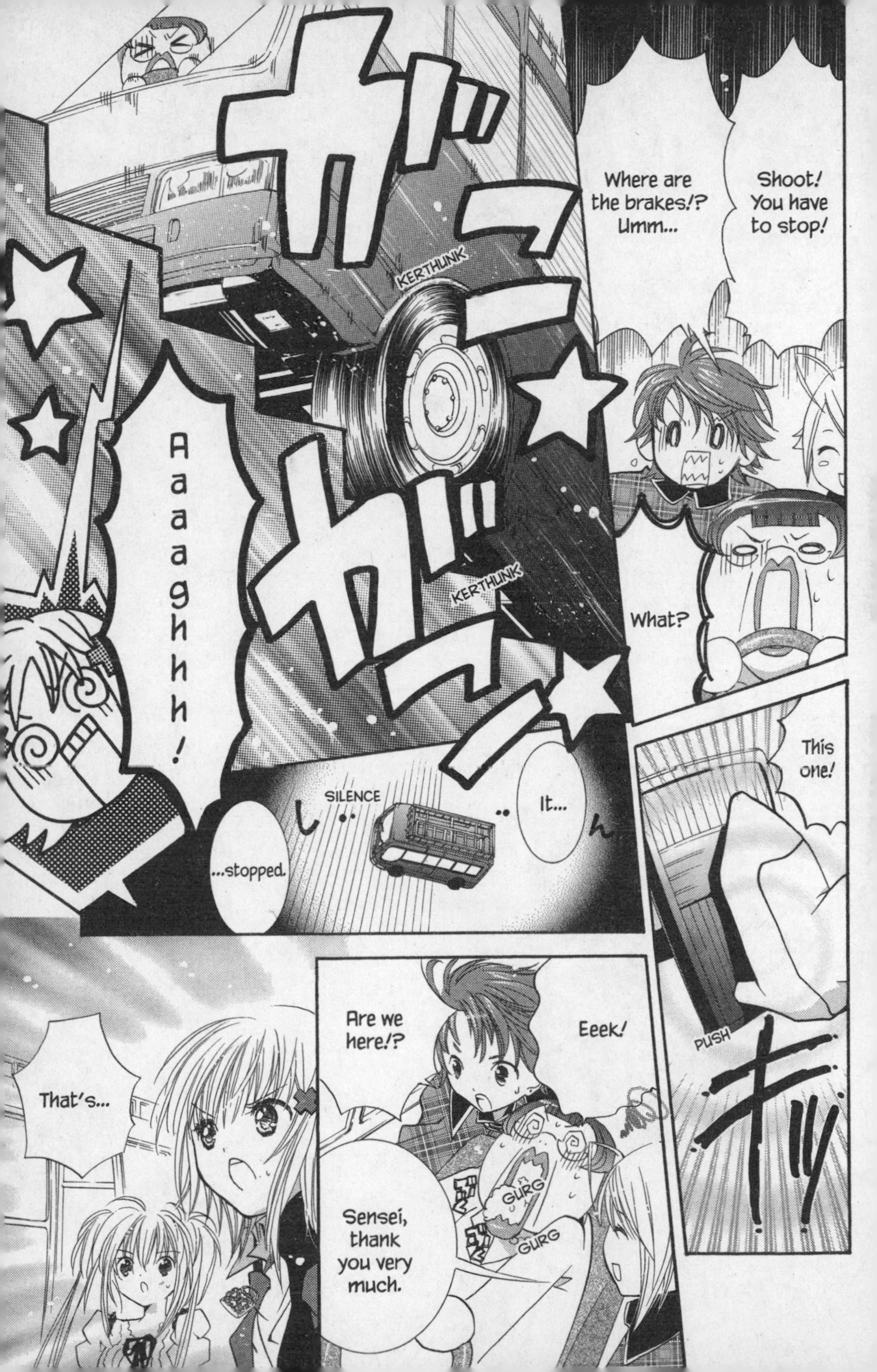
Shoot! You have to stop!
Where are the brakes!? Umm...
What?
This one!
PUSH
KERTHUNK
KERTHUNK
Aaaaghhh!
It...
SILENCE
...stopped.
Eeek!
Are we here!?
GURG
GURG
Sensei, thank you very much.
That's...

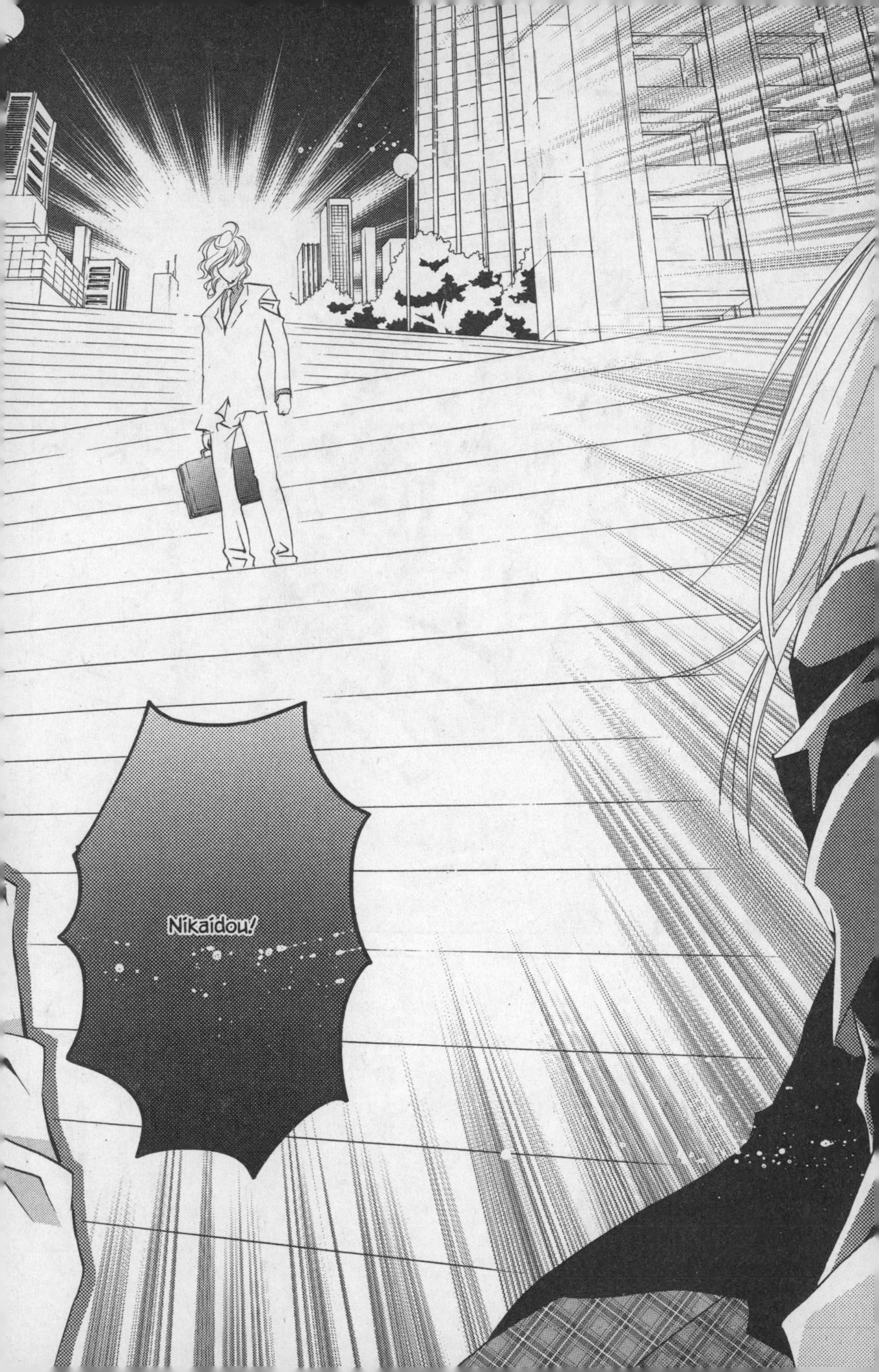
Nikaidou!

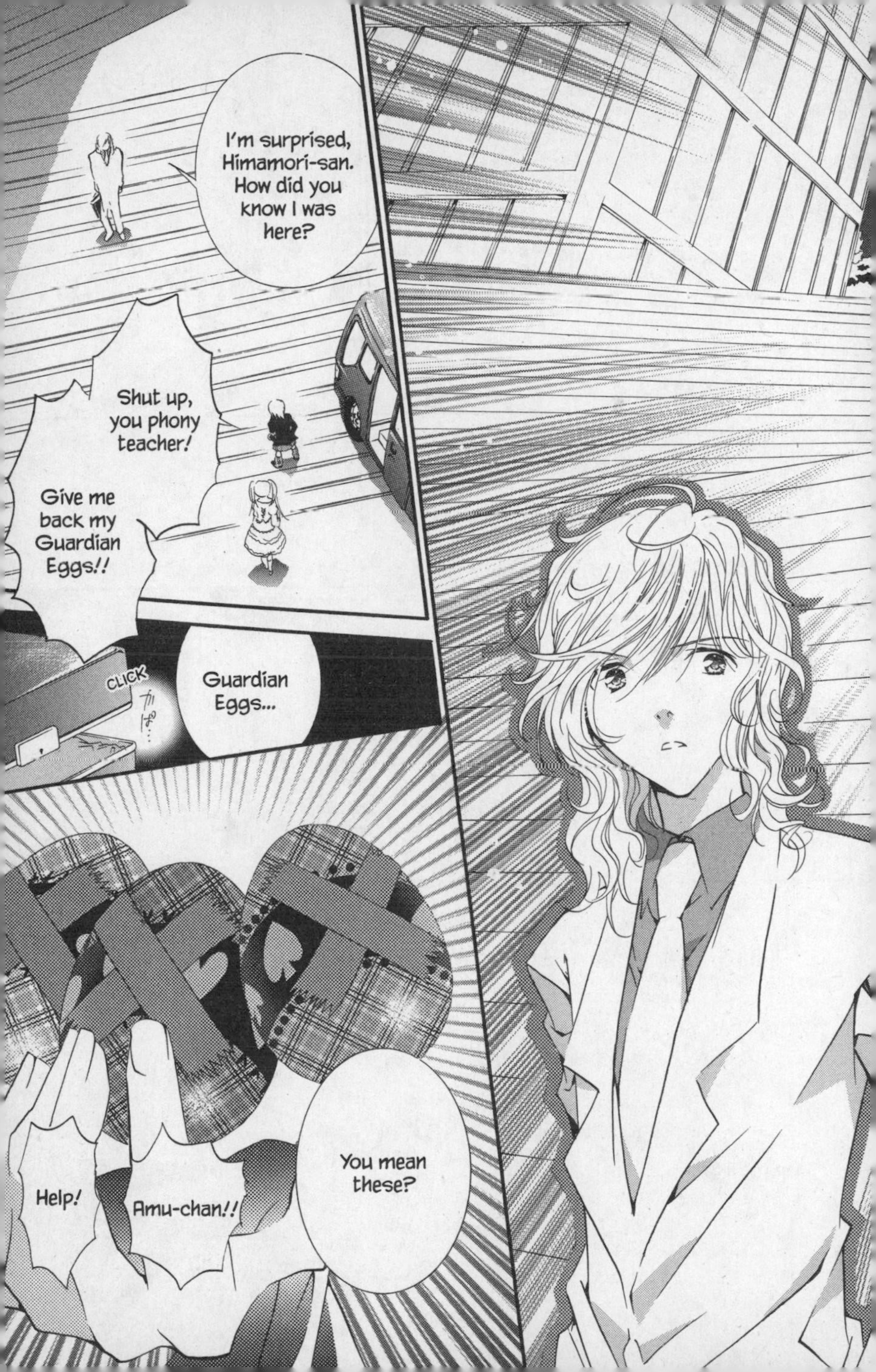
I'm surprised, Himamori-san. How did you know I was here?
Shut up, you phony teacher!
Give me back my Guardian Eggs!!
Guardian Eggs...
CLICK
You mean these?
Amu-chan!!
Help!

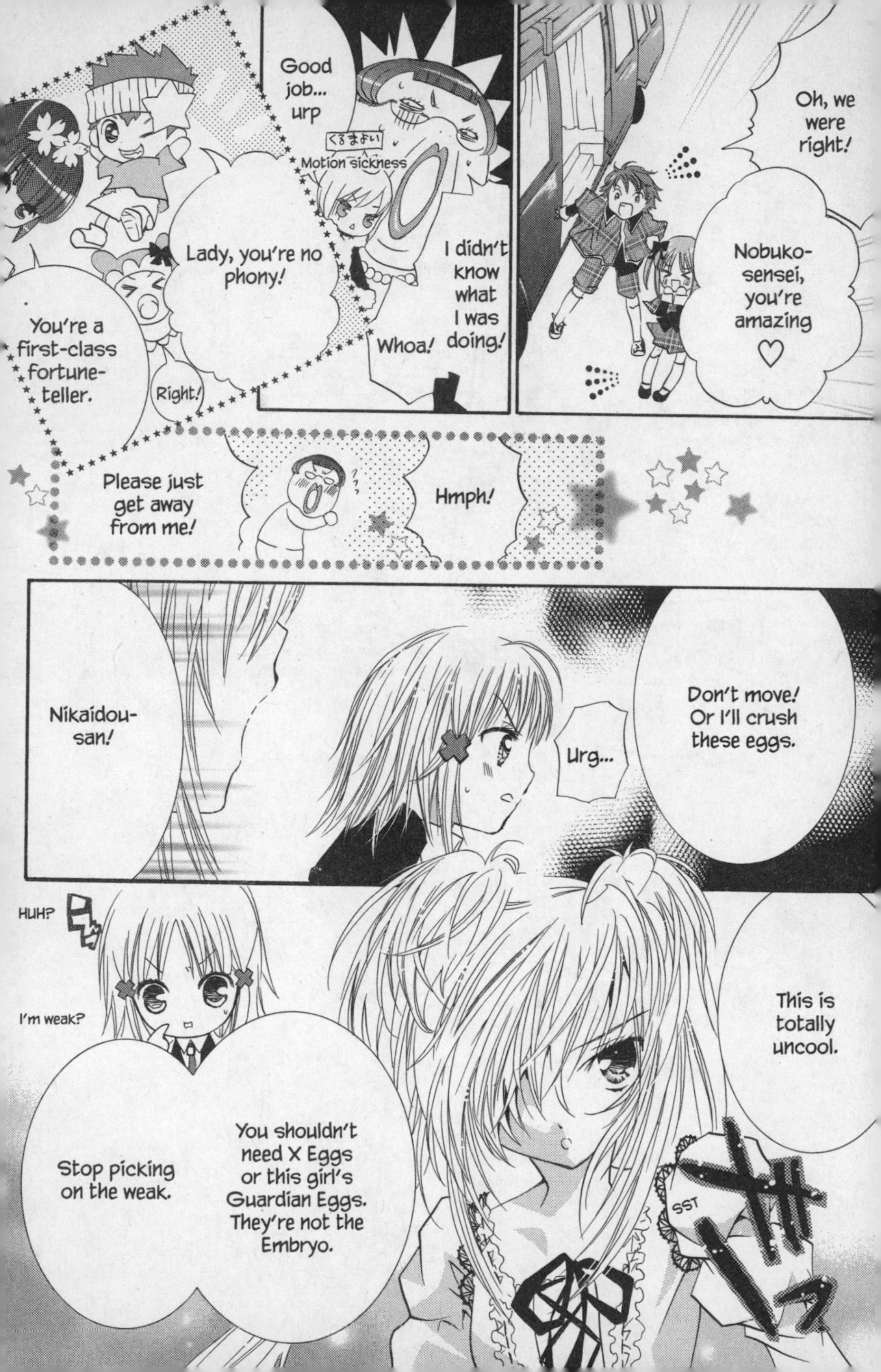
Oh, we were right!
Nobuko-sensei, you're amazing ♡
Good job... urp
くるまよい
Motion sickness
I didn't know what I was doing!
Whoa!
Lady, you're no phony!
You're a first-class fortune-teller.
Right!
Hmph!
Please just get away from me!
Don't move! Or I'll crush these eggs.
Urg...
Nikaidou-san!
This is totally uncool.
SST
You shouldn't need X Eggs or this girl's Guardian Eggs. They're not the Embryo.
Stop picking on the weak.
HUH?
I'm weak?

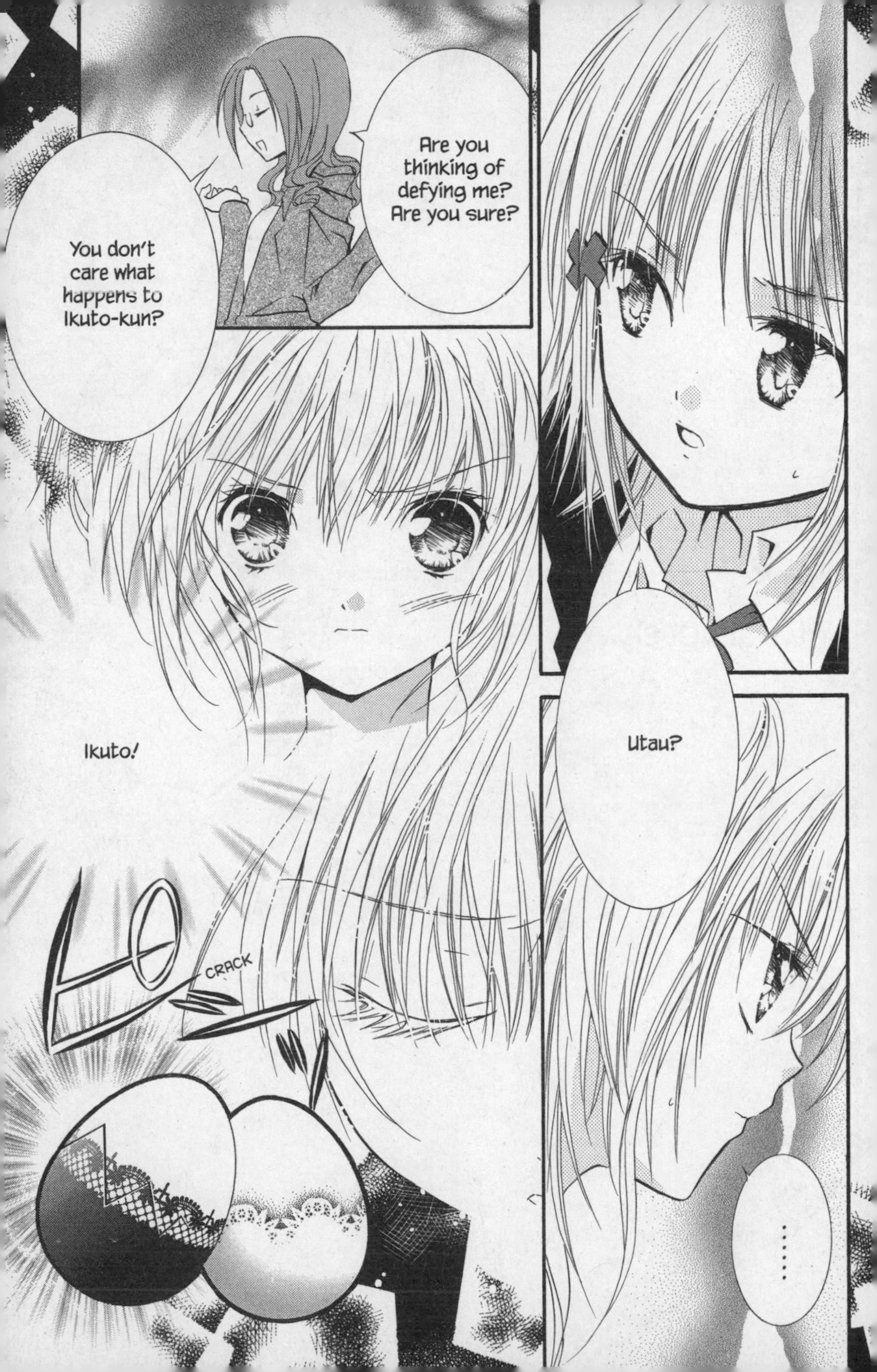
Are you thinking of defying me? Are you sure?
You don't care what happens to Ikuto-kun?
Ikuto!
CRACK
Utau?
......

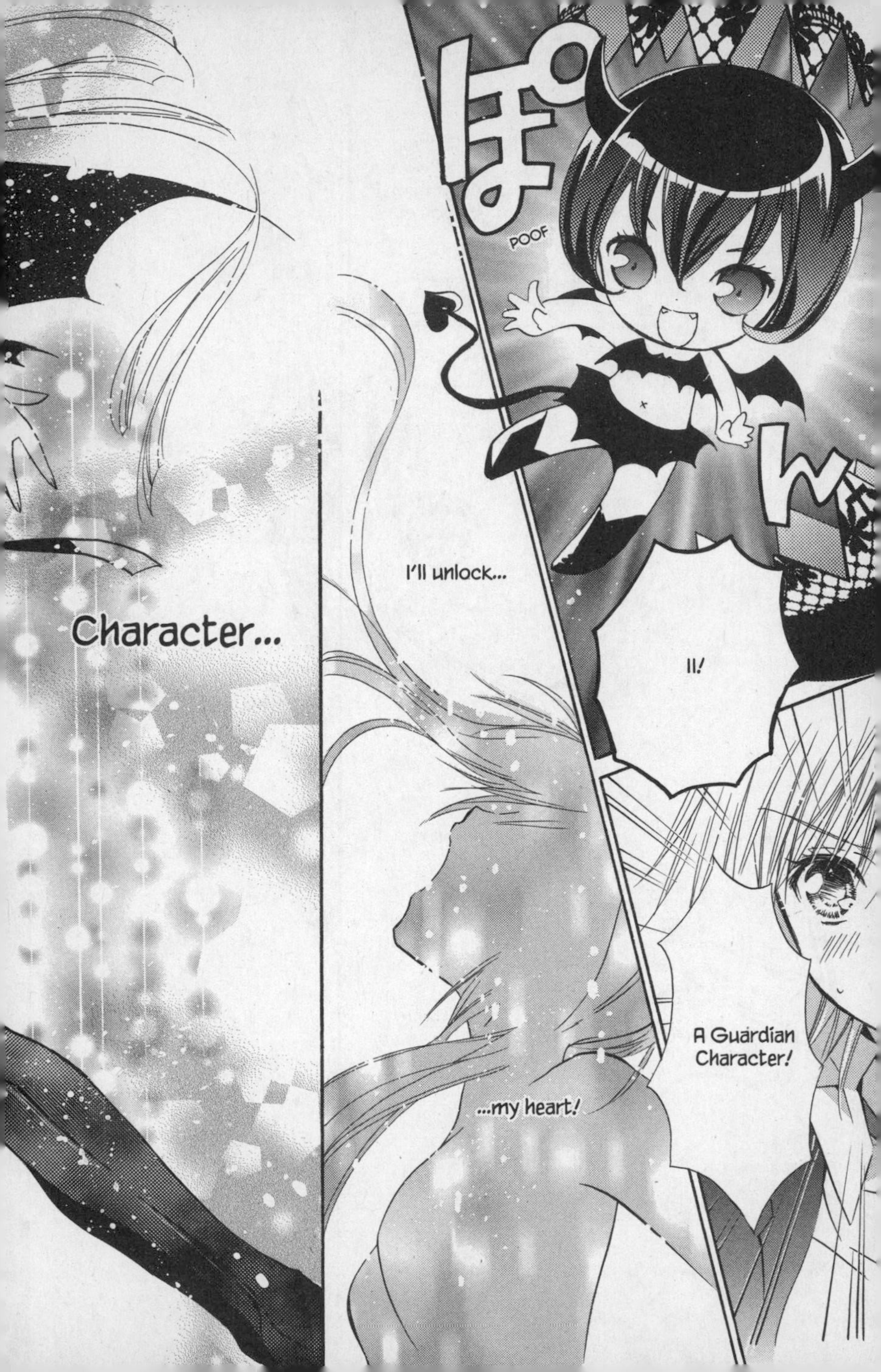
ぽん
POOF
!!
A Guardian Character!
I'll unlock...
...my heart!
Character...

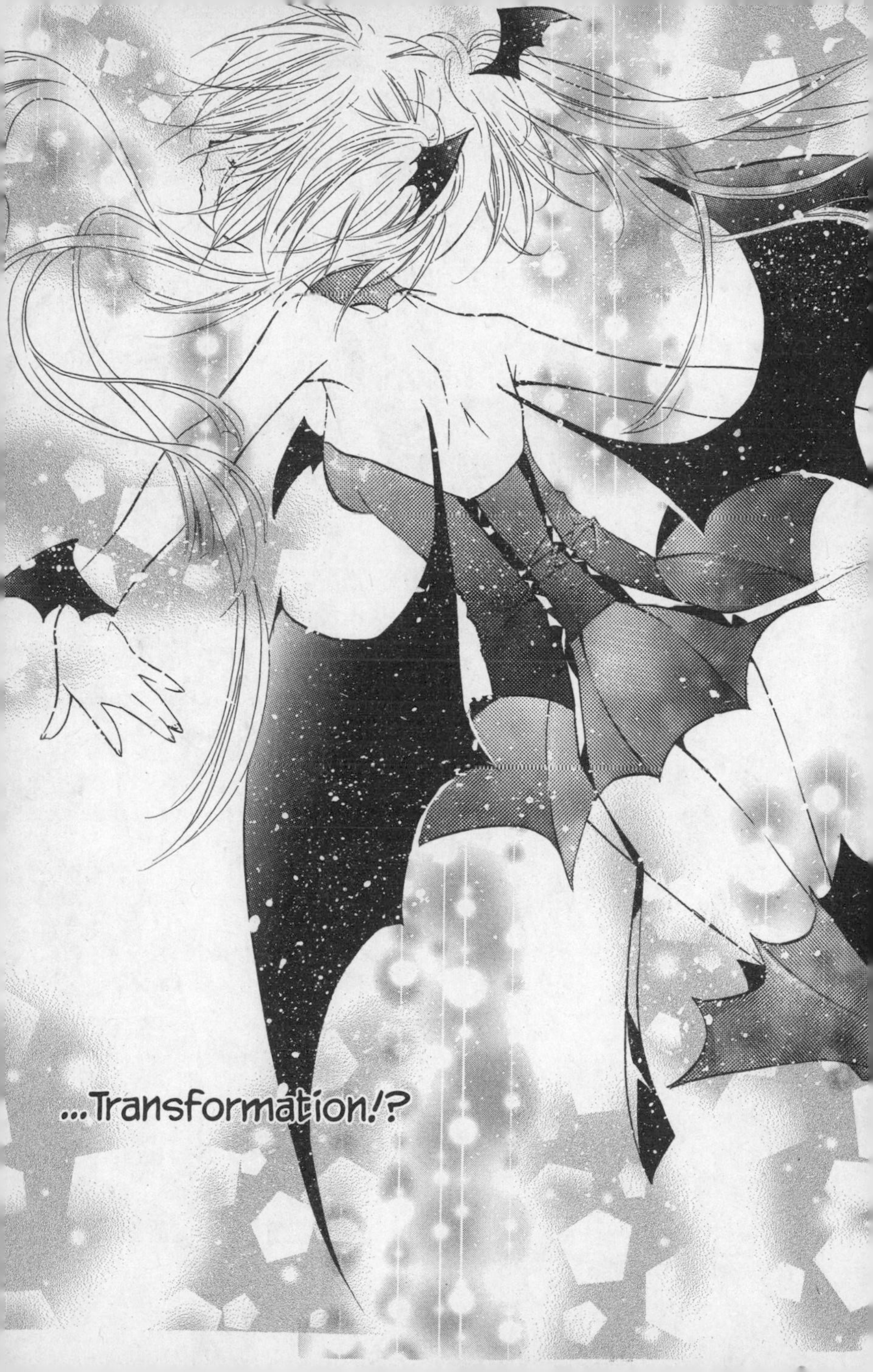
...Transformation!?

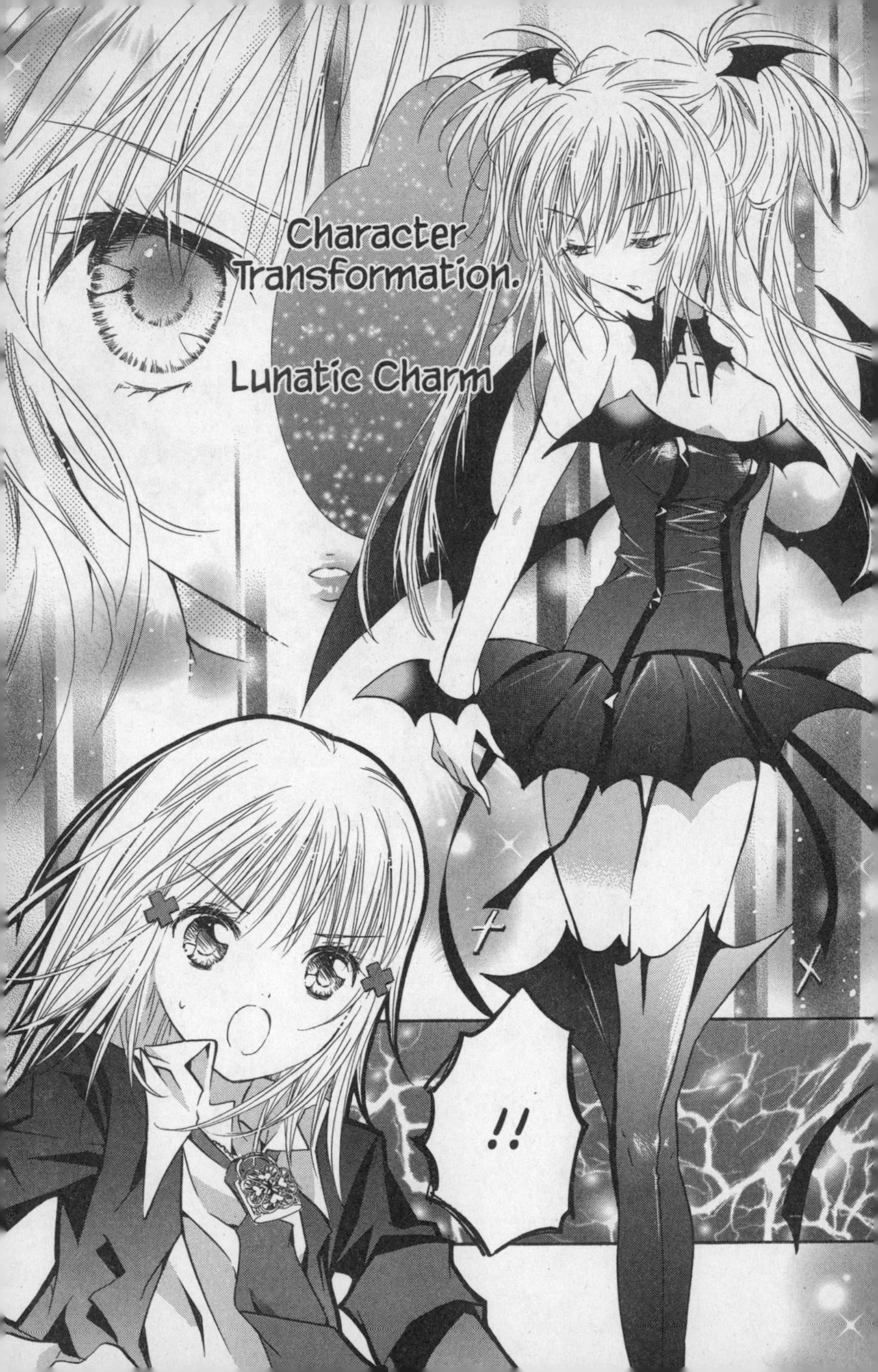
Character Transformation.
Lunatic Charm
!!

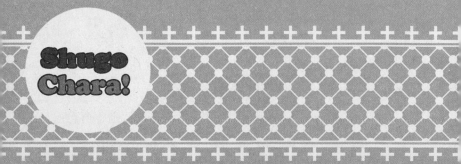
Shugo Chara!

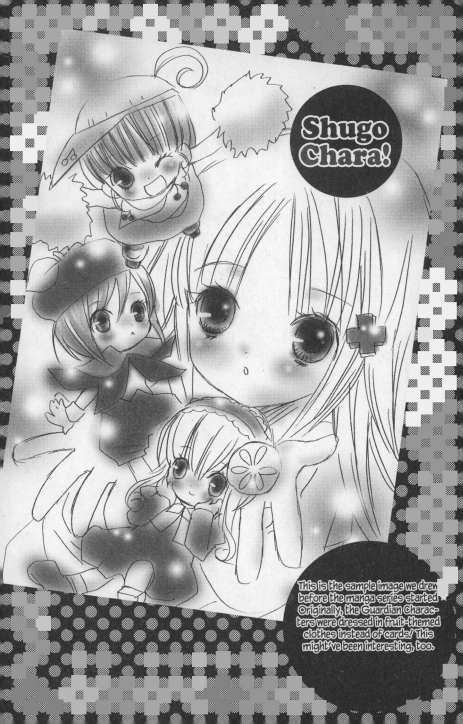

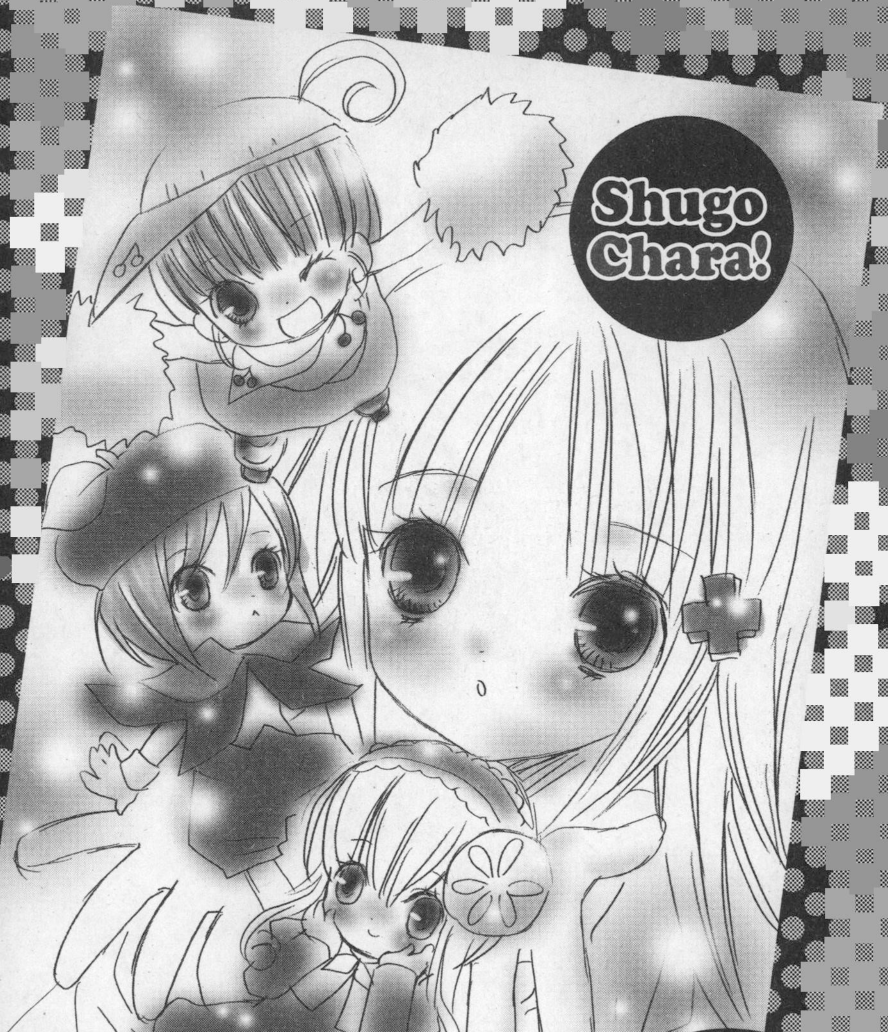
Shugo
Chara!

This is the sample image we drew before the manga series started★ Originally, the Guardian Characters were dressed in fruit-themed clothes instead of cards! This might've been interesting, too.

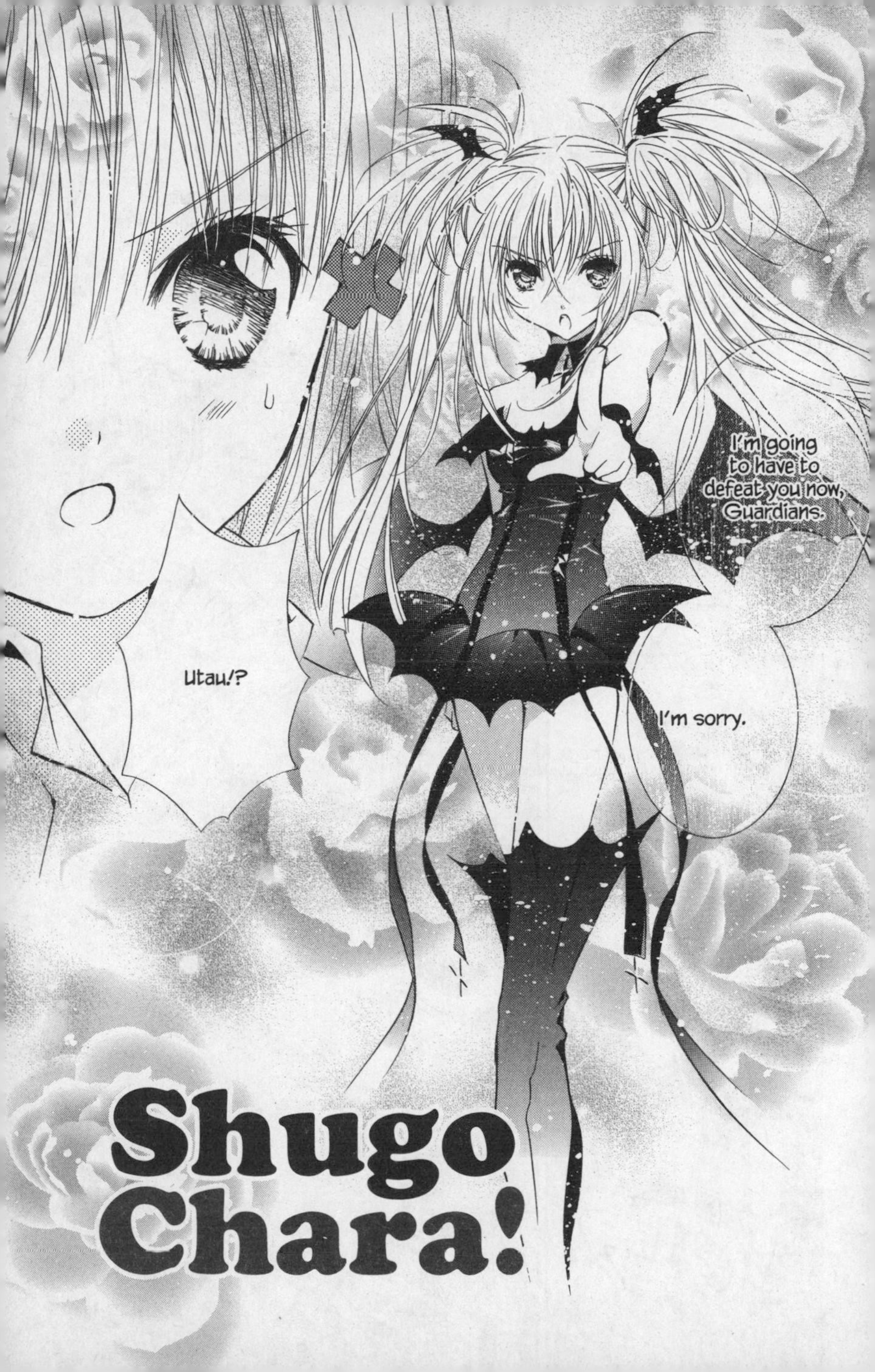

I'm going to have to defeat you now, Guardians.
I'm sorry.
Utau!?
Shugo Chara!

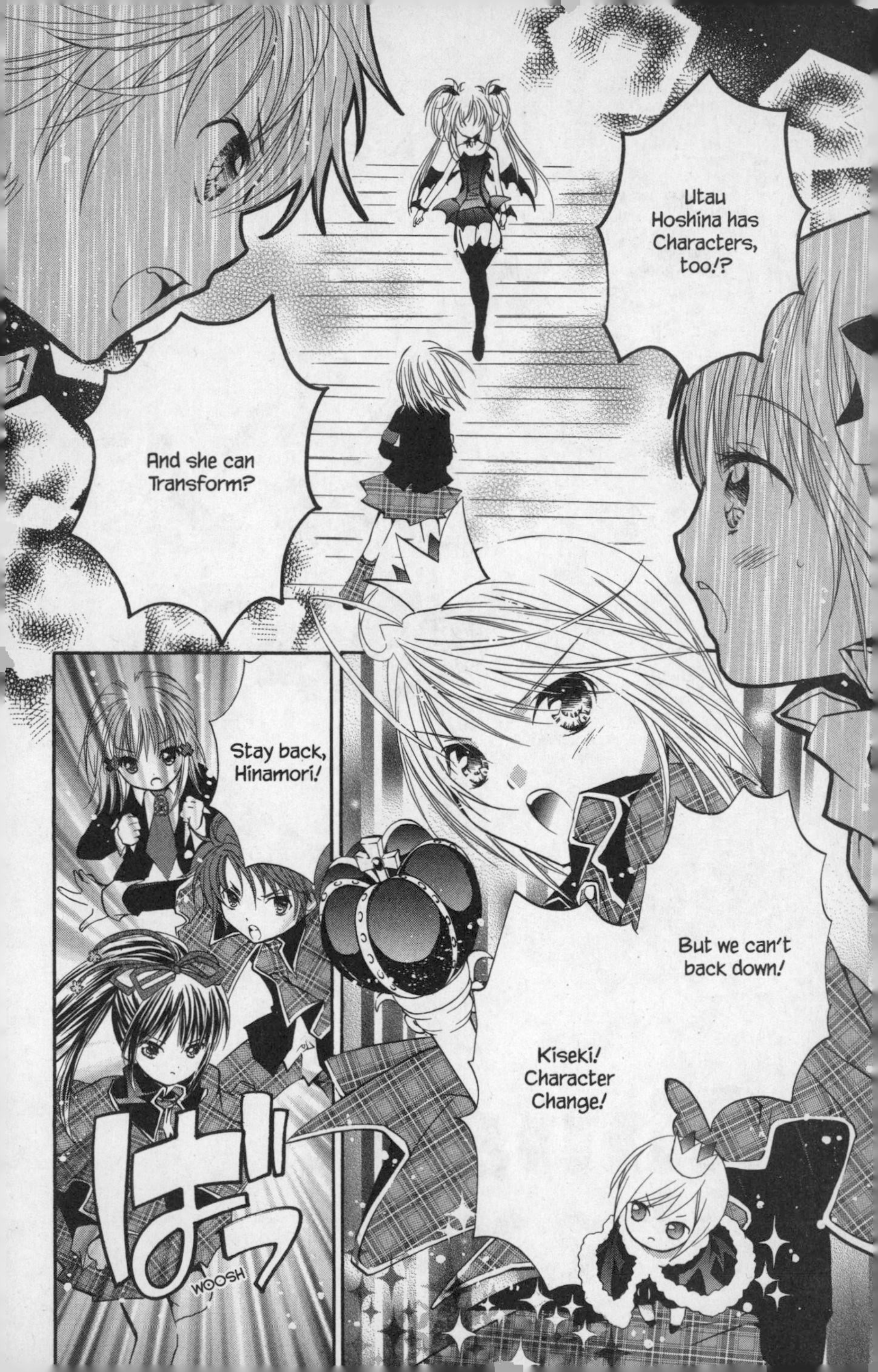
Utau Hoshina has Characters, too!?
And she can Transform?
But we can't back down!
Kiseki! Character Change!
Stay back, Hinamori!
WOOSH

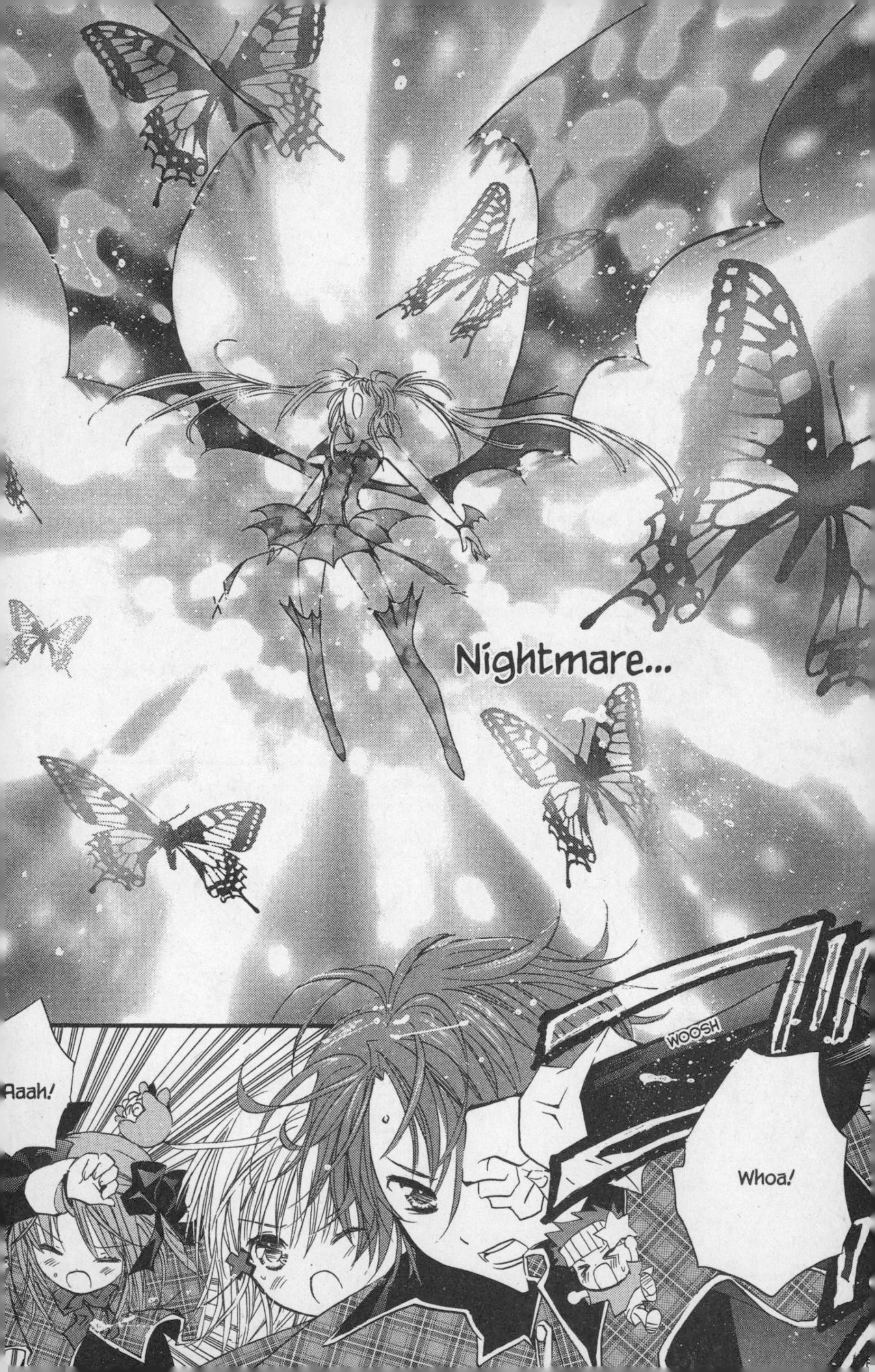
Nightmare...
WOOSH
Whoa!
Aaah!

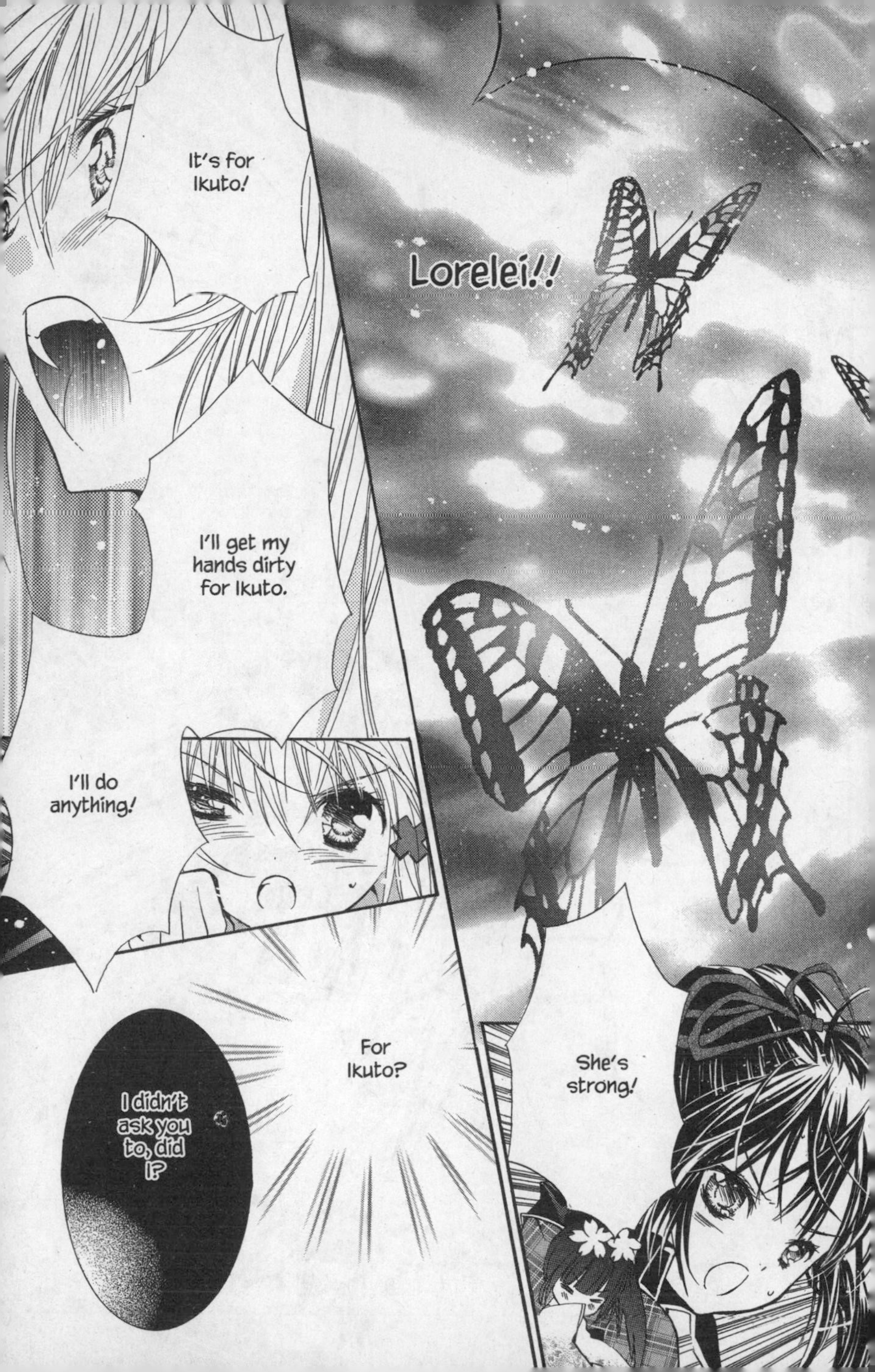
Lorelei!!
She's strong!
It's for Ikuto!
I'll get my hands dirty for Ikuto.
I'll do anything!
For Ikuto?
I didn't ask you to, did I?

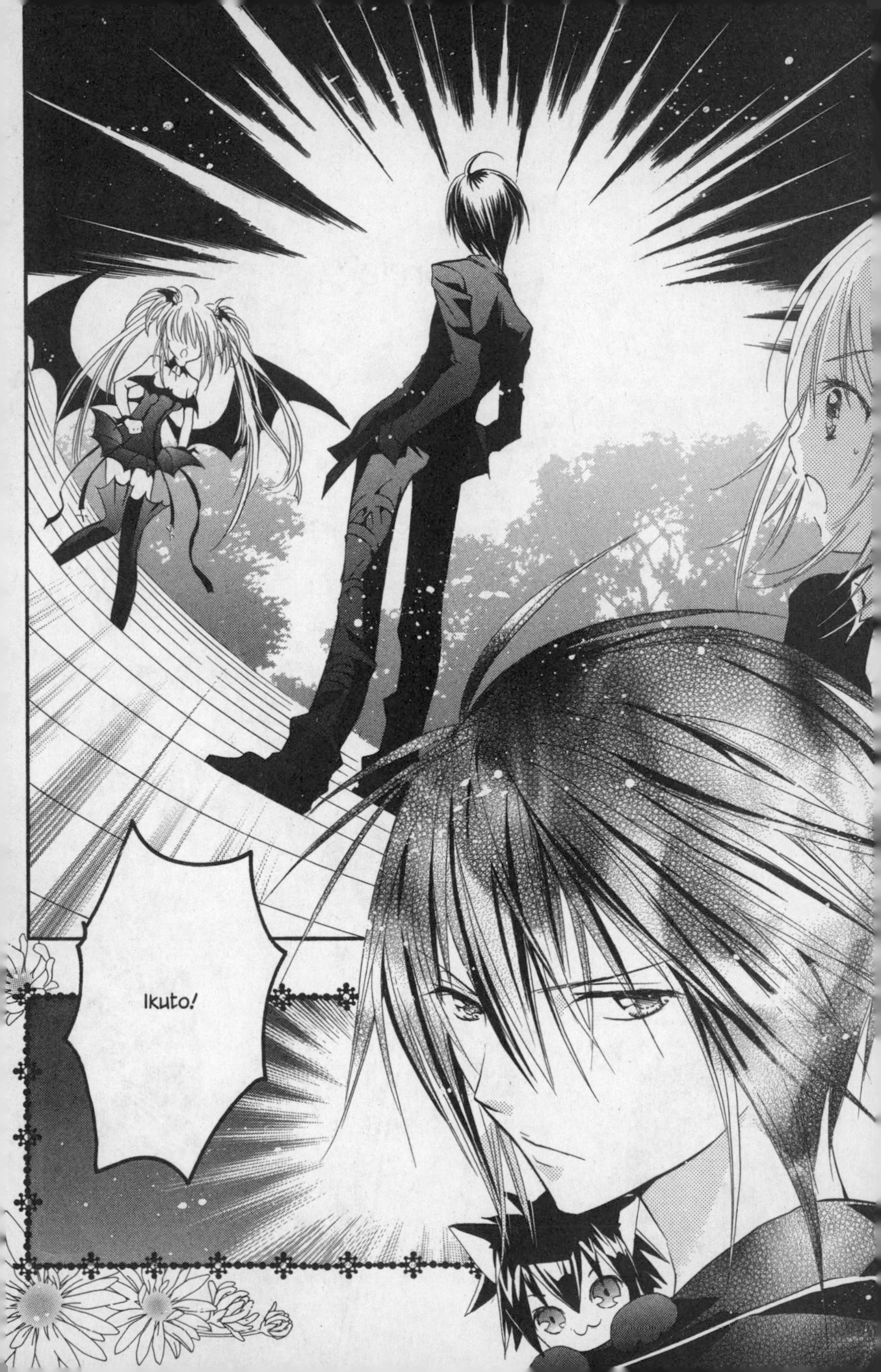
Ikuto!

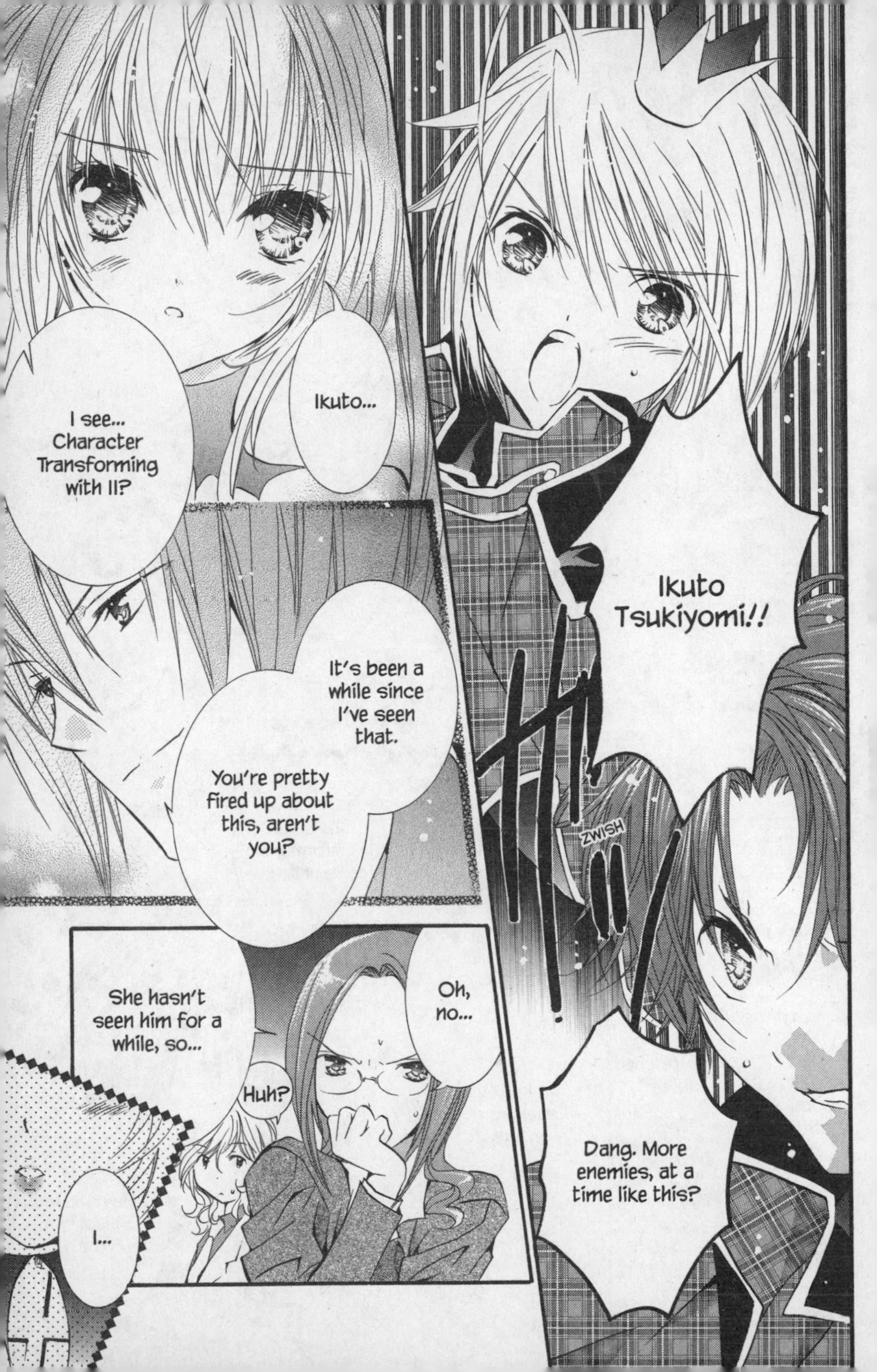
Ikuto Tsukiyomi!!
ZWISH
Dang. More enemies, at a time like this?
Ikuto...
I see... Character Transforming with II?
It's been a while since I've seen that.
You're pretty fired up about this, aren't you?
Oh, no...
She hasn't seen him for a while, so...
Huh?
I...

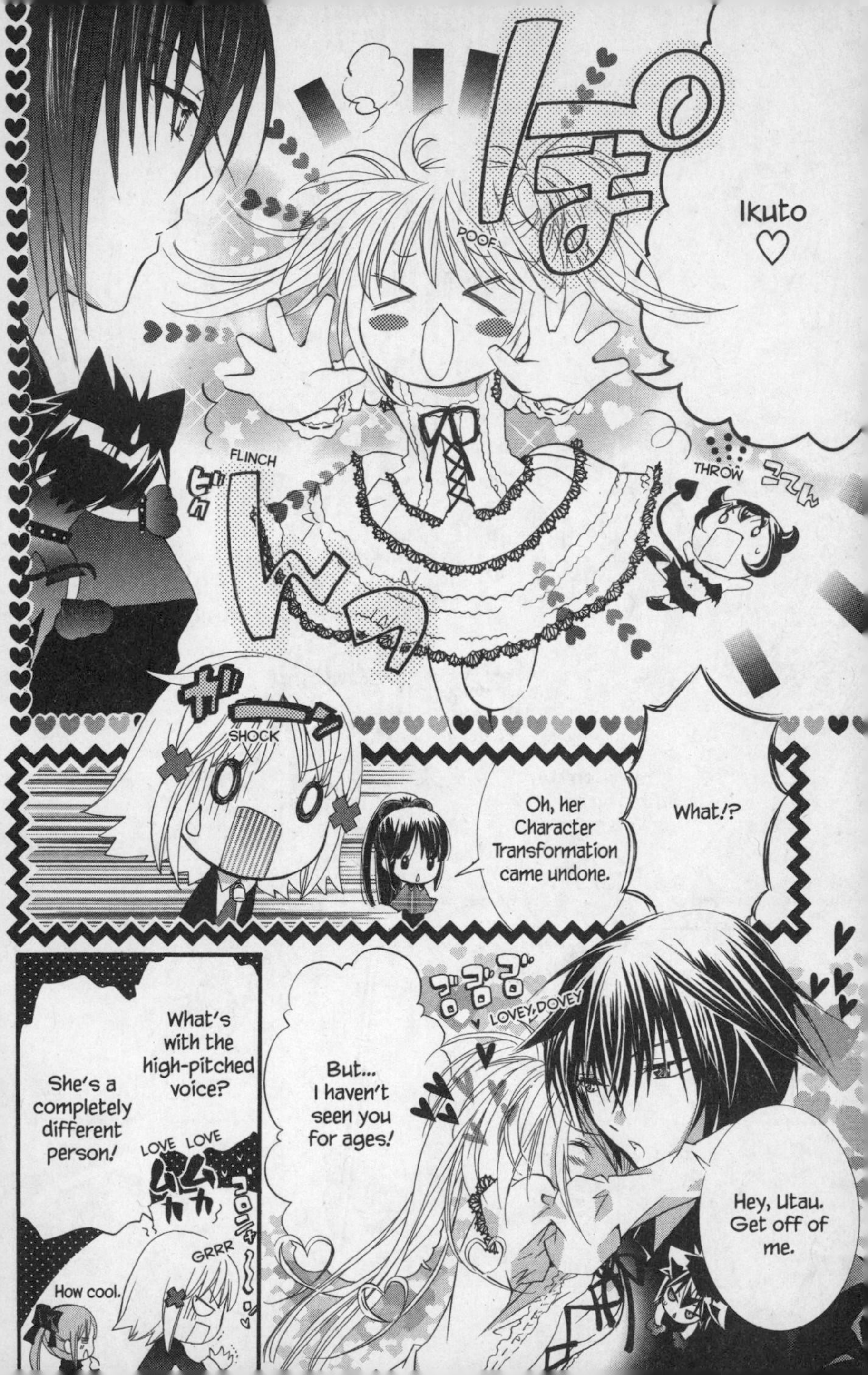
Ikuto ♡
POOF
THROW
FLINCH
What!?
Oh, her Character Transformation came undone.
SHOCK
Hey, Utau. Get off of me.
But... I haven't seen you for ages!
LOVEY DOVEY
What's with the high-pitched voice?
She's a completely different person!
LOVE LOVE
GRRR
How cool.

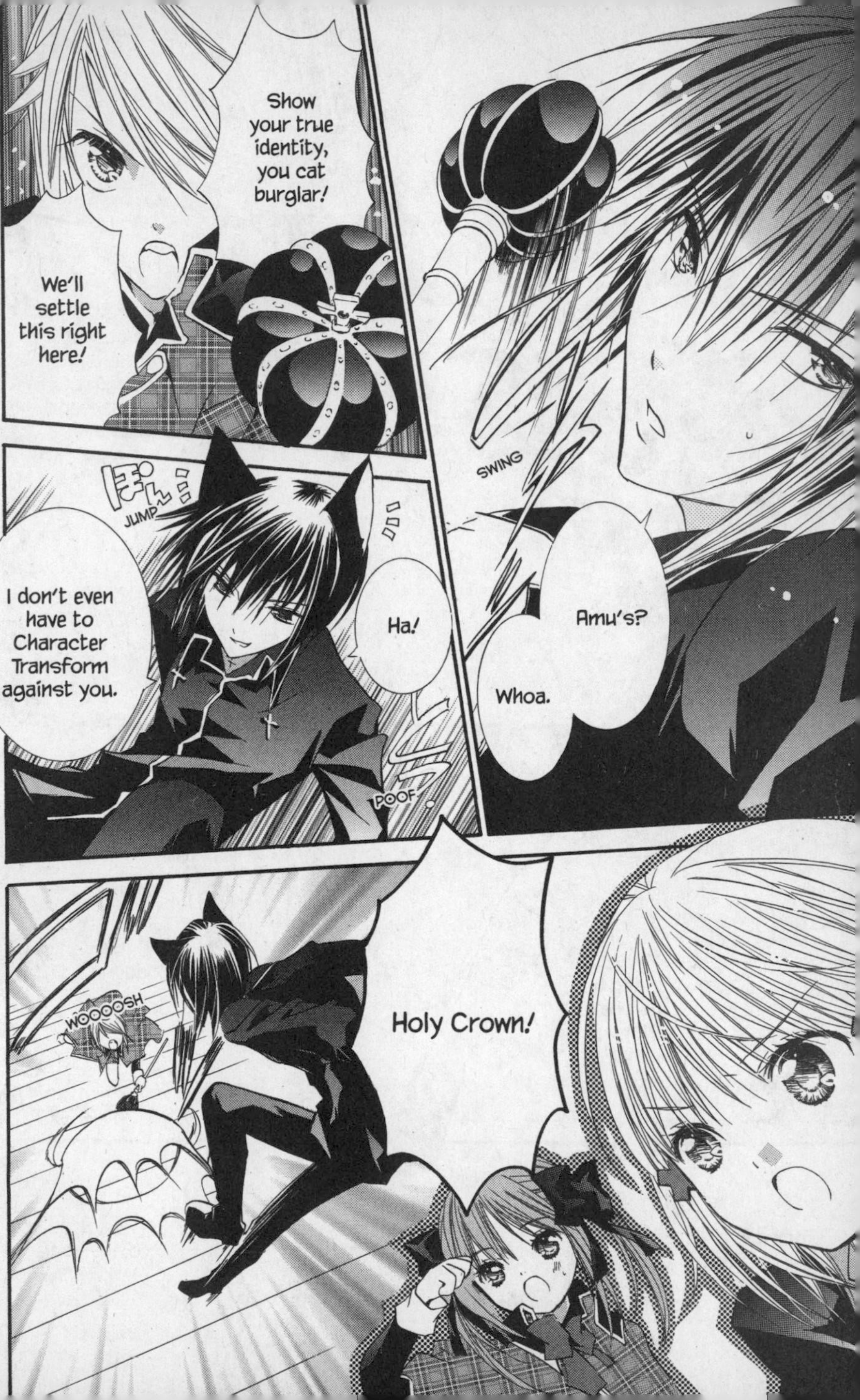
SWING
Amu's?
Whoa.
Show your true identity, you cat burglar!
We'll settle this right here!
Ha!
ぽん
JUMP
I don't even have to Character Transform against you.
POOF
Holy Crown!
WOOOOSH

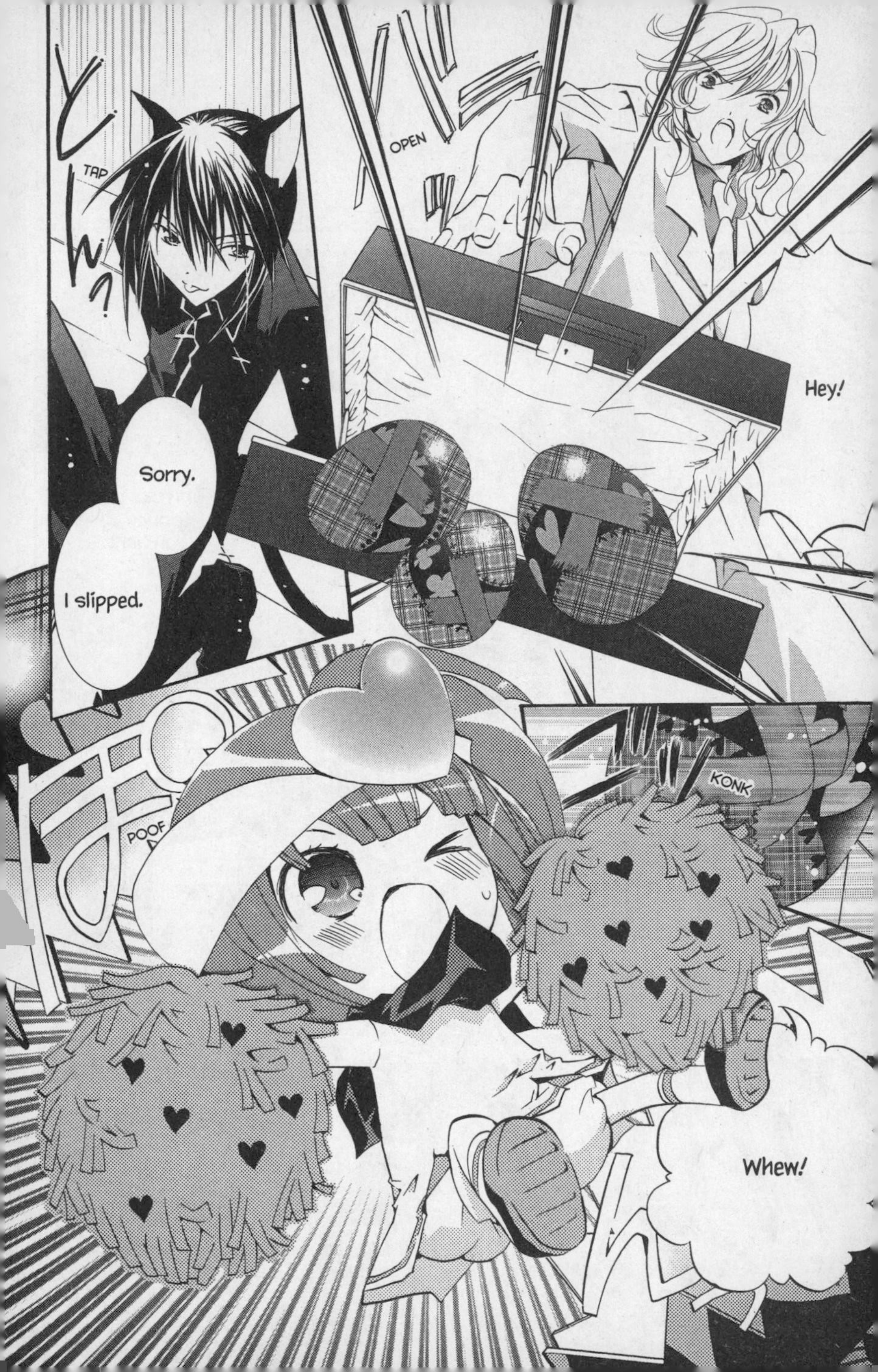
OPEN
Hey!
TAP
Sorry.
I slipped.
KONK
POOF
Whew!

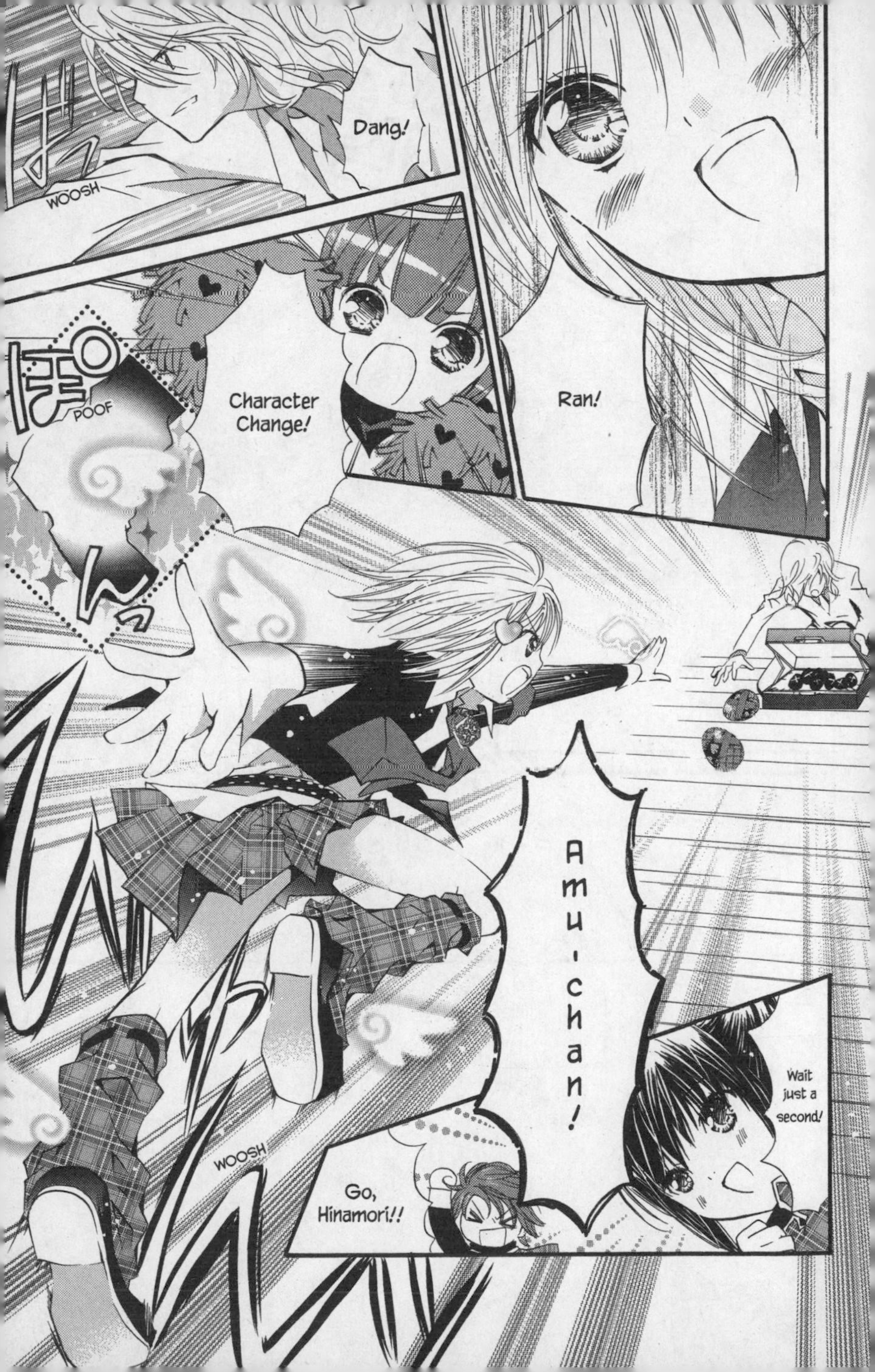
Ran!
Dang!
WOOSH
Character Change!
POOF
Amu-chan!
WOOSH
Wait just a second!
Go, Hinamori!!

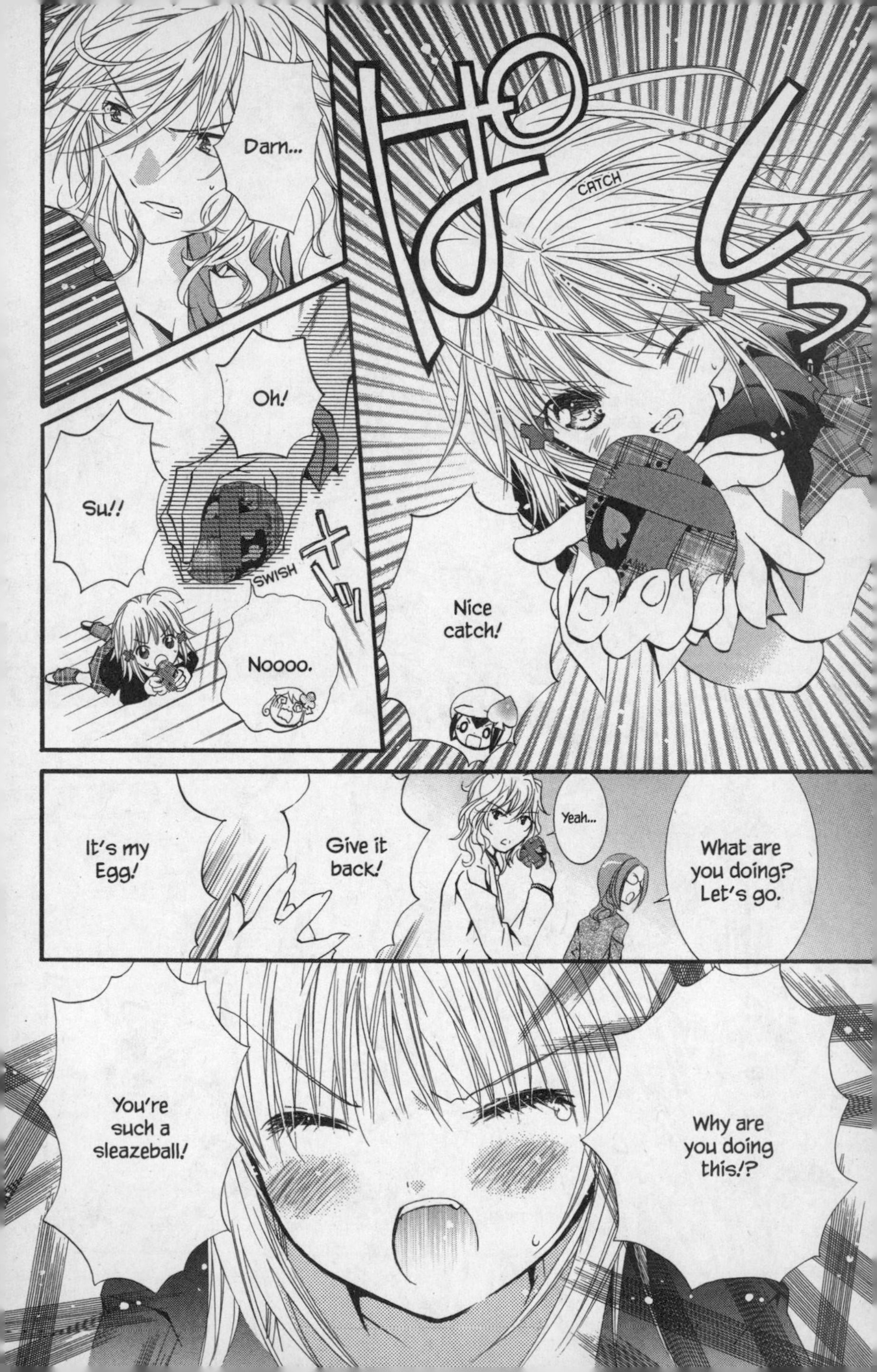
ぱしっ
CATCH
Nice catch!
Darn...
Oh!
Su!!
SWISH
Noooo.
What are you doing? Let's go.
Yeah...
Give it back!
It's my Egg!
Why are you doing this!?
You're such a sleazeball!

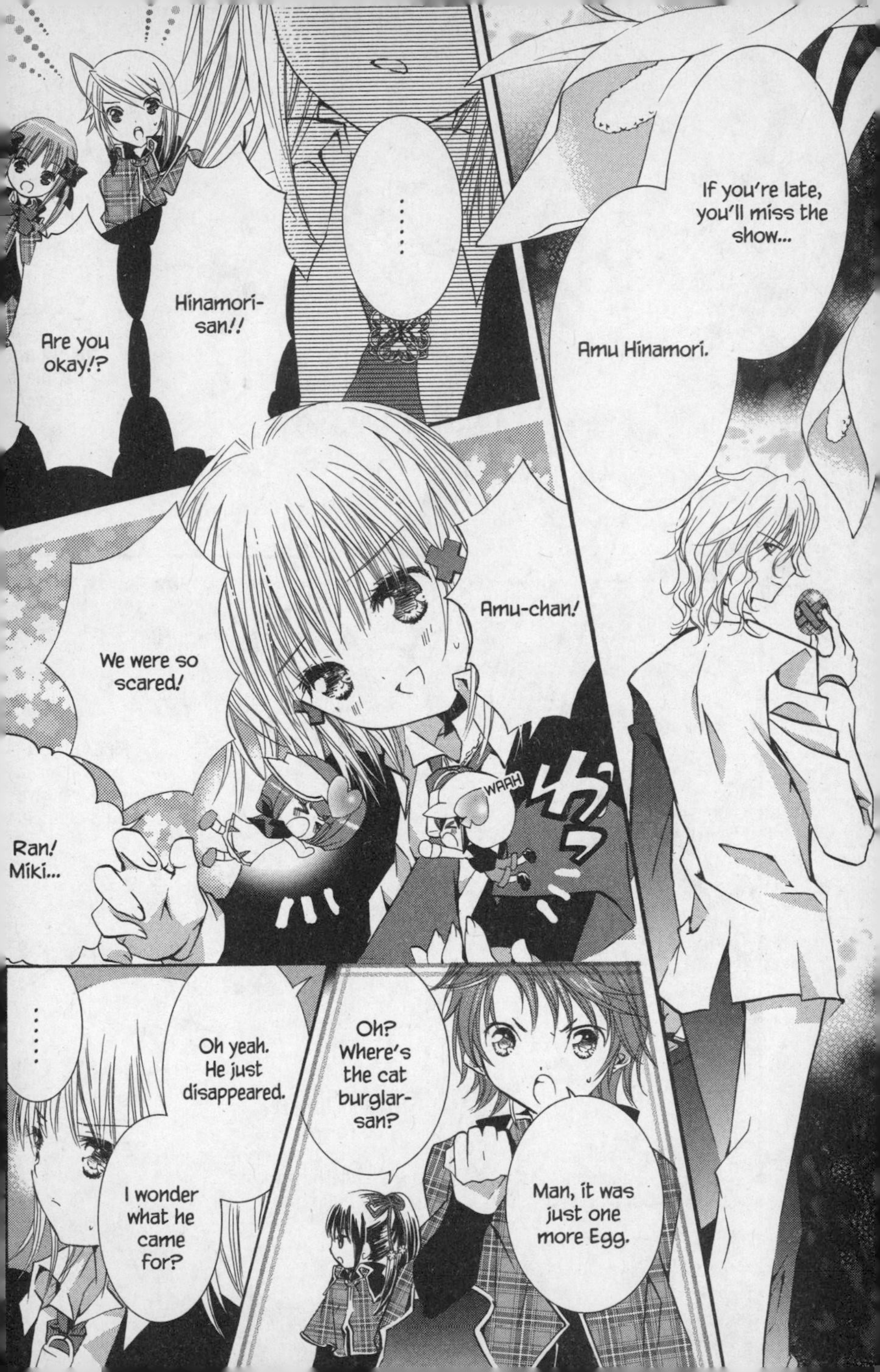
If you're late, you'll miss the show...
Amu Hinamori.
......
Hinamori-san!!
Are you okay!?
Amu-chan!
We were so scared!
WAAH
Ran! Miki...
Oh? Where's the cat burglar-san?
Man, it was just one more Egg.
Oh yeah. He just disappeared.
I wonder what he came for?
......

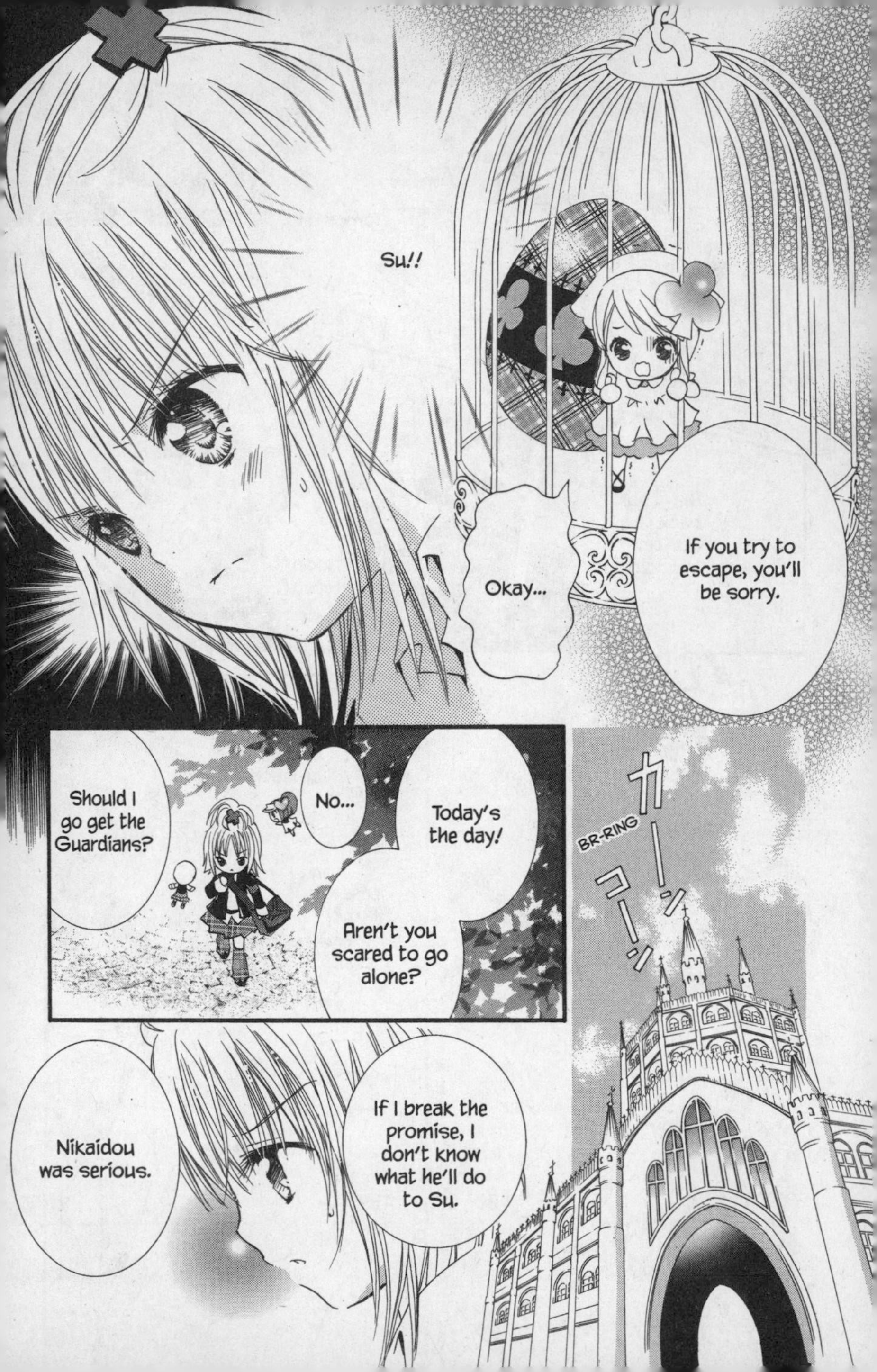
If you try to escape, you'll be sorry.
Okay...
Su!!
カーン
BR-RING
コーン
Today's the day!
Aren't you scared to go alone?
No...
Should I go get the Guardians?
If I break the promise, I don't know what he'll do to Su.
Nikaidou was serious.

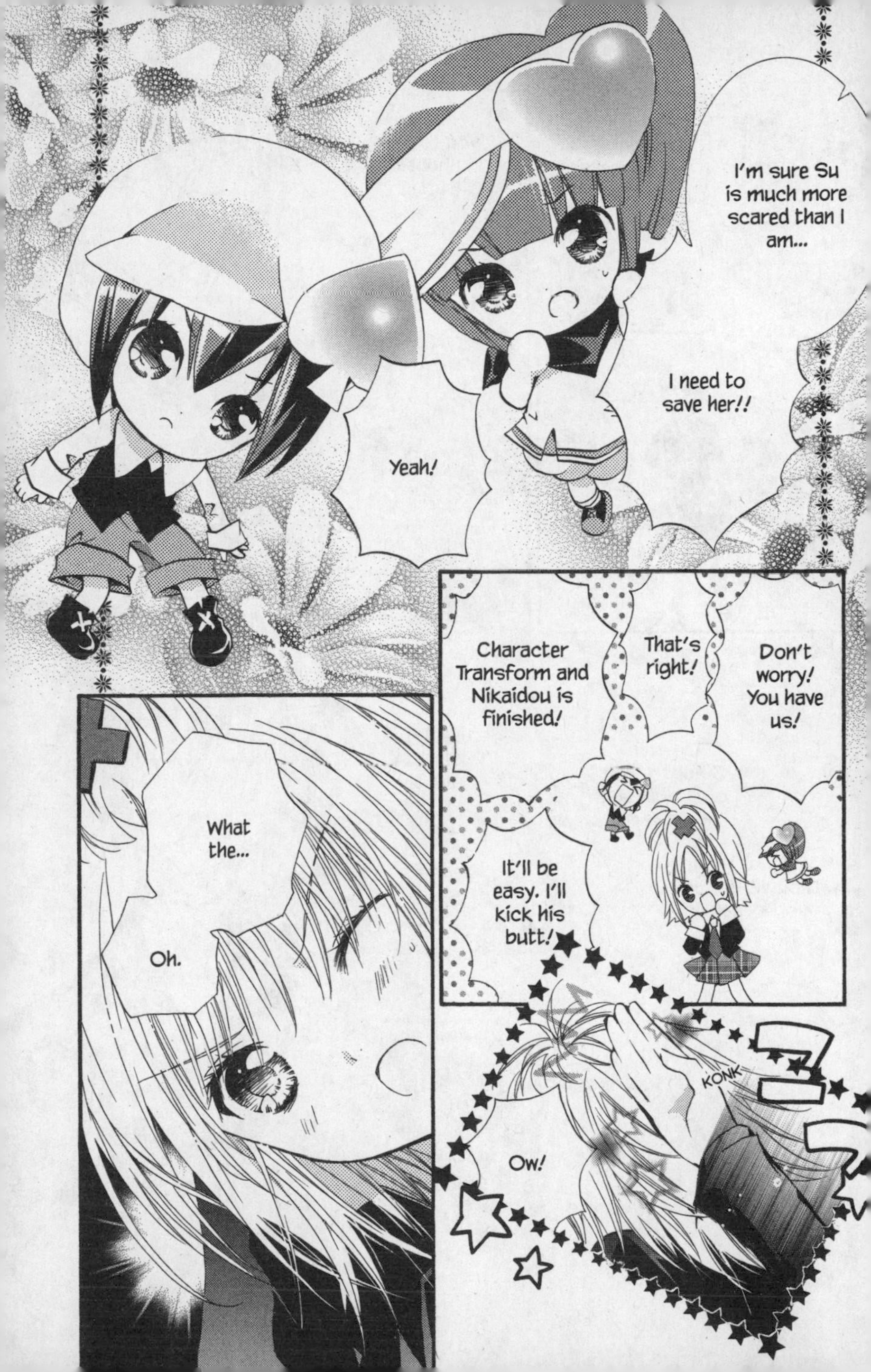
I'm sure Su is much more scared than I am...
I need to save her!!
Yeah!
Don't worry! You have us!
That's right!
Character Transform and Nikaidou is finished!
It'll be easy. I'll kick his butt!
KONK
Ow!
What the...
Oh.

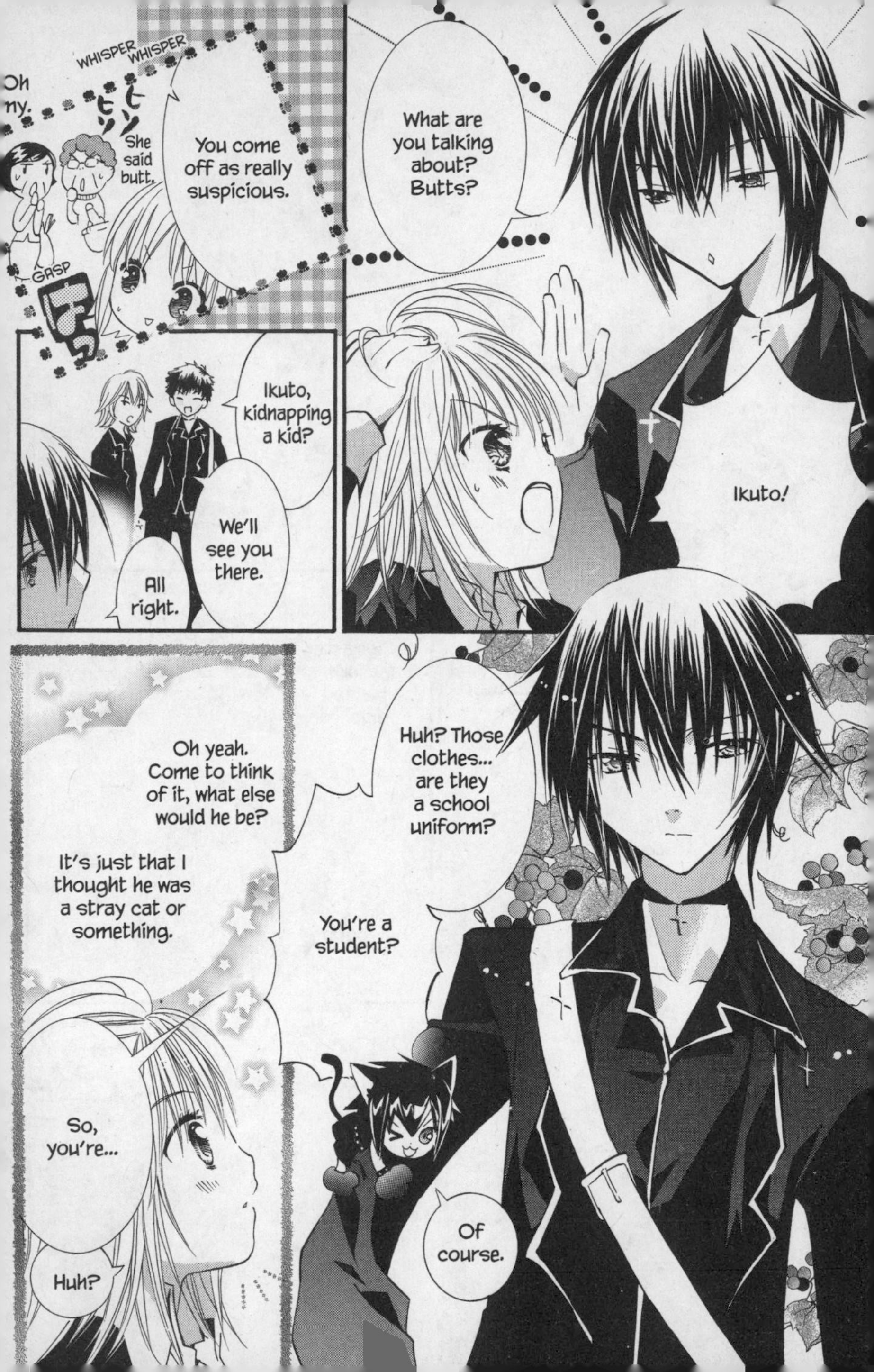
What are you talking about? Butts?
Ikuto!
WHISPER WHISPER
You come off as really suspicious.
Oh ny.
She said butt.
GASP
Ikuto, kidnapping a kid?
We'll see you there.
All right.
Huh? Those clothes... are they a school uniform?
You're a student?
Of course.
Oh yeah. Come to think of it, what else would he be?
It's just that I thought he was a stray cat or something.
So, you're...
Huh?

You're going to Nikaidou's place, right?

How do you know?

Did you come to stop me?

He is part of Easter!

You were just talking about it out loud.

I'm telling you...

...he's not listening!

SHOCK

DRZED

CHIRP

The former employee dorm for Easter is currently vacant.

Research? For what?

Actually...

Why is he telling me all of this?

Oh!

Don't know.

Nikaidou rented it.

To use as his "research lab."

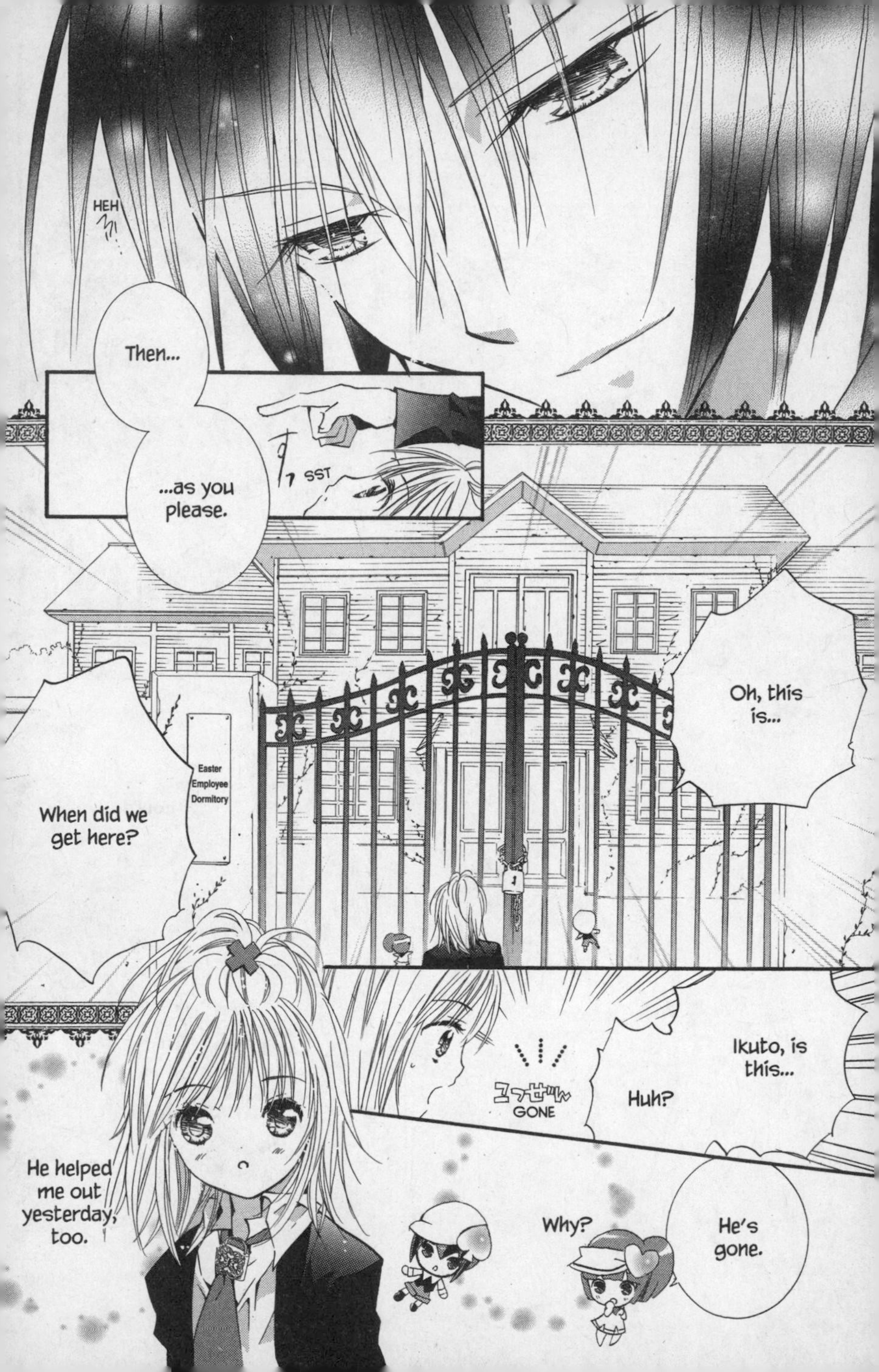

HEH
Then...
...as you please.
SST
Oh, this is...
Easter Employee Dormitory
When did we get here?
Ikuto, is this...
Huh?
GONE
He's gone.
Why?
He helped me out yesterday, too.

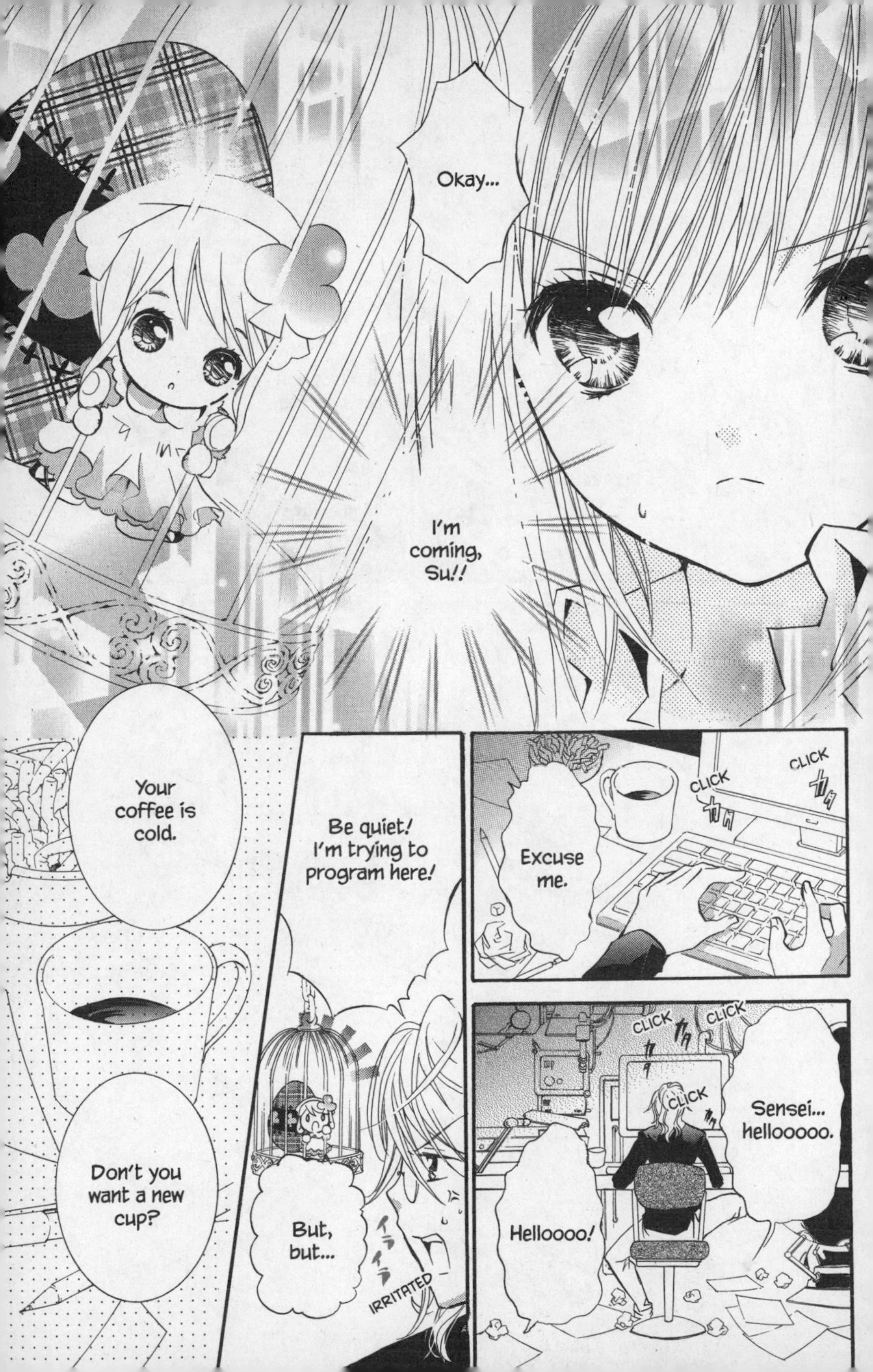
Okay...
I'm coming, Su!!
CLICK
CLICK
Excuse me.
CLICK
CLICK
Sensei... hellooooo.
CLICK
Helloooo!
Be quiet! I'm trying to program here!
But, but...
IRRITATED
Your coffee is cold.
Don't you want a new cup?

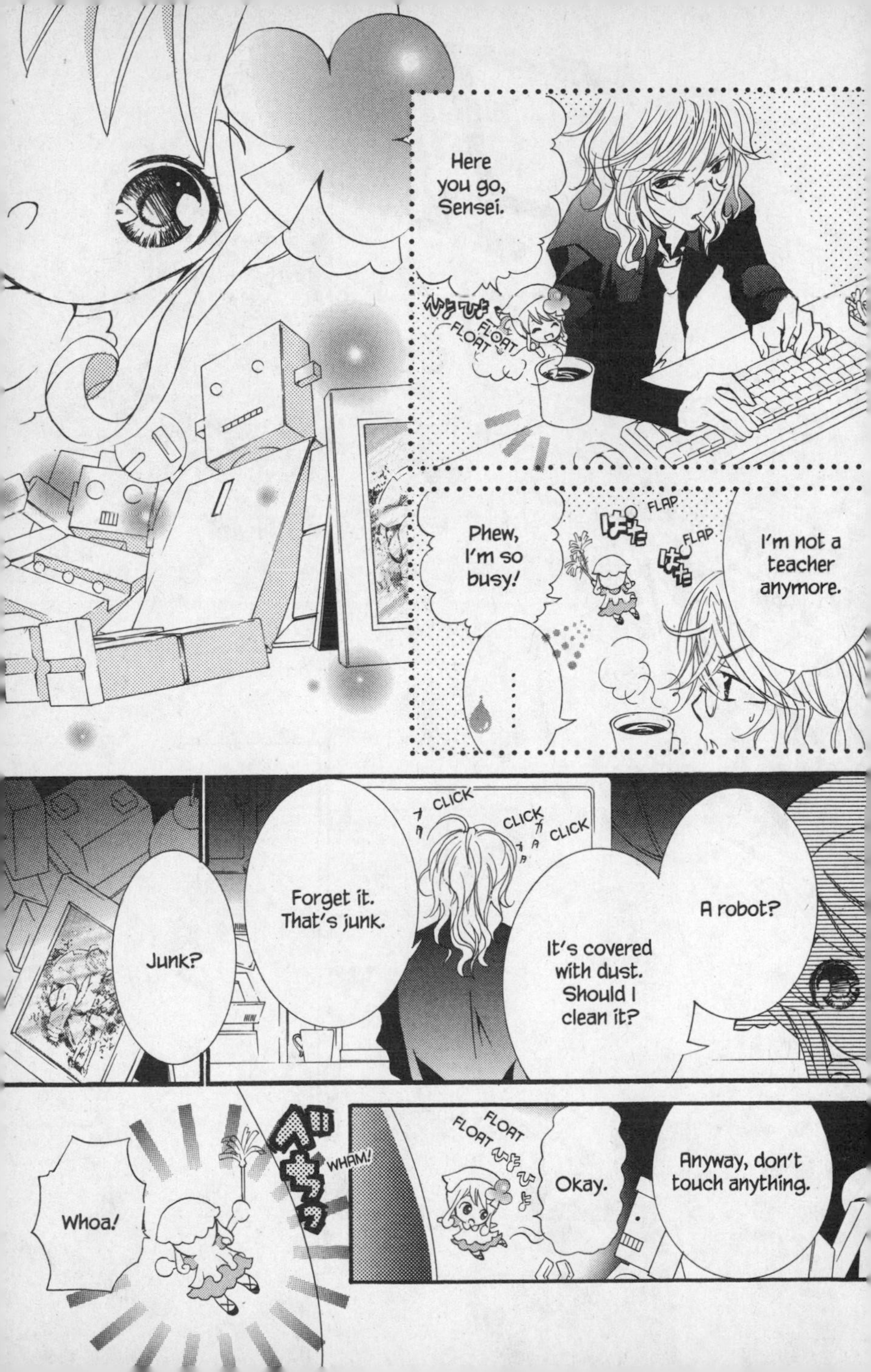
Here you go, Sensei.
FLOAT FLOAT
I'm not a teacher anymore.
FLAP FLAP
Phew, I'm so busy!
...
A robot?
It's covered with dust. Should I clean it?
CLICK CLICK CLICK
Forget it. That's junk.
Junk?
Anyway, don't touch anything.
Okay.
FLOAT FLOAT
WHAM!
Whoa!

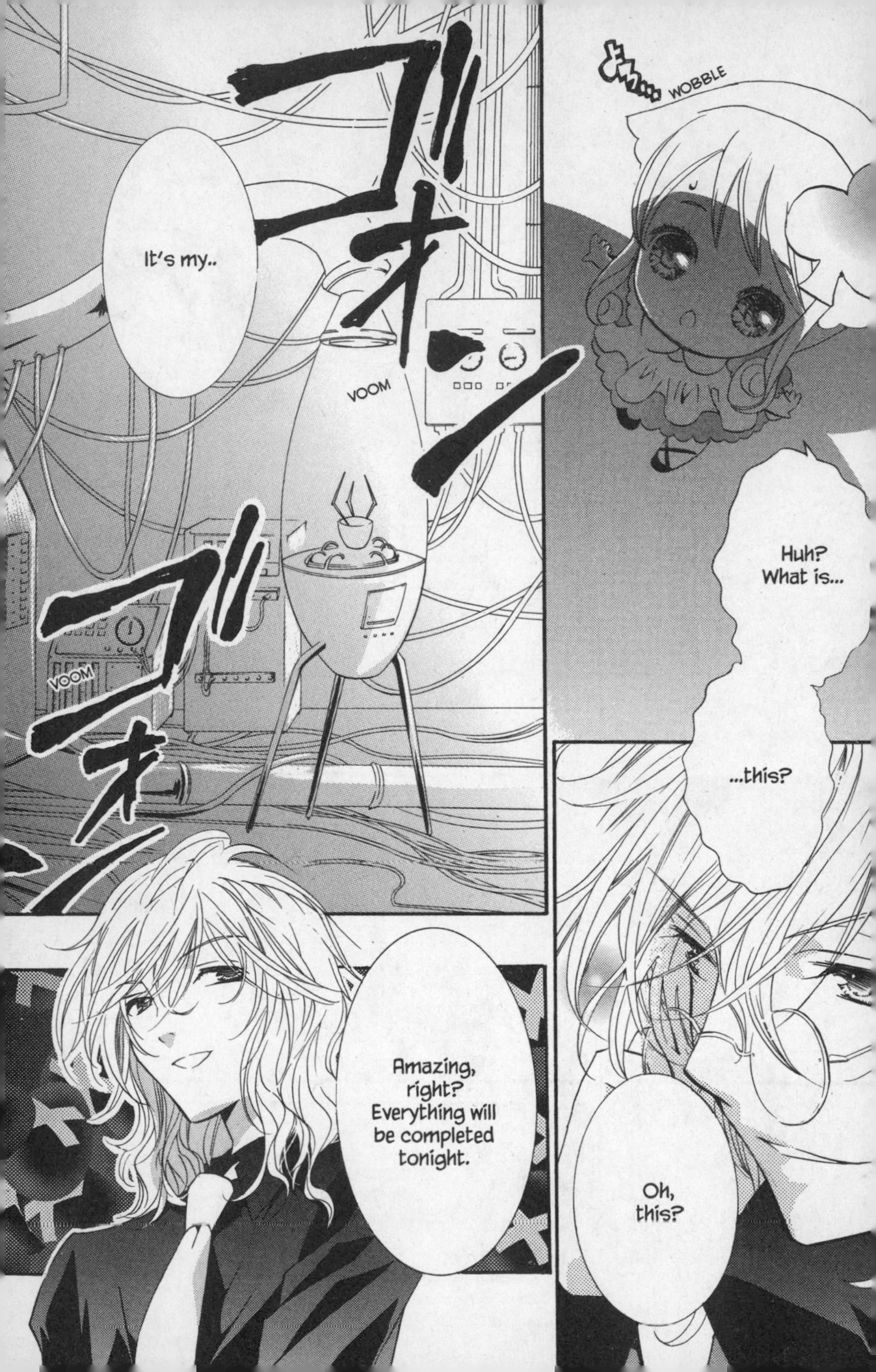
WOBBLE
Huh? What is...
...this?
Oh, this?
It's my..
VOOM
VOOM
Amazing, right? Everything will be completed tonight.

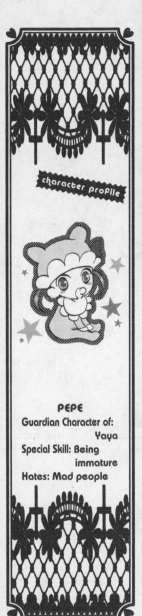

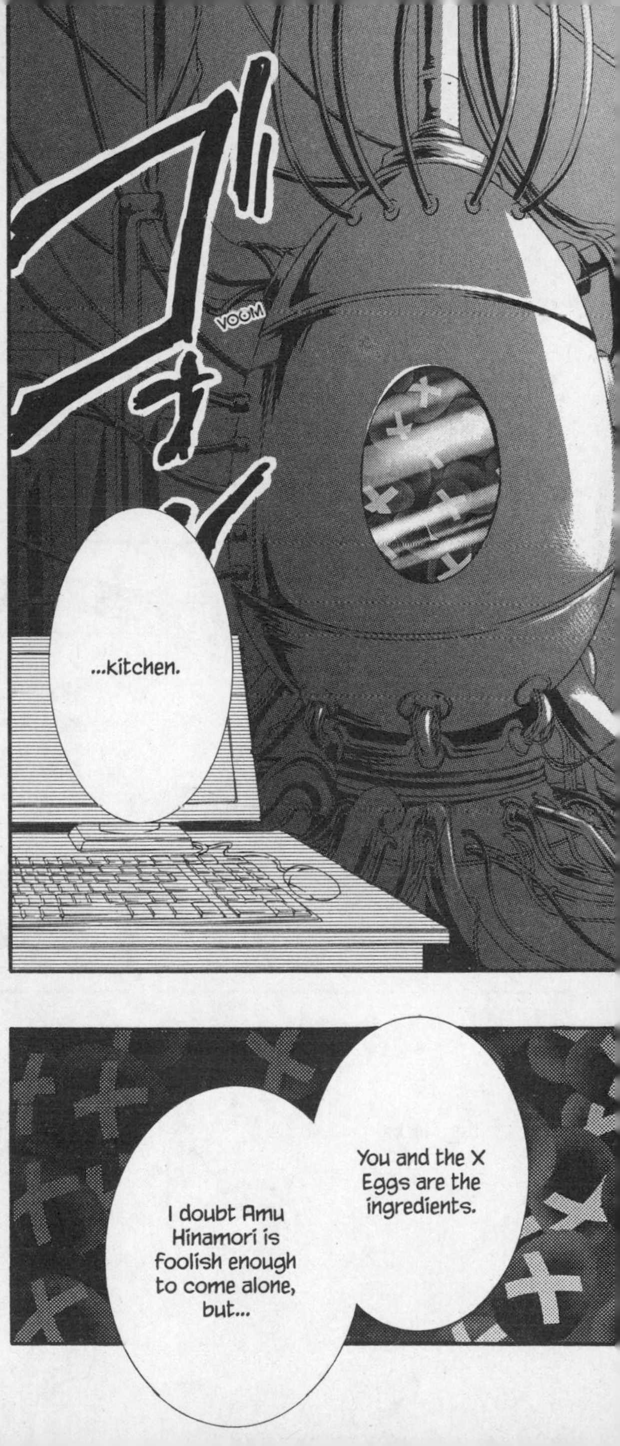
VOOM
...kitchen.
You and the X Eggs are the ingredients.
I doubt Amu Hinamori is foolish enough to come alone, but...

character profile

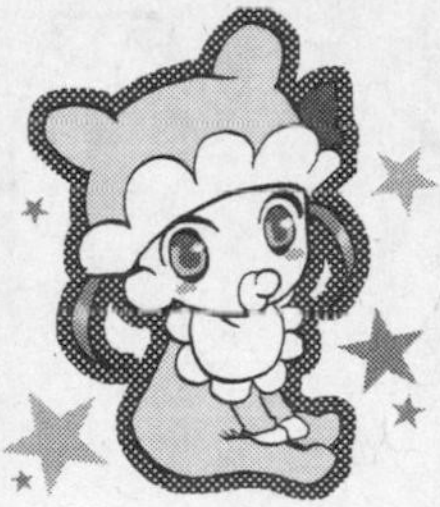

PEPE

Guardian Character of: Yaya

Special Skill: Being immature

Hates: Mad people

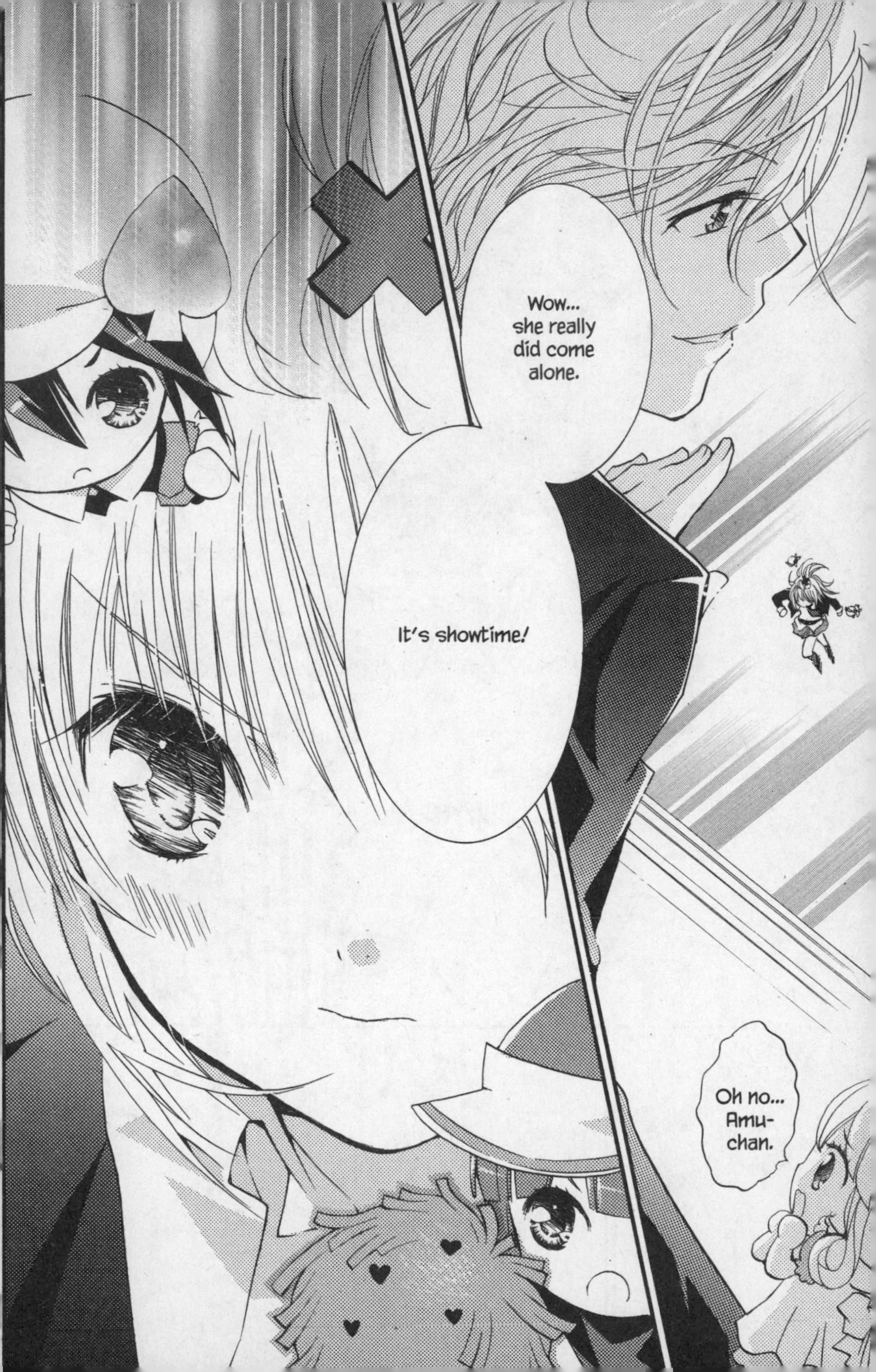
Wow... she really did come alone.
It's showtime!
Oh no... Amu-chan.

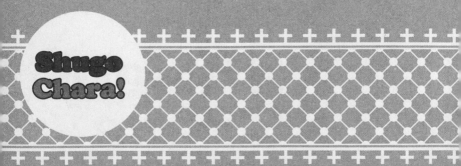

Shugo
Chara!

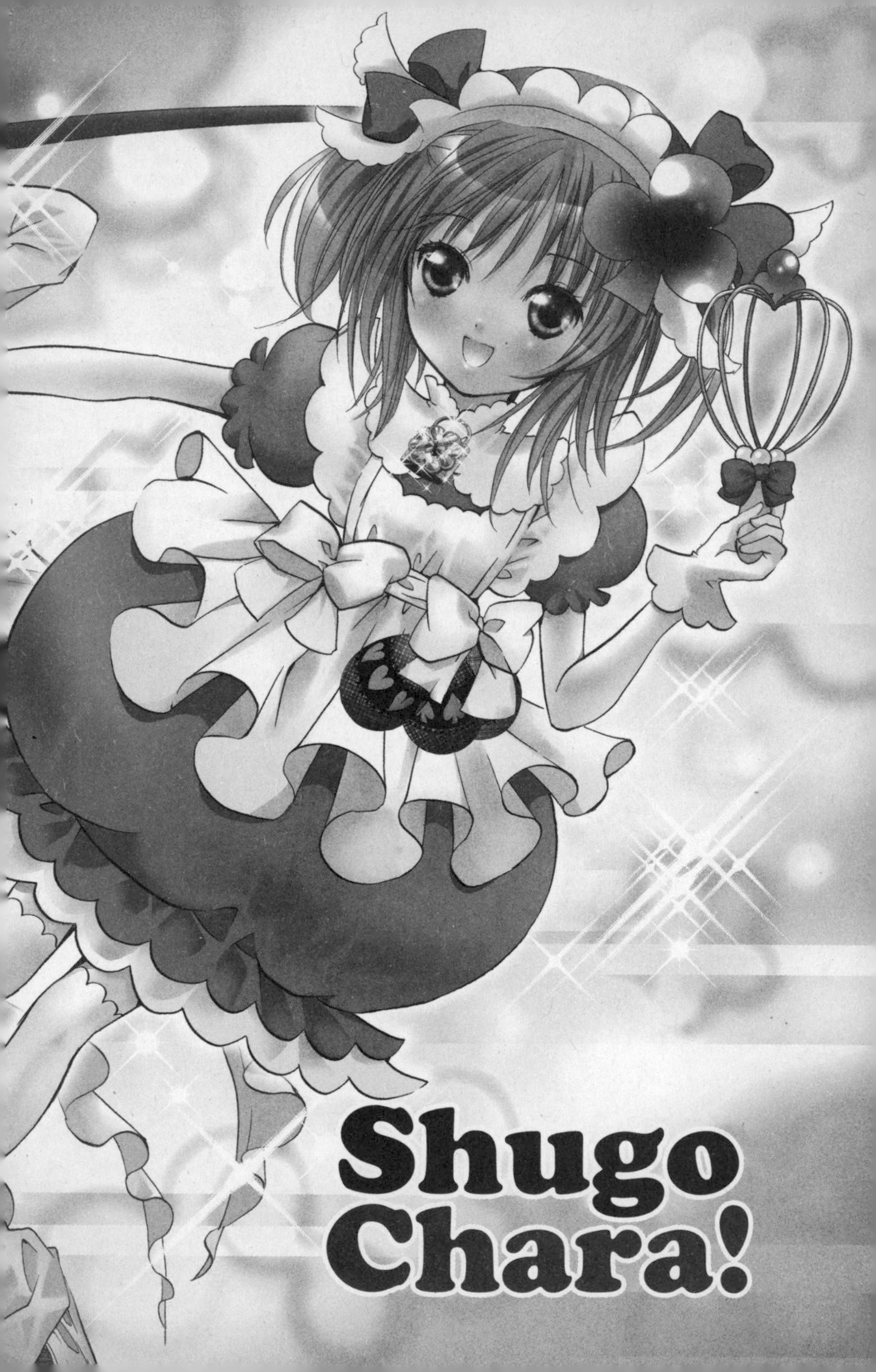
Shugo
Chara!

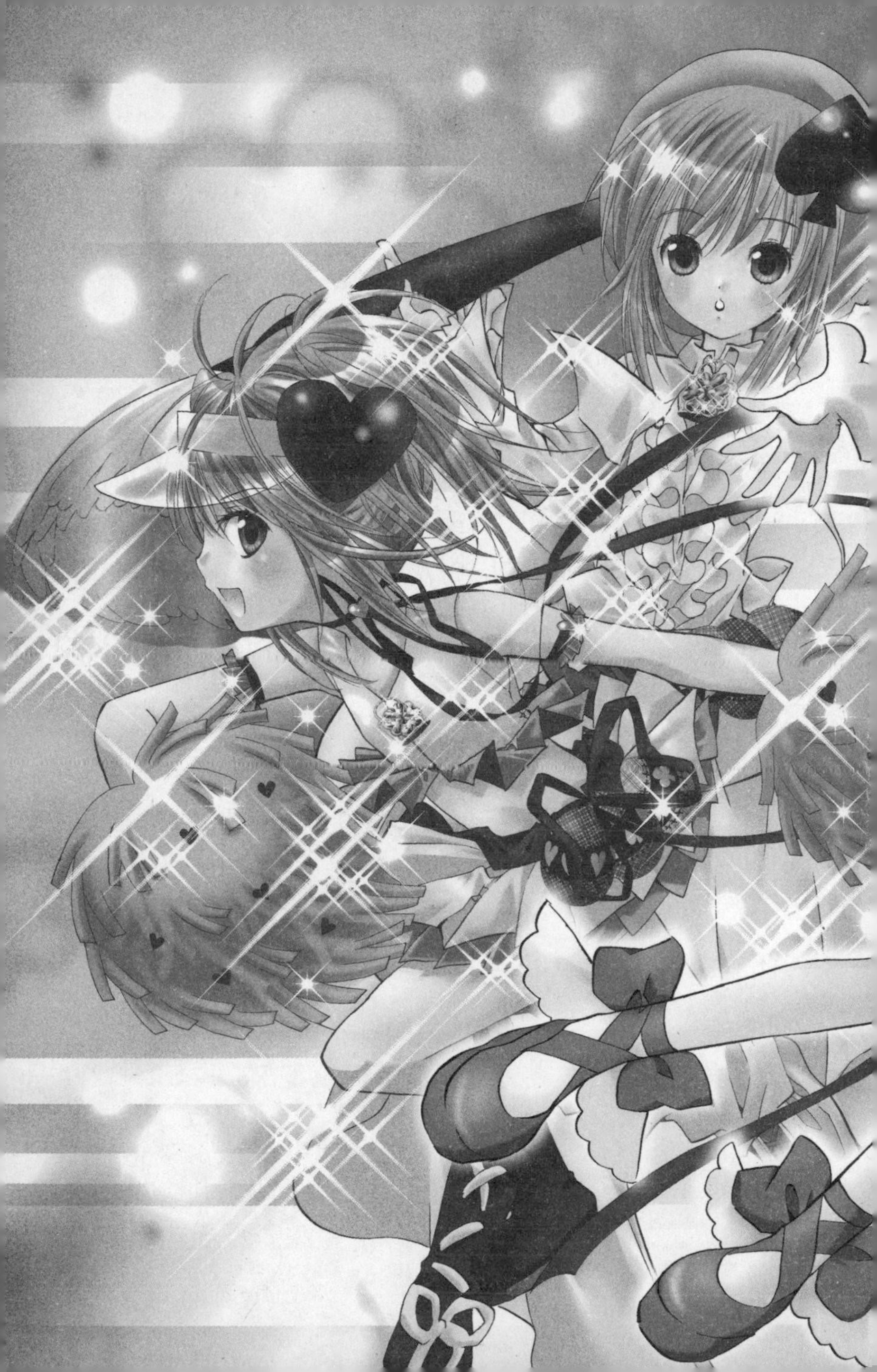

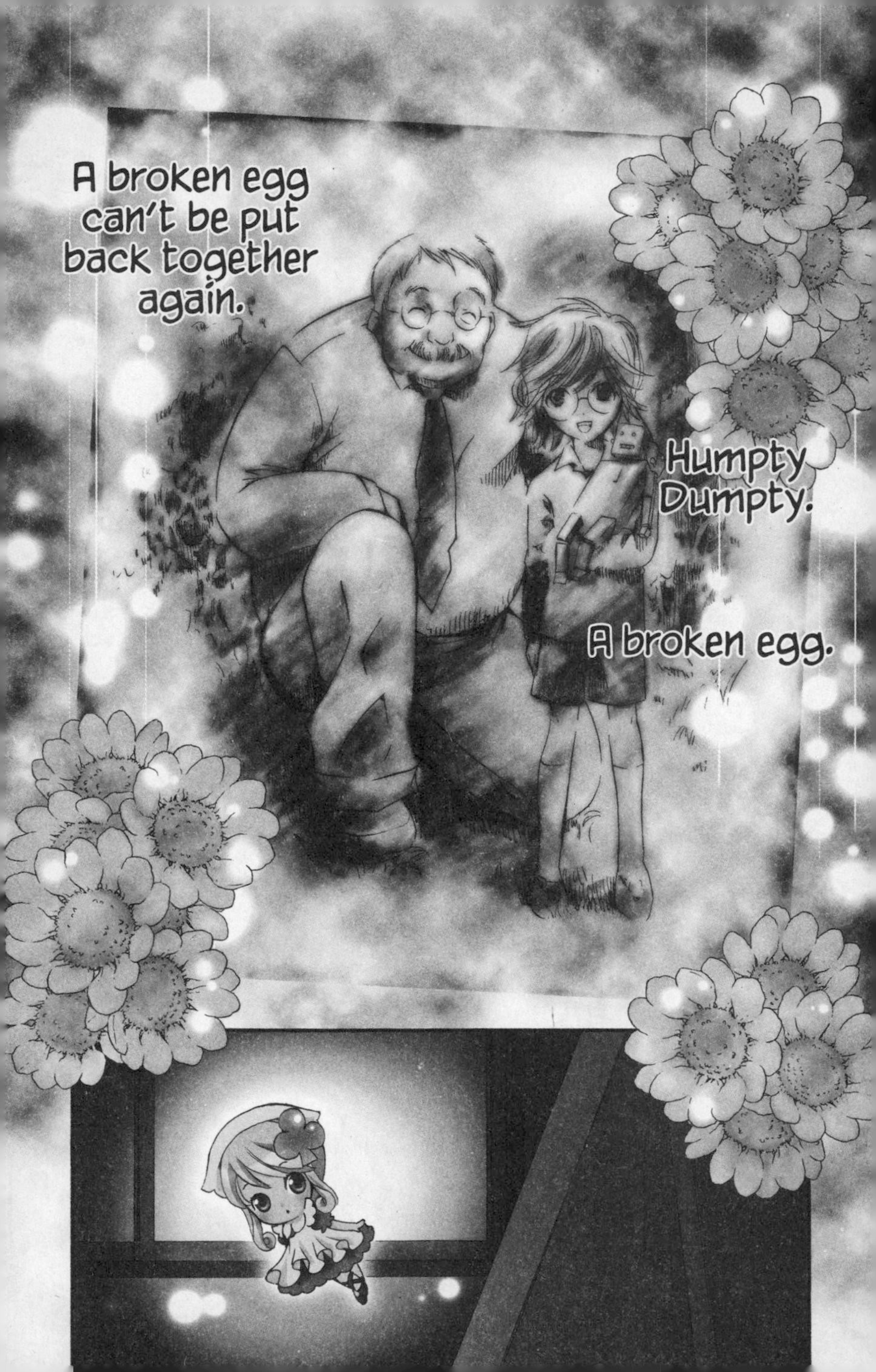
Humpty Dumpty.
A broken egg.
A broken egg can't be put back together again.

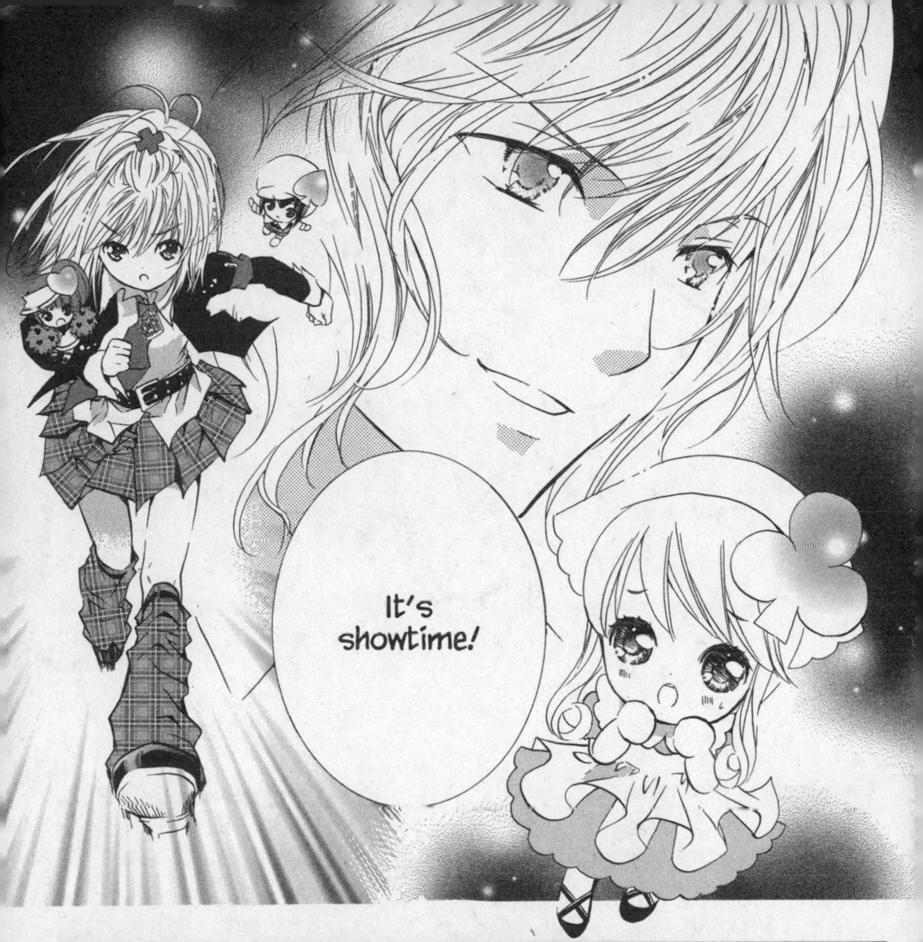
It's showtime!

Q2: What clubs were you in at school? I'm on the volleyball team!
A2: How nice and sporty! Ebara was in the Drama Club, and Sendo wasn't in anything. Both of us were bad at sports, and we were amazed by our friends who were on sports teams.
Q3: Where are you from?
A3: We're both from the Chiba prefecture.
Q4: What's ajitama?
A4: Ajitama are flavored eggs. They're a ramen topping ♡
You can try making them with your mom!

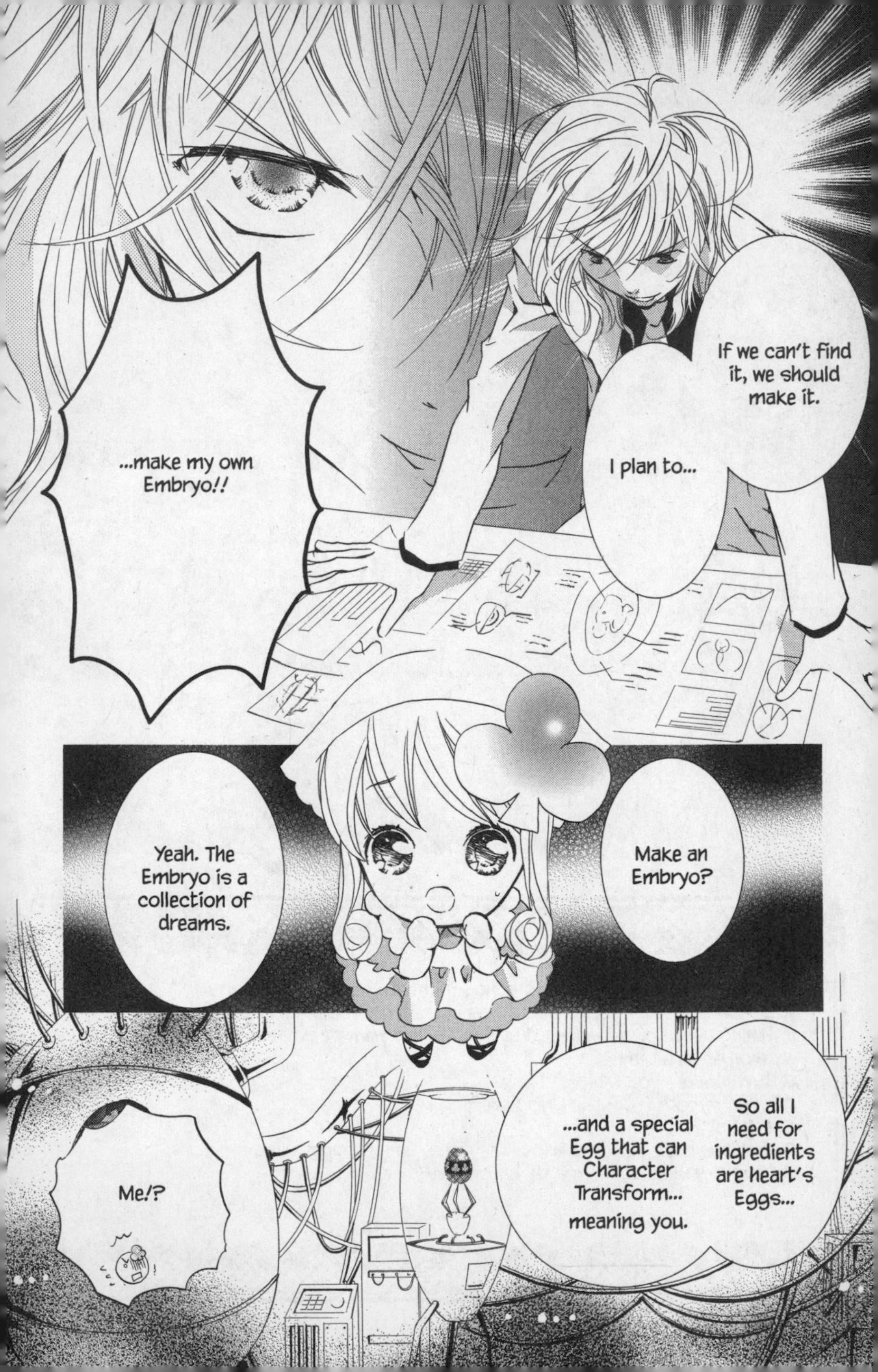
If we can't find it, we should make it.
I plan to...
...make my own Embryo!!
Make an Embryo?
Yeah. The Embryo is a collection of dreams.
So all I need for ingredients are heart's Eggs...
...and a special Egg that can Character Transform... meaning you.
Me!?

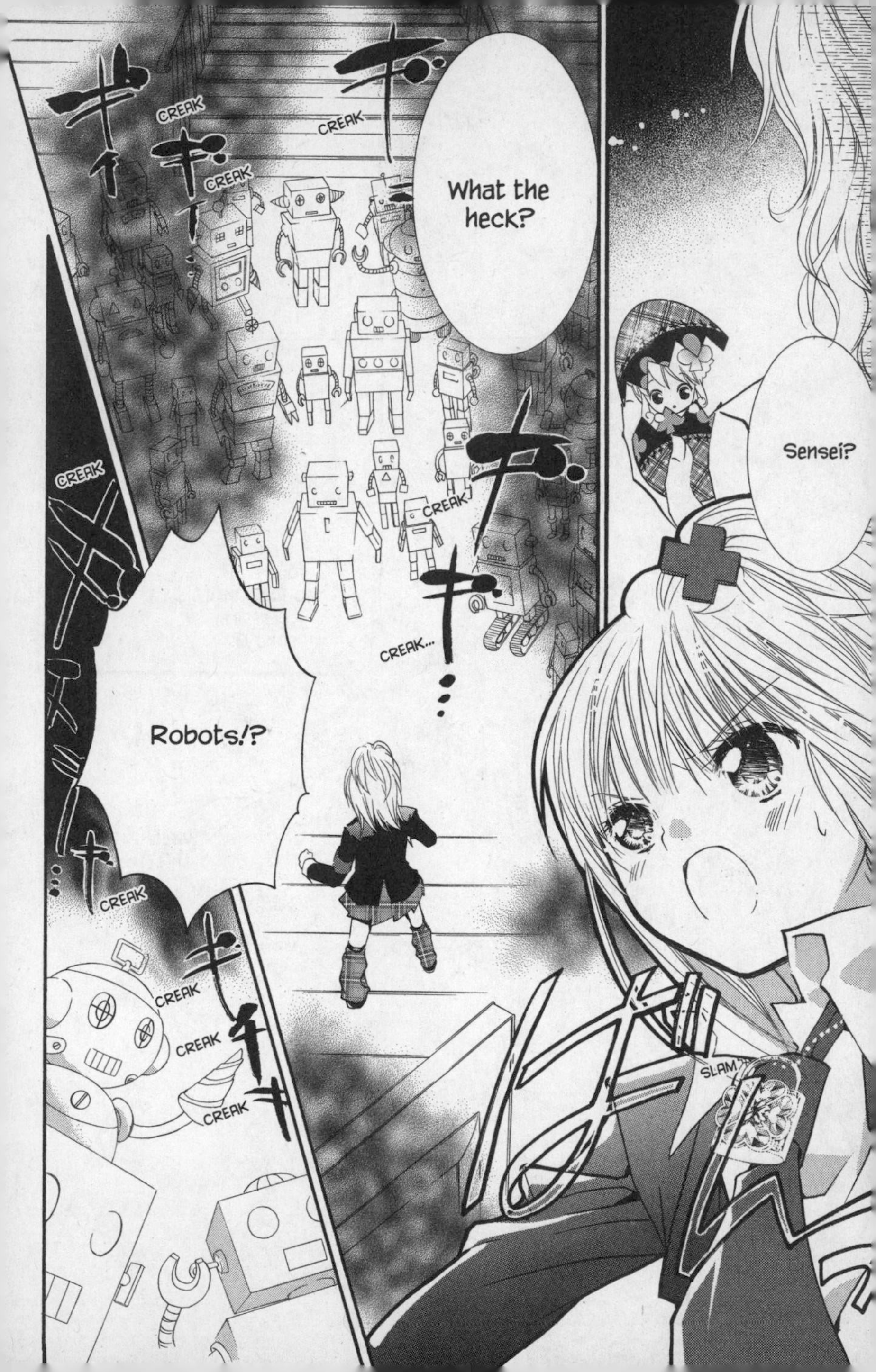
Sensei?
SLAM
What the heck?
CREAK
CREAK
CREAK
CREAK
CREAK...
CREAK
Robots!?
CREAK
CREAK
CREAK
CREAK

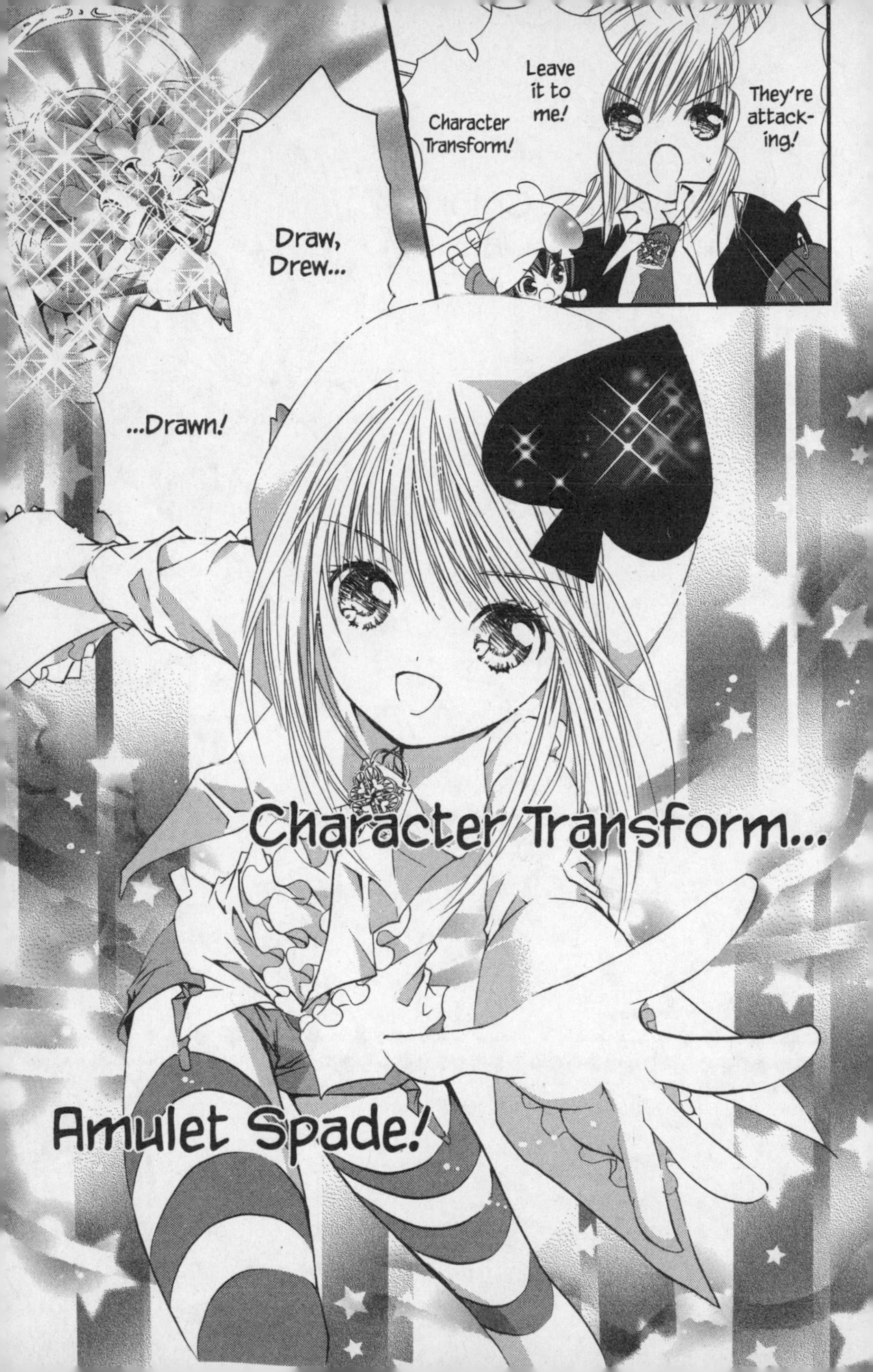
They're attack-ing!
Leave it to me!
Character Transform!
Draw, Drew...
...Drawn!
Character Transform...
Amulet Spade!

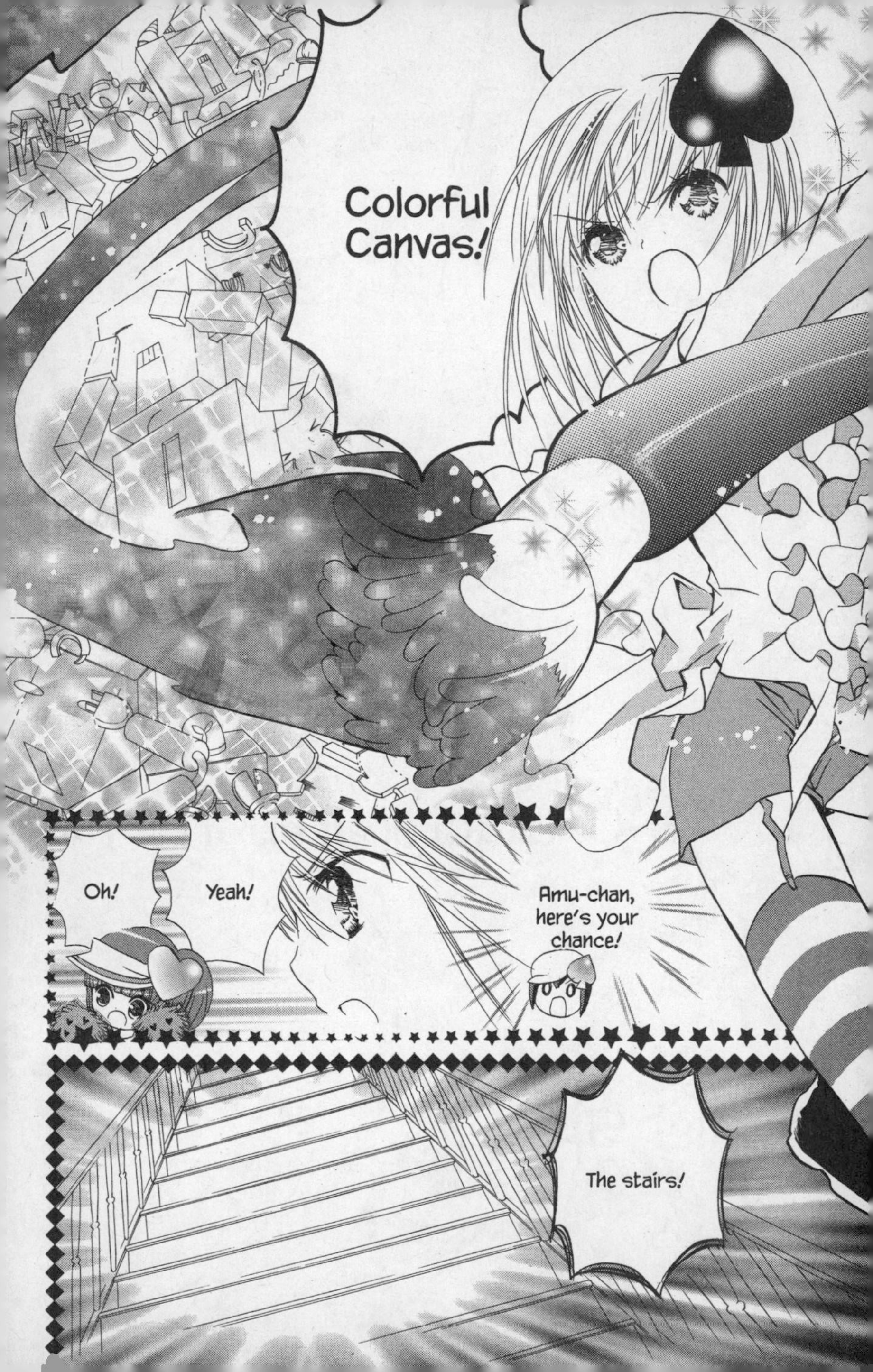
Colorful Canvas!
Amu-chan, here's your chance!
Yeah!
Oh!
The stairs!

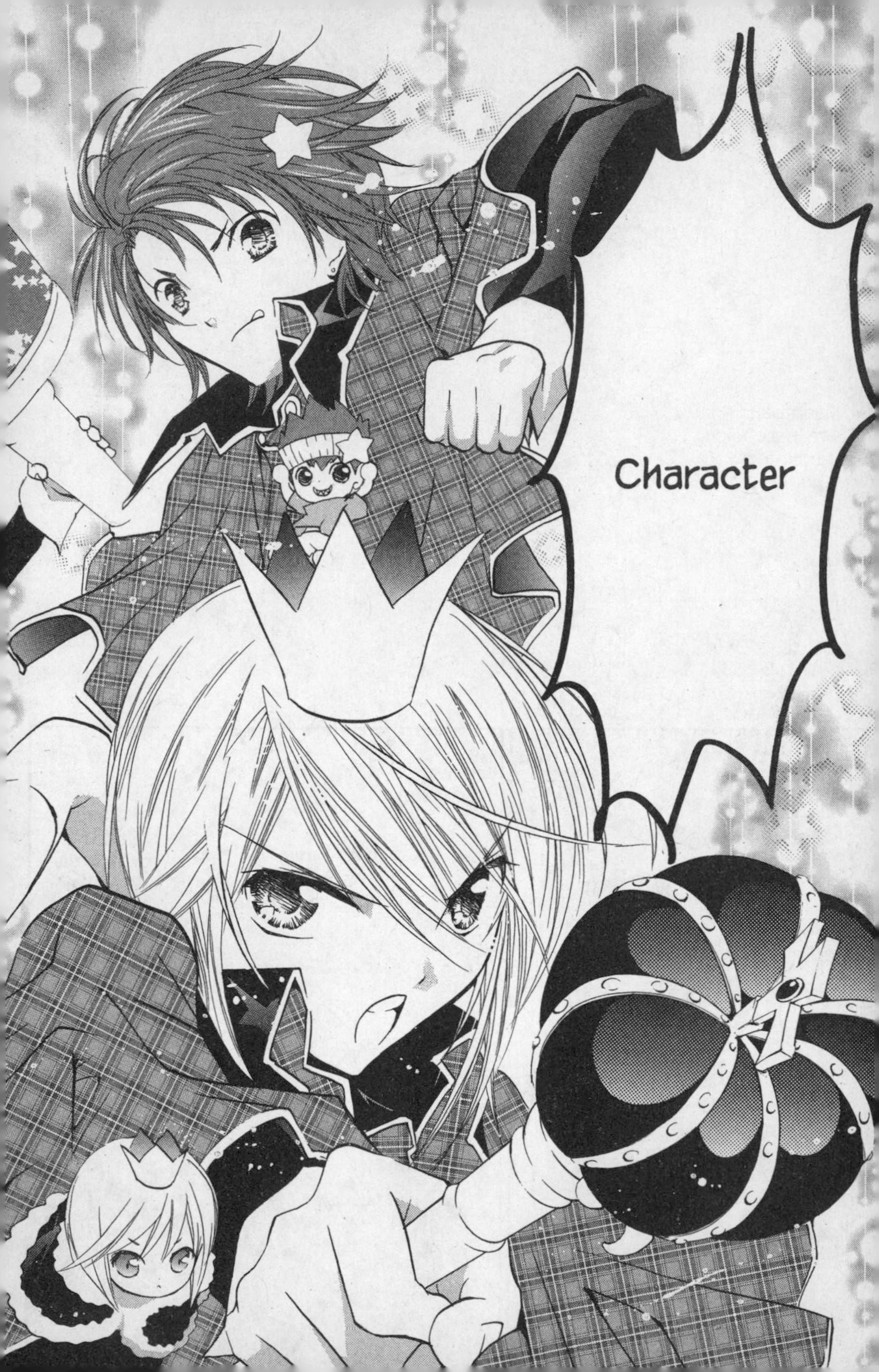
Character

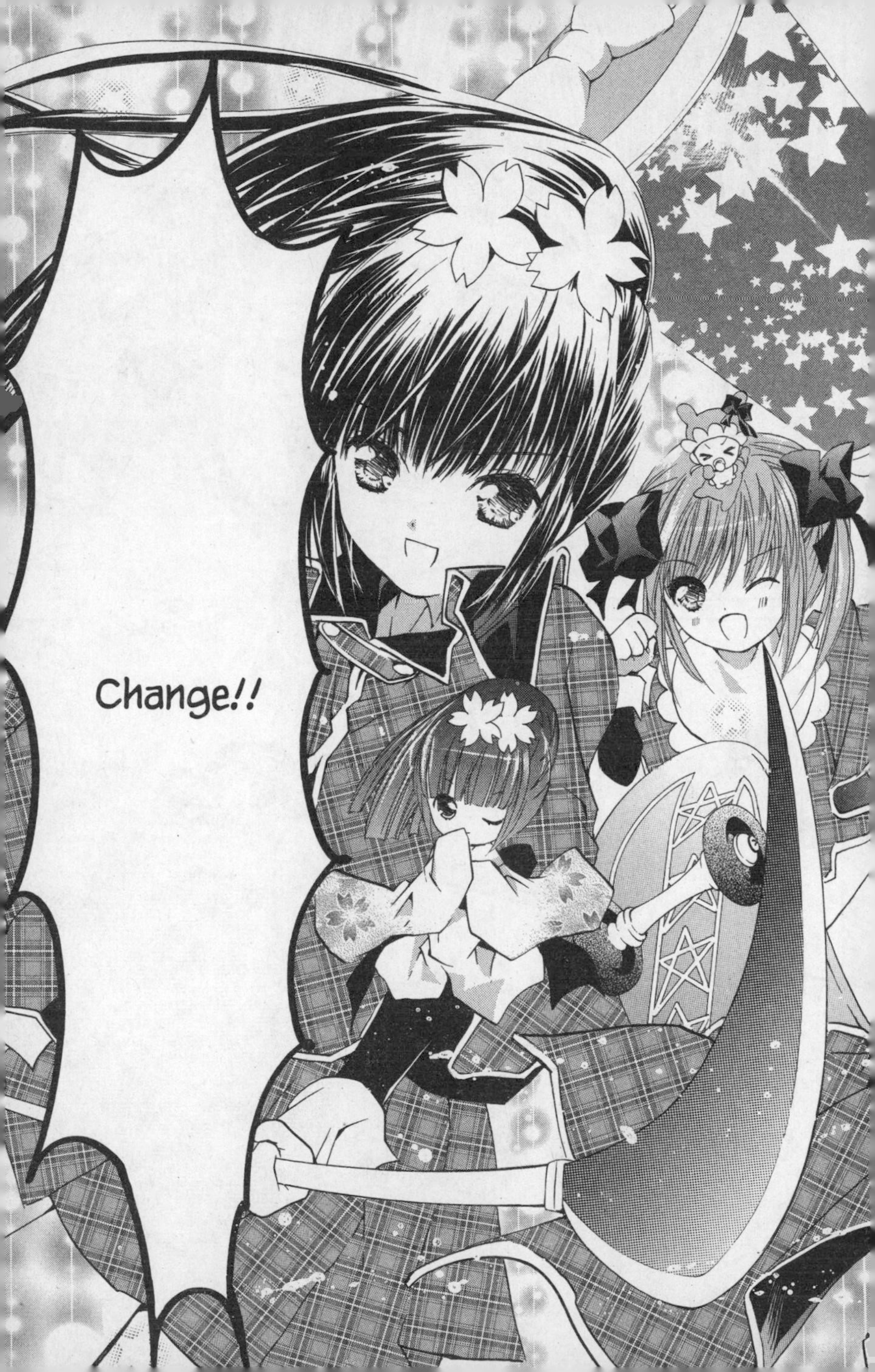
Change!!

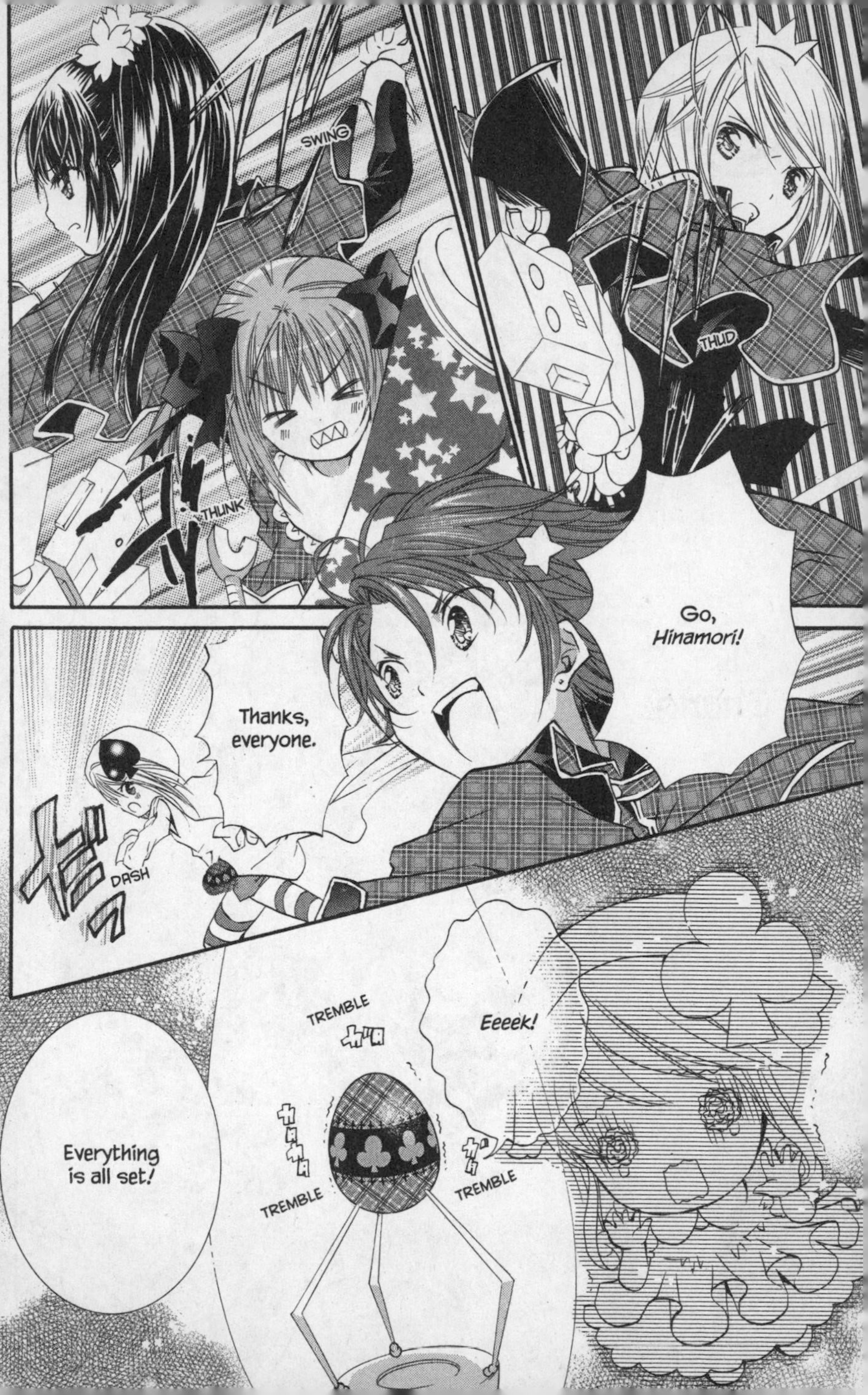
THUD
SWING
THUNK
Go, Hinamori!
Thanks, everyone.
DASH
Eeeek!
TREMBLE
TREMBLE
TREMBLE
Everything is all set!

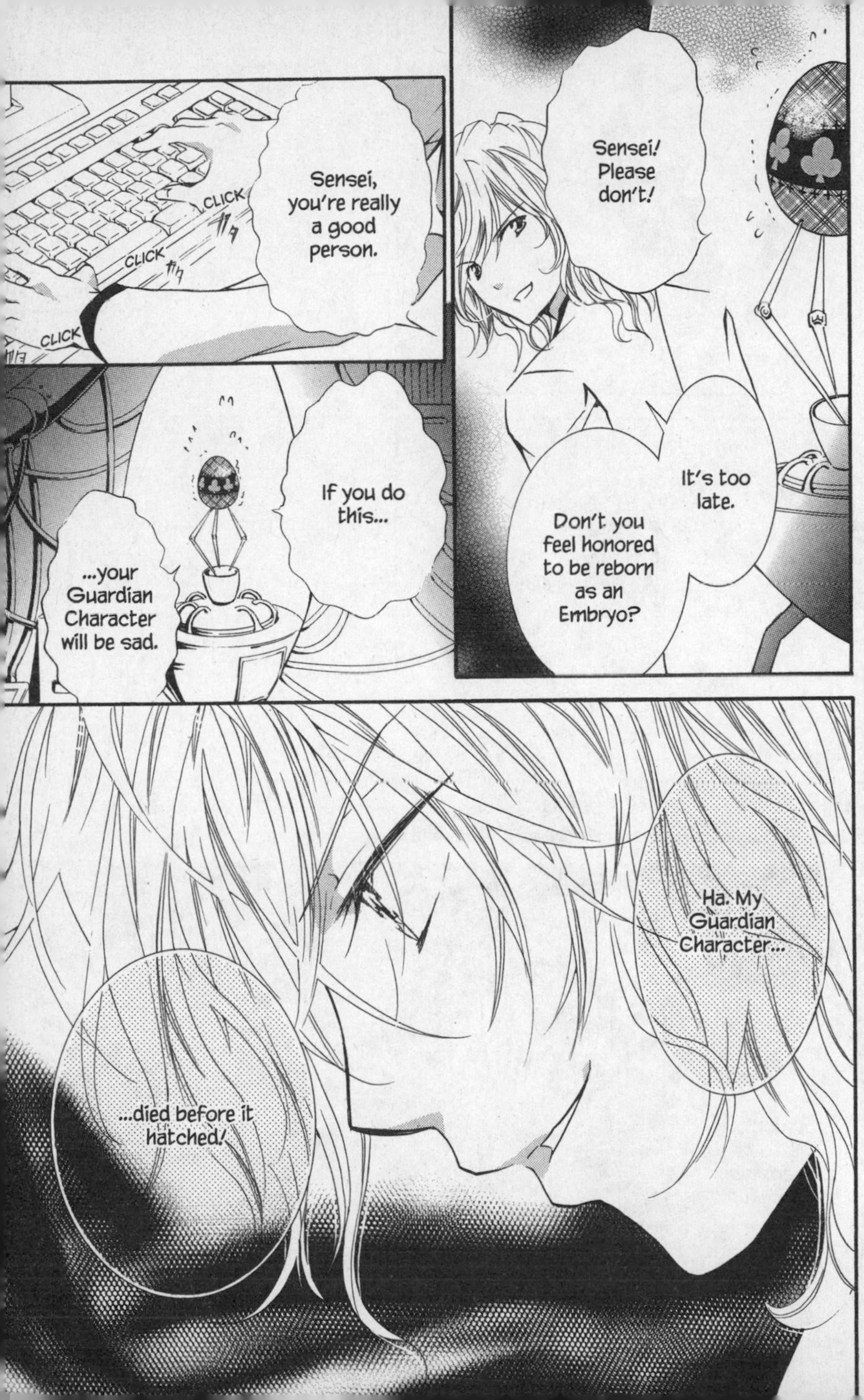
Sensei! Please don't!
It's too late.
Don't you feel honored to be reborn as an Embryo?
CLICK
CLICK
CLICK
Sensei, you're really a good person.
If you do this...
...your Guardian Character will be sad.
Ha. My Guardian Character...
...died before it hatched!

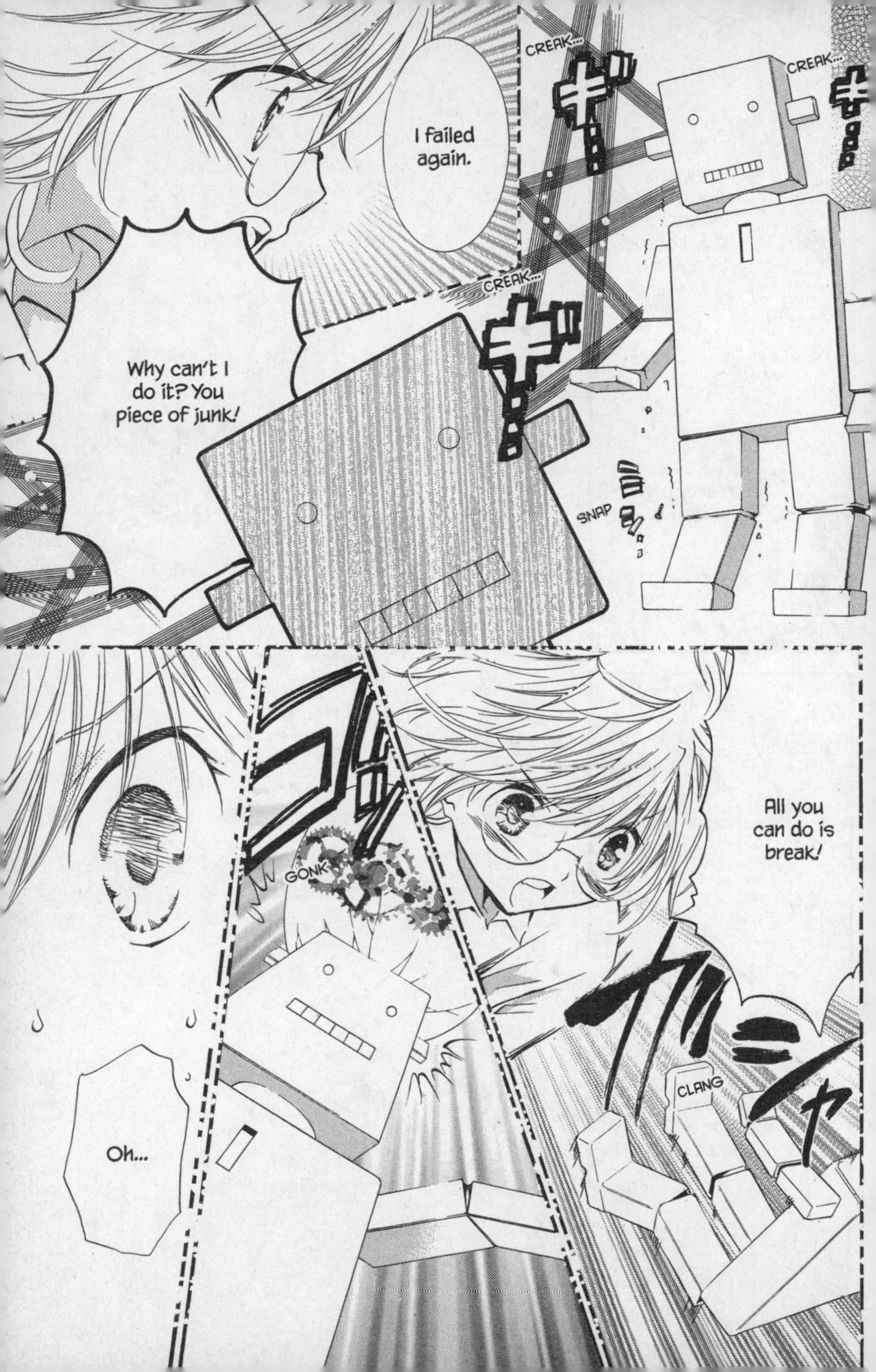
CREAK...
CREAK...
CREAK...
SNAP
I failed again.
Why can't I do it? You piece of junk!
All you can do is break!
CLANG
GONK
Oh...

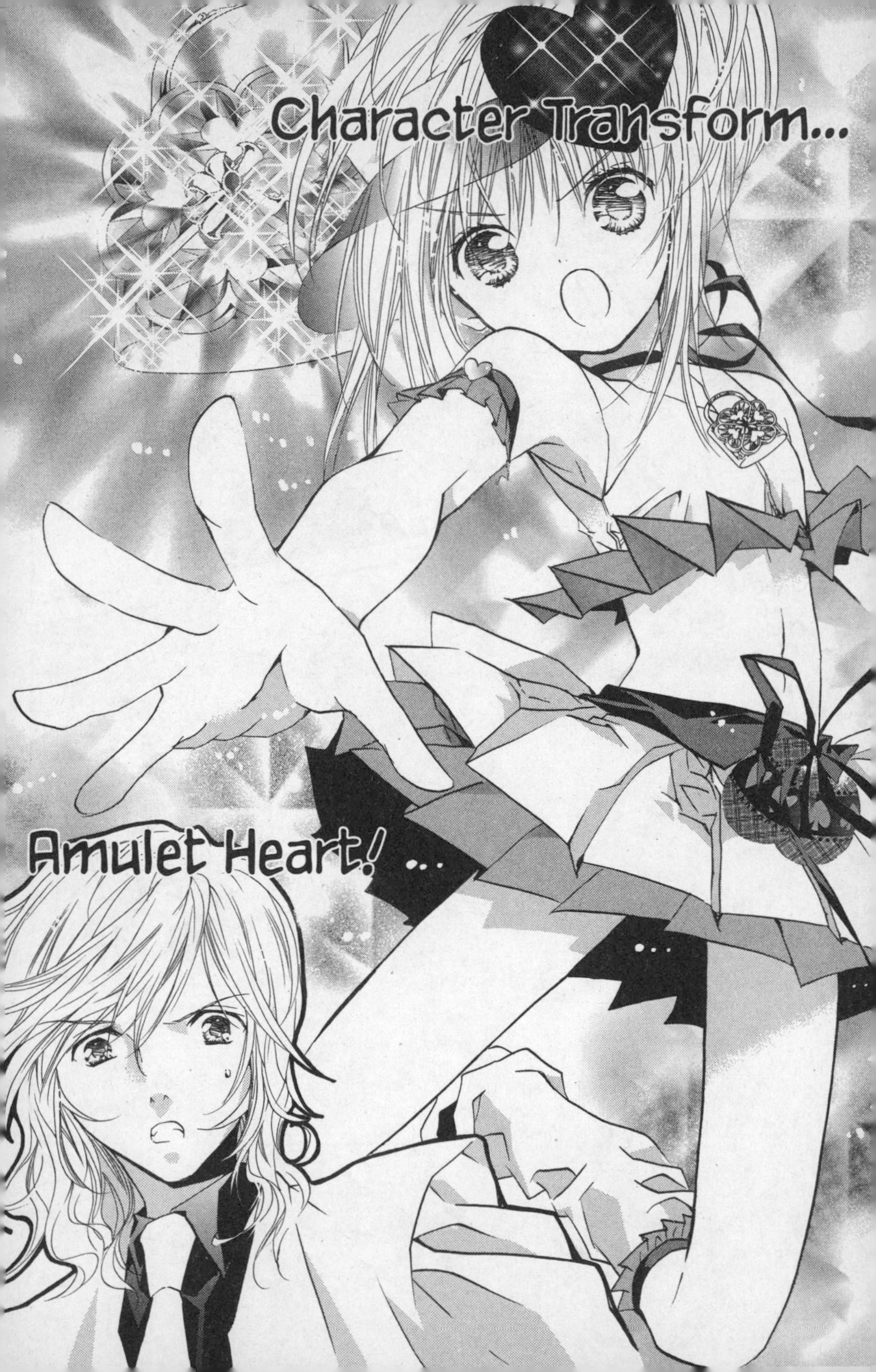
Character Transform...
Amulet Heart!
...

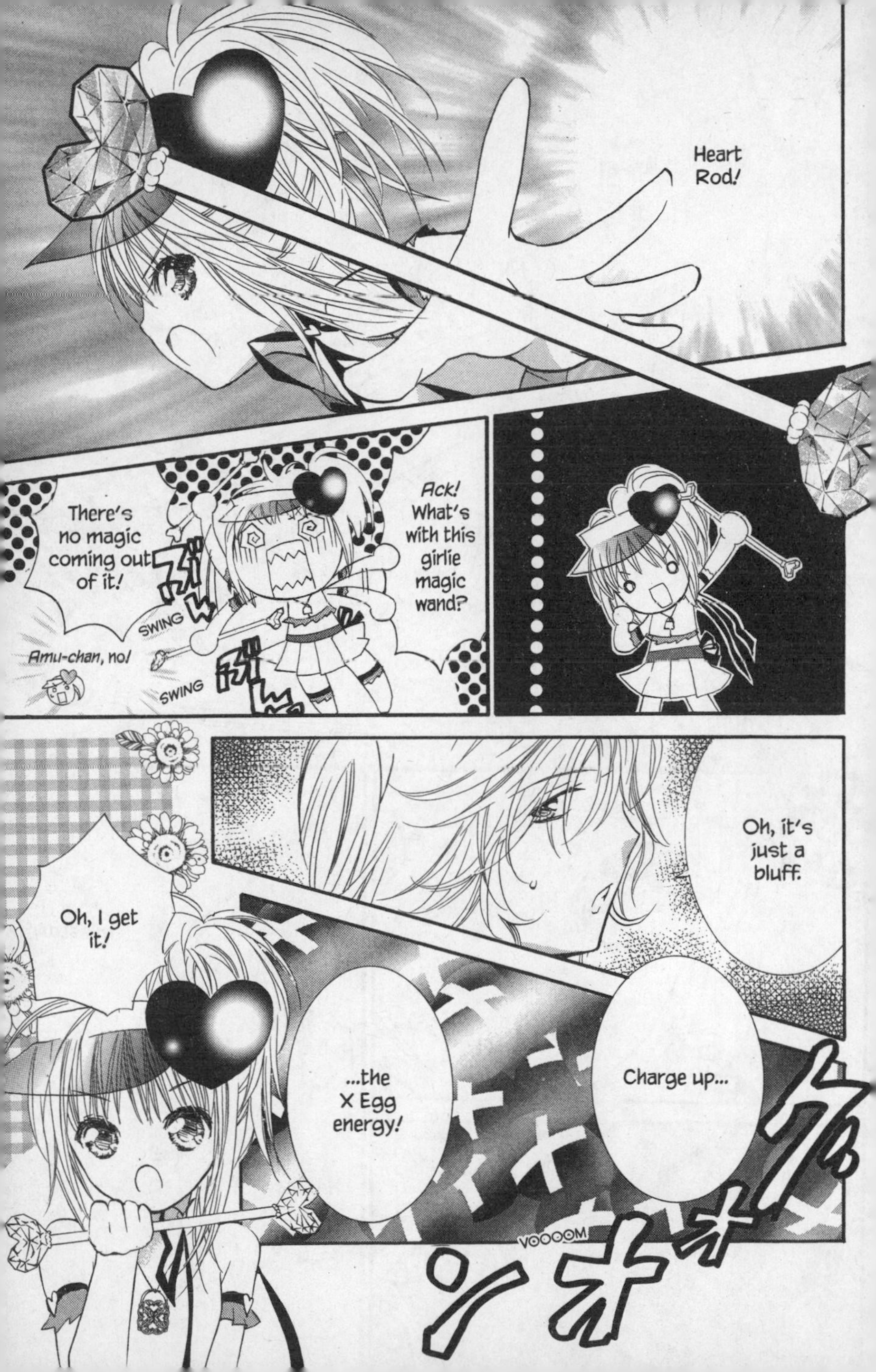
Heart Rod!
Ack! What's with this girlie magic wand?
There's no magic coming out of it!
SWING
SWING
Amu-chan, no!
Oh, it's just a bluff.
Oh, I get it!
Charge up...
...the X Egg energy!
VOOOOM

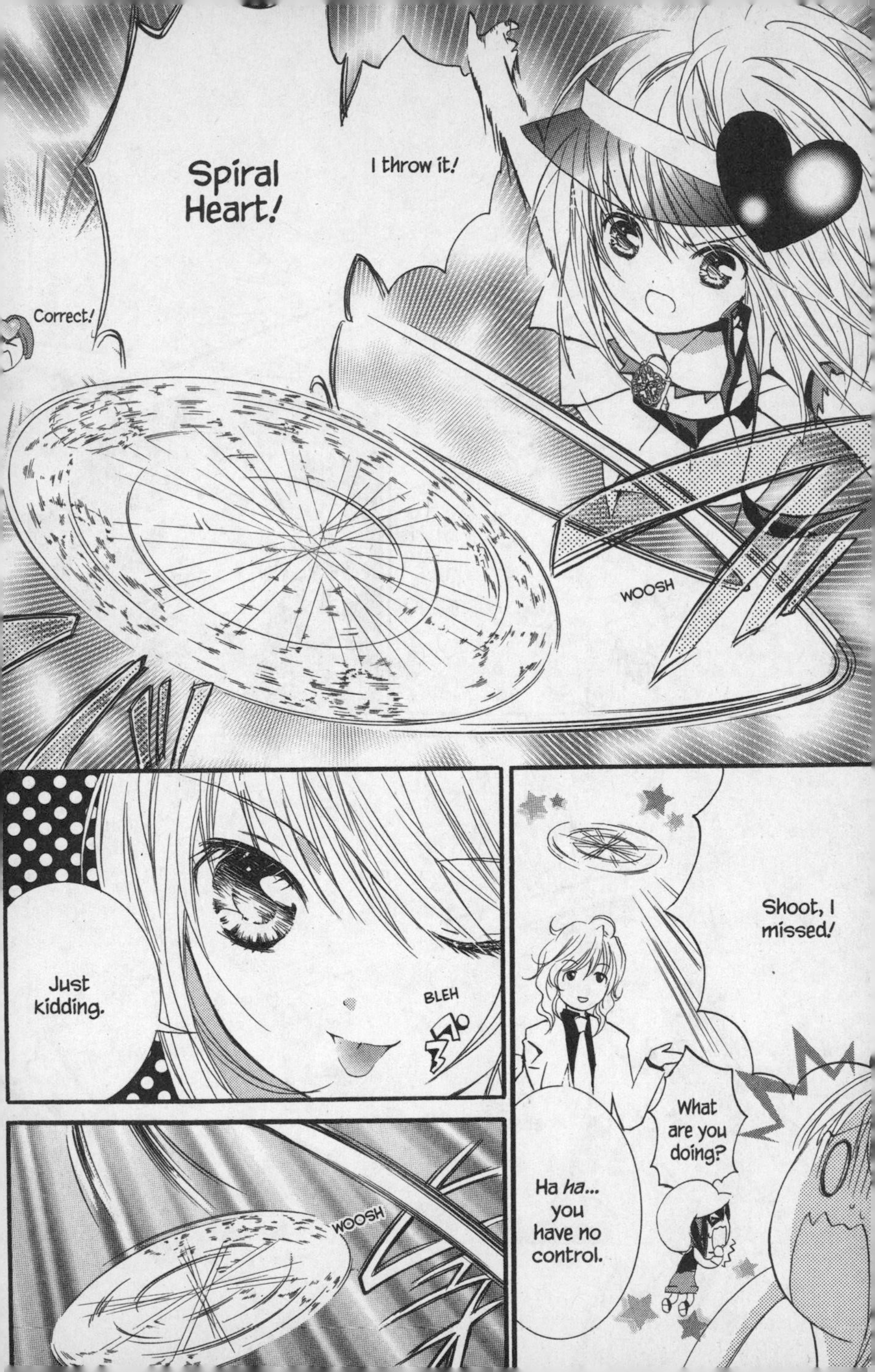
I throw it!
Spiral Heart!
Correct!
WOOSH
Shoot, I missed!
What are you doing?
Ha *ha*... you have no control.
Just kidding.
BLEH
WOOSH

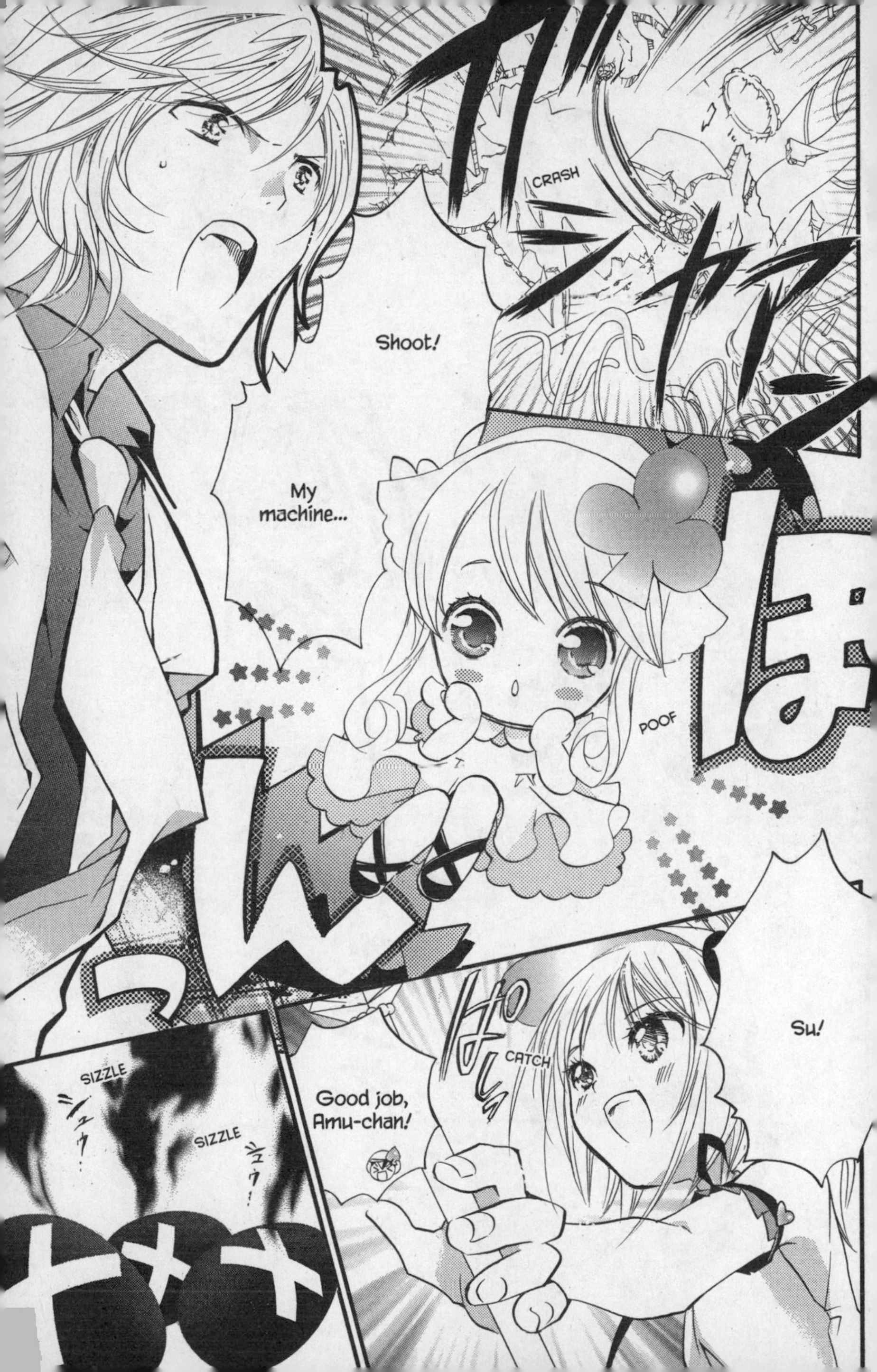
CRASH
Shoot!
POOF
My machine...
Su!
CATCH
Good job, Amu-chan!
SIZZLE
SIZZLE

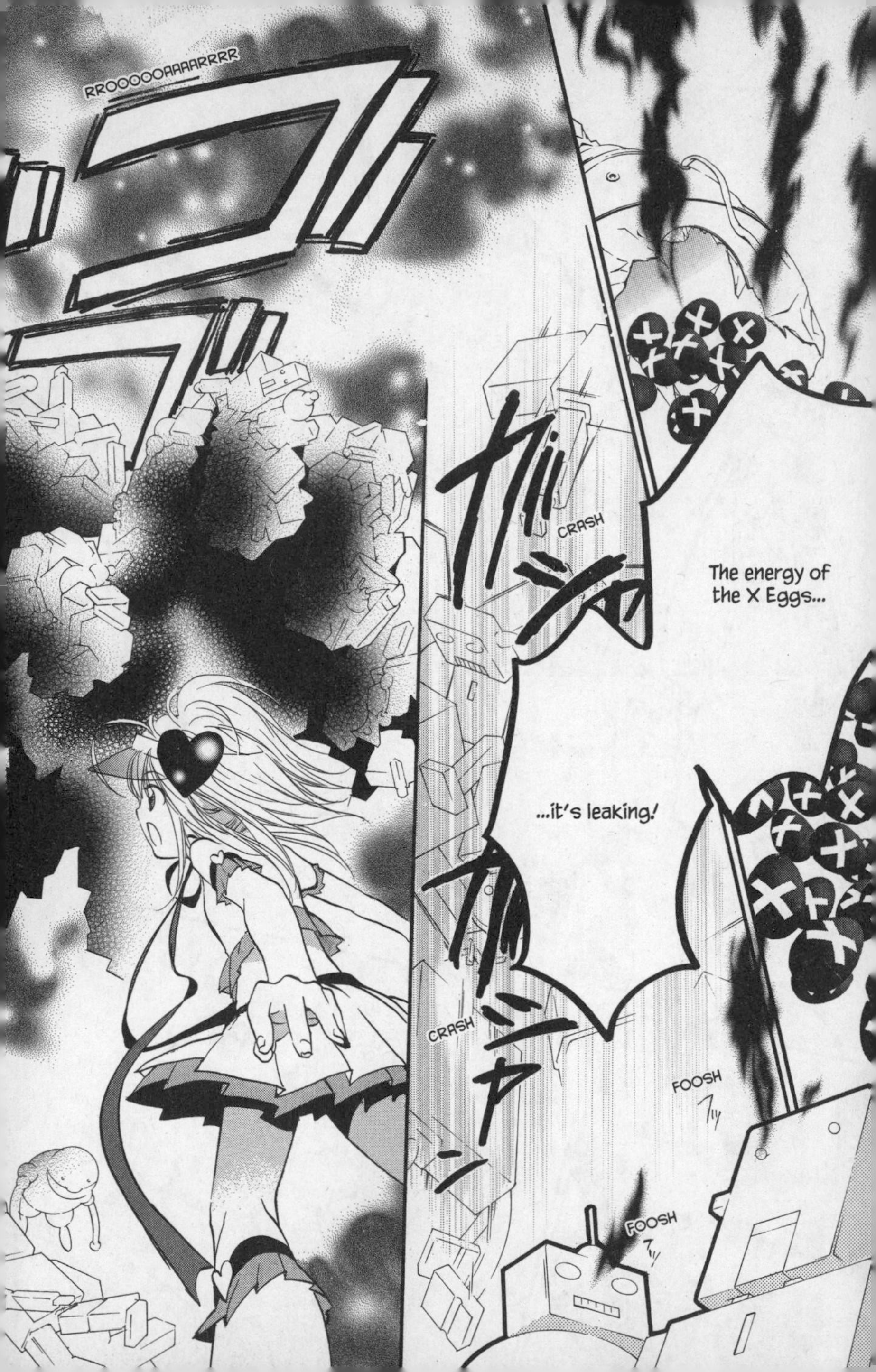
CRASH
The energy of the X Eggs...
...it's leaking!
CRASH
FOOSH
FOOSH
RROOOOOAAAARRRR

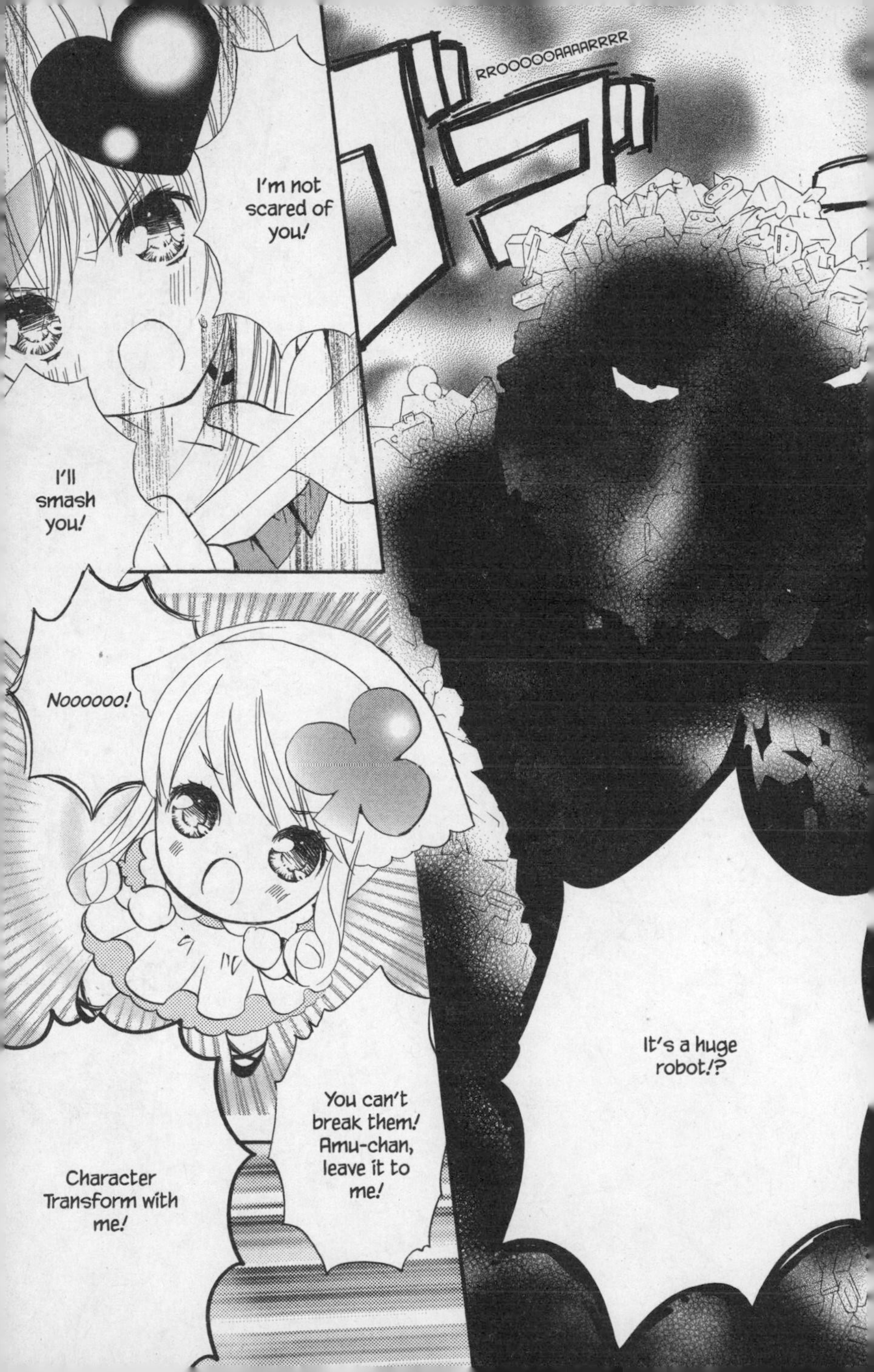
I'm not scared of you!
I'll smash you!
RROOOOOAAAARRRR
It's a huge robot!?
Nooooooo!
You can't break them! Amu-chan, leave it to me!
Character Transform with me!

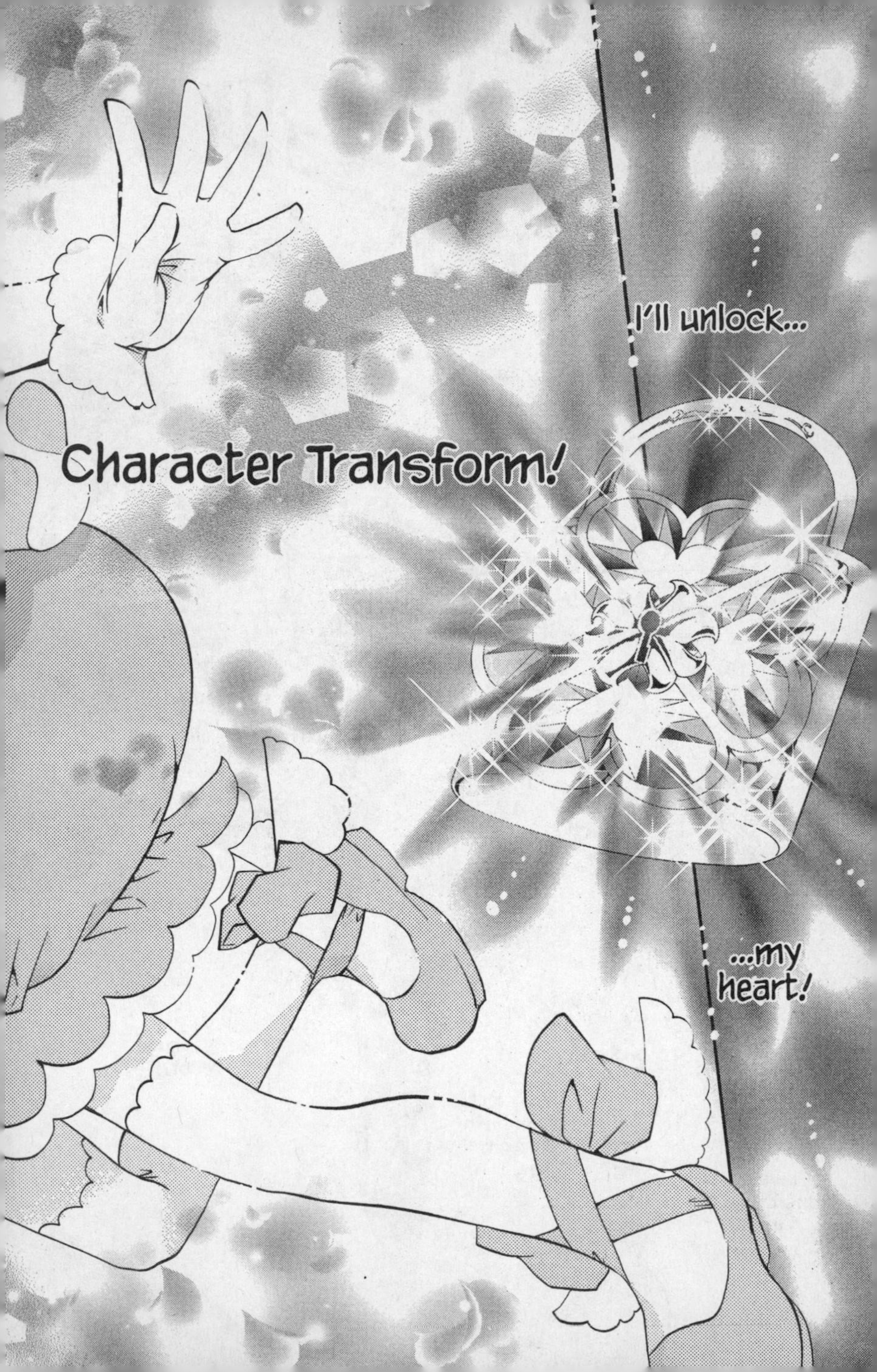
I'll unlock...
...my heart!
Character Transform!

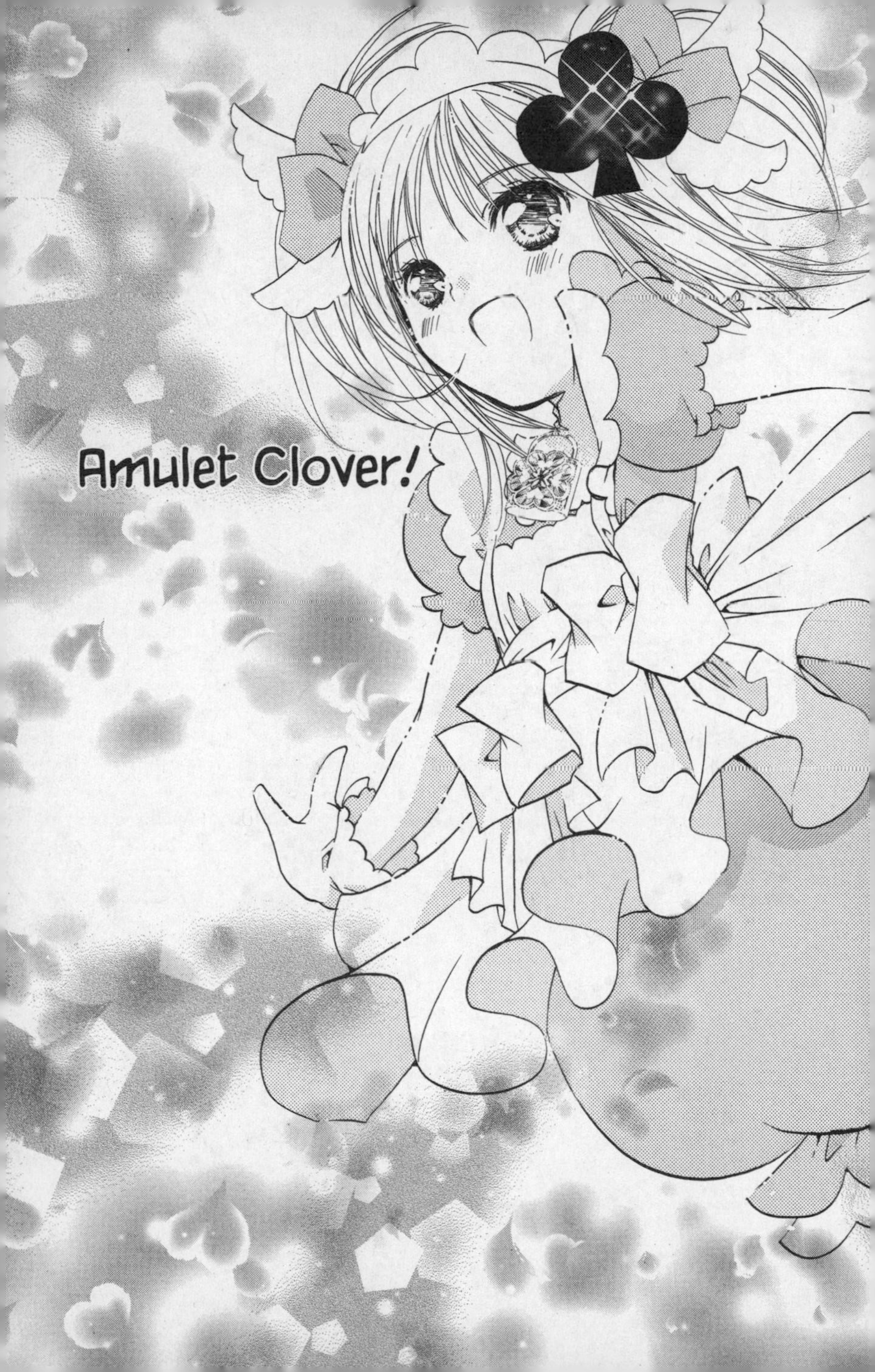
Amulet Clover!

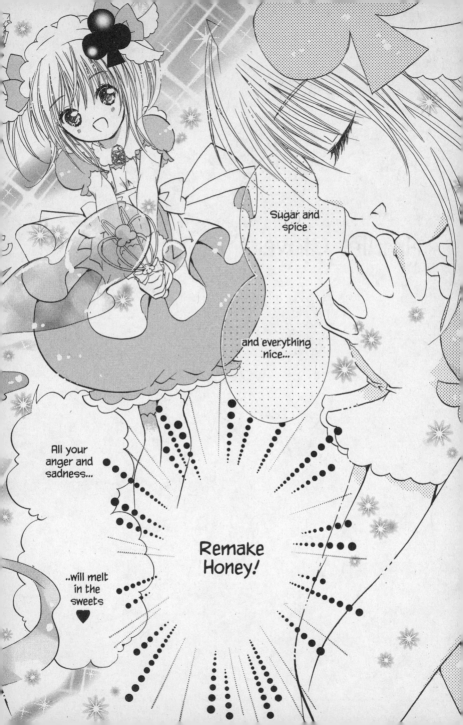

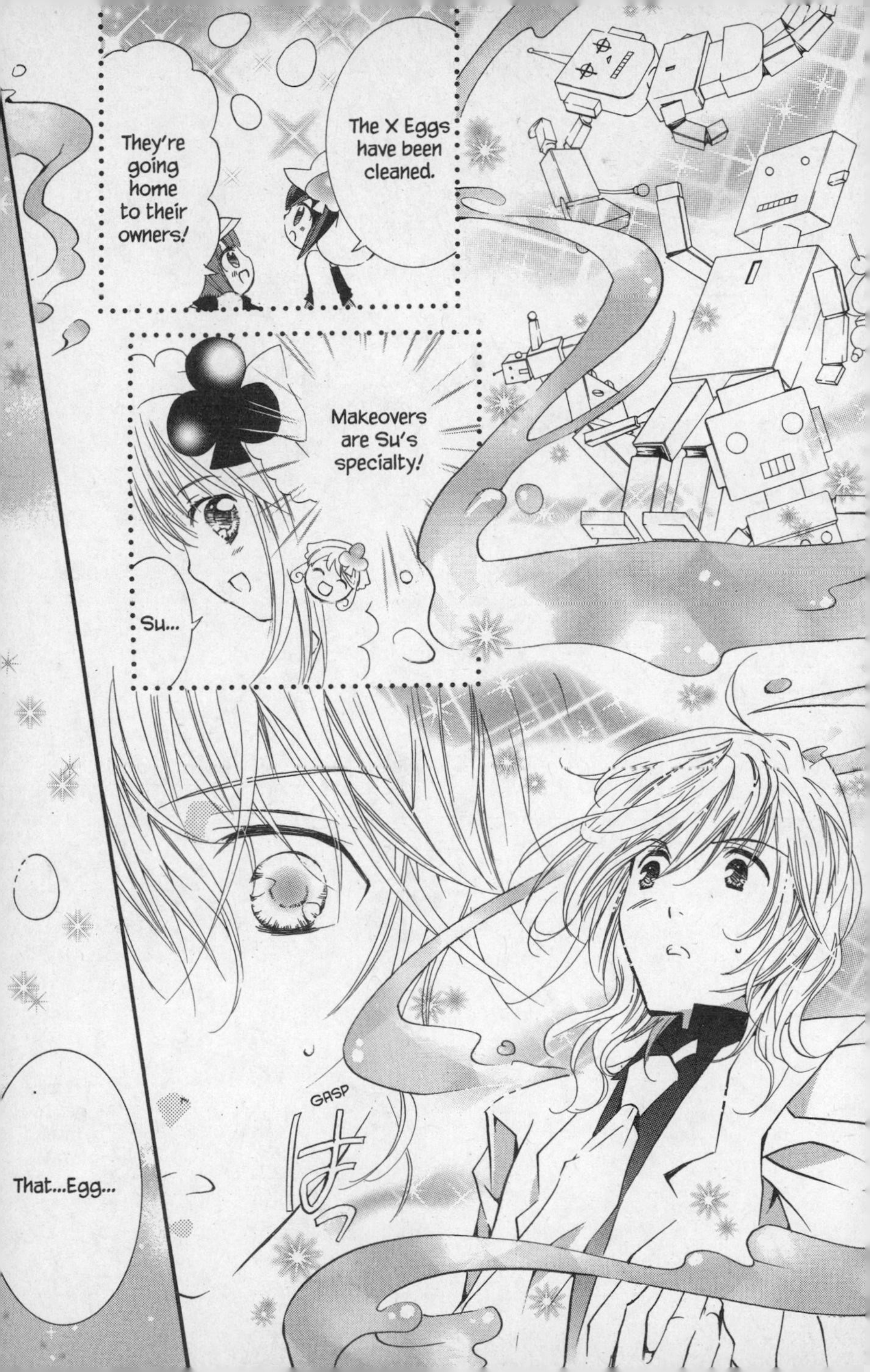
The X Eggs have been cleaned.
They're going home to their owners!
Makeovers are Su's specialty!
Su...
GASP
That...Egg...

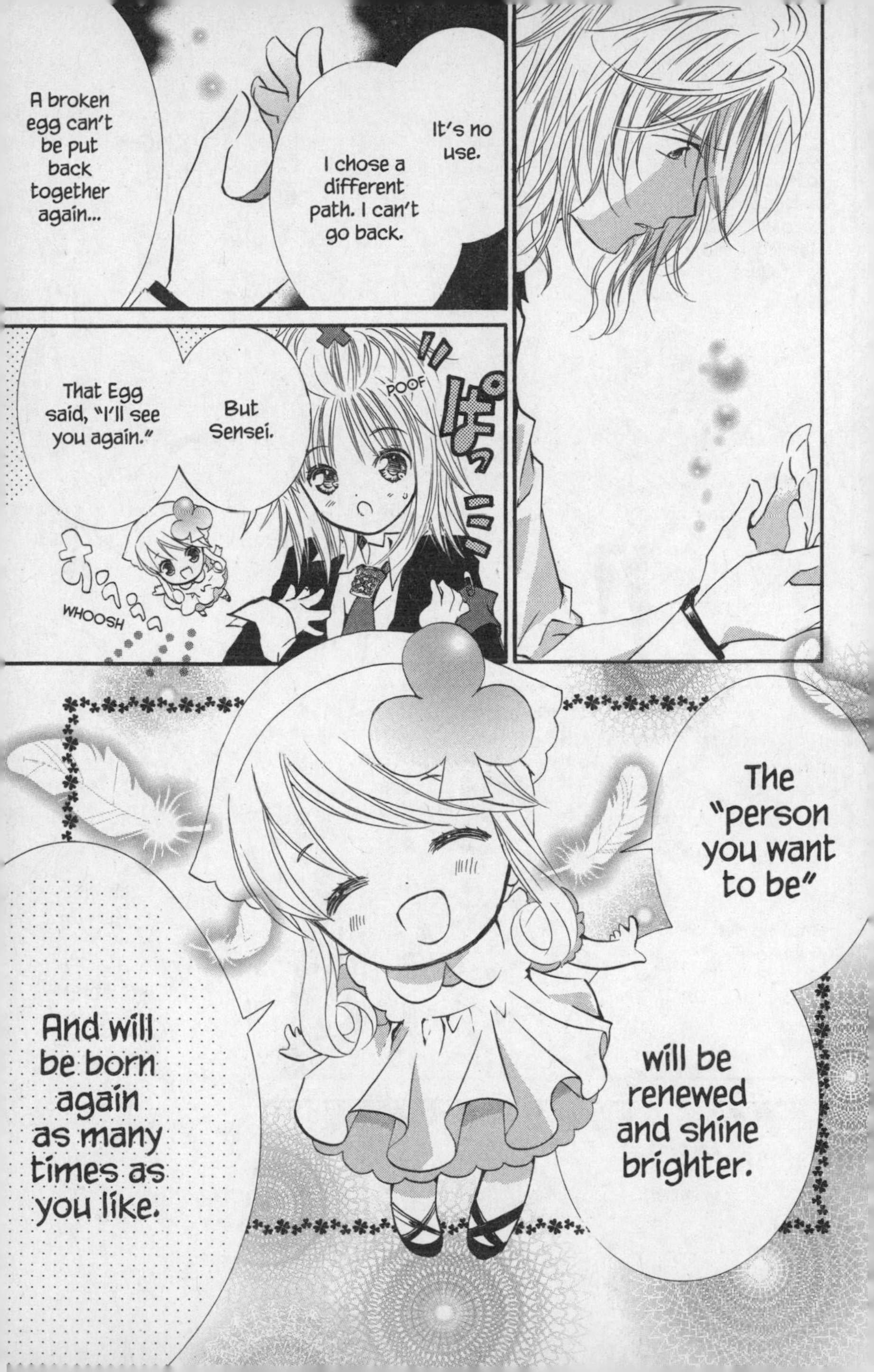
It's no use.
I chose a different path. I can't go back.
A broken egg can't be put back together again...
But Sensei.
POOF
That Egg said, "I'll see you again."
WHOOSH
The "person you want to be"
will be renewed and shine brighter.
And will be born again as many times as you like.

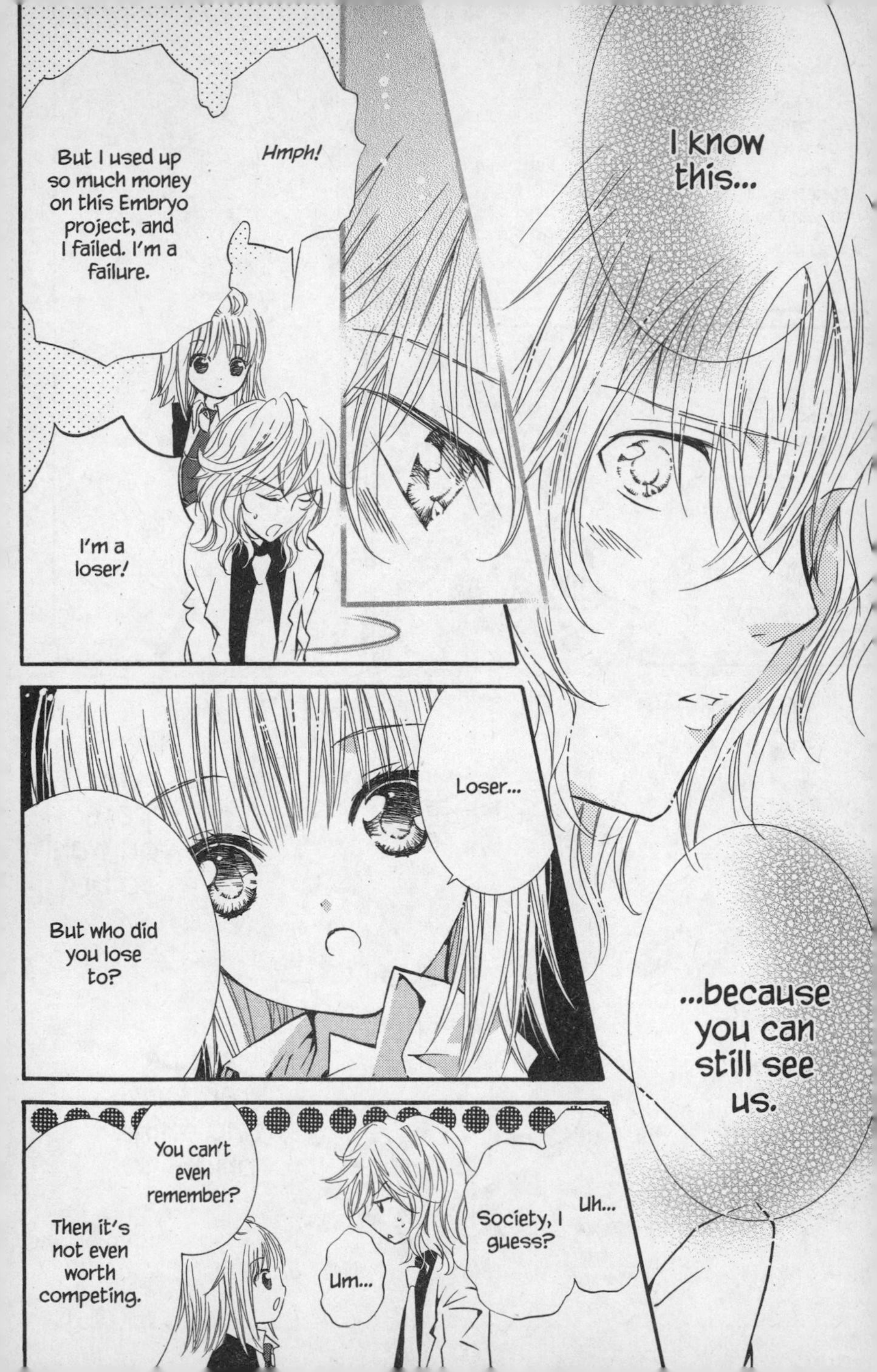
I know this...
...because you can still see us.
Hmph!
But I used up so much money on this Embryo project, and I failed. I'm a failure.
I'm a loser!
Loser...
But who did you lose to?
Uh...
Society, I guess?
Um...
You can't even remember?
Then it's not even worth competing.

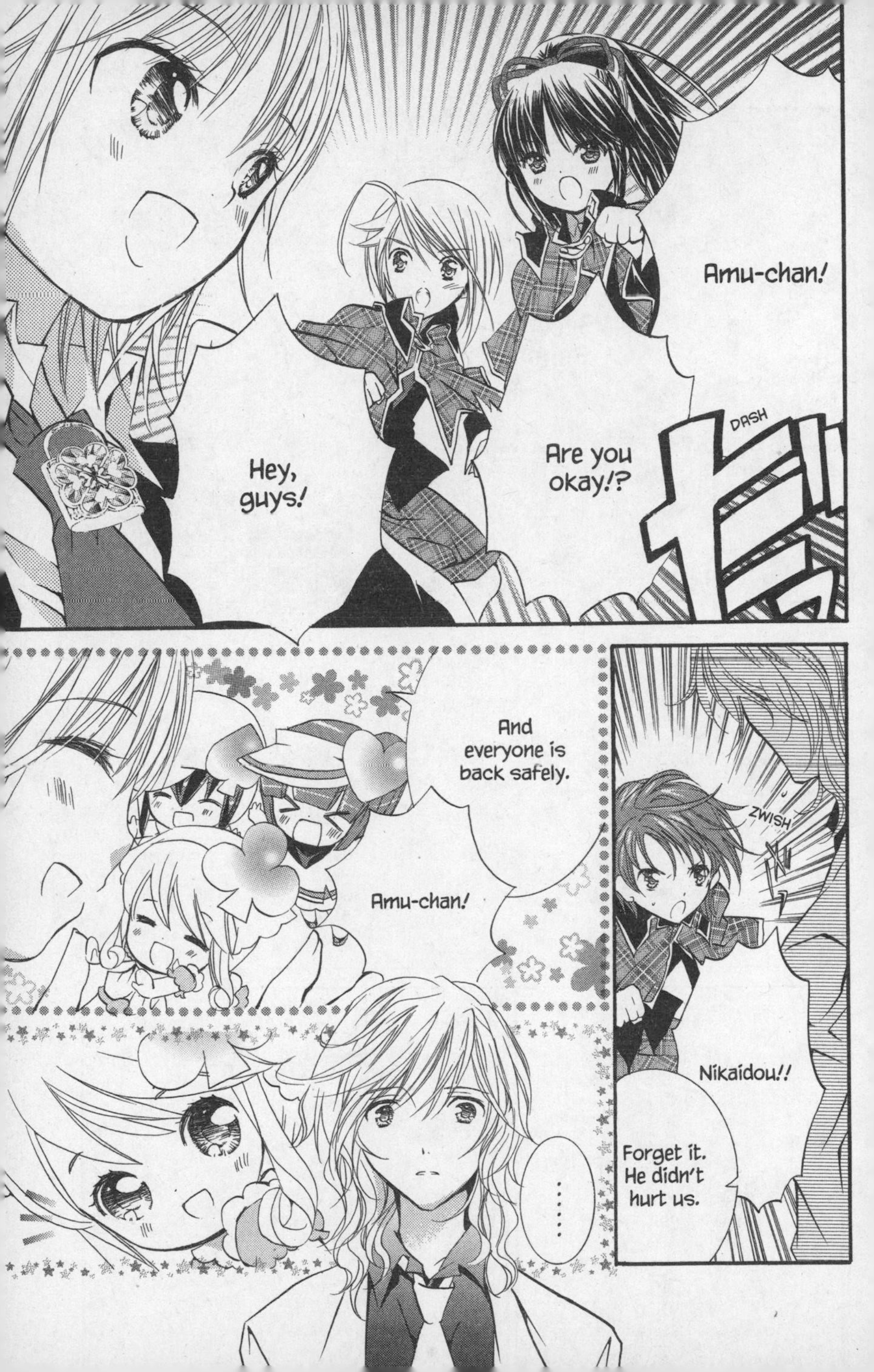
Amu-chan!
DASH
Are you okay!?
Hey, guys!
ZWISH
Nikaidou!!
Forget it. He didn't hurt us.
And everyone is back safely.
Amu-chan!
......

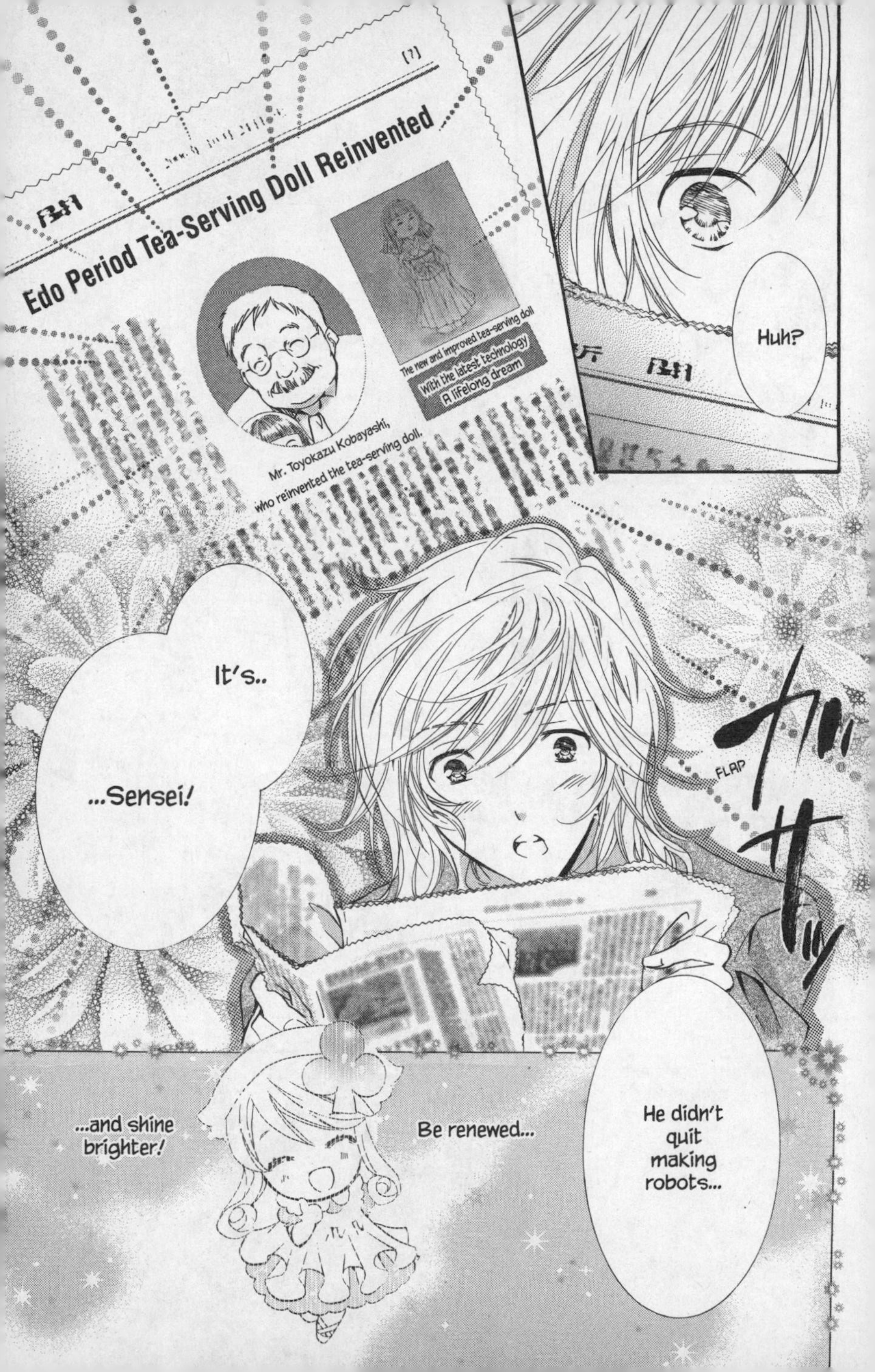
Huh?
[7]
Edo Period Tea-Serving Doll Reinvented
The new and improved tea-serving doll
With the latest technology
A lifelong dream
Mr. Toyokazu Kobayashi, who reinvented the tea-serving doll.
FLAP
It's..
...Sensei!
He didn't quit making robots...
Be renewed...
...and shine brighter!

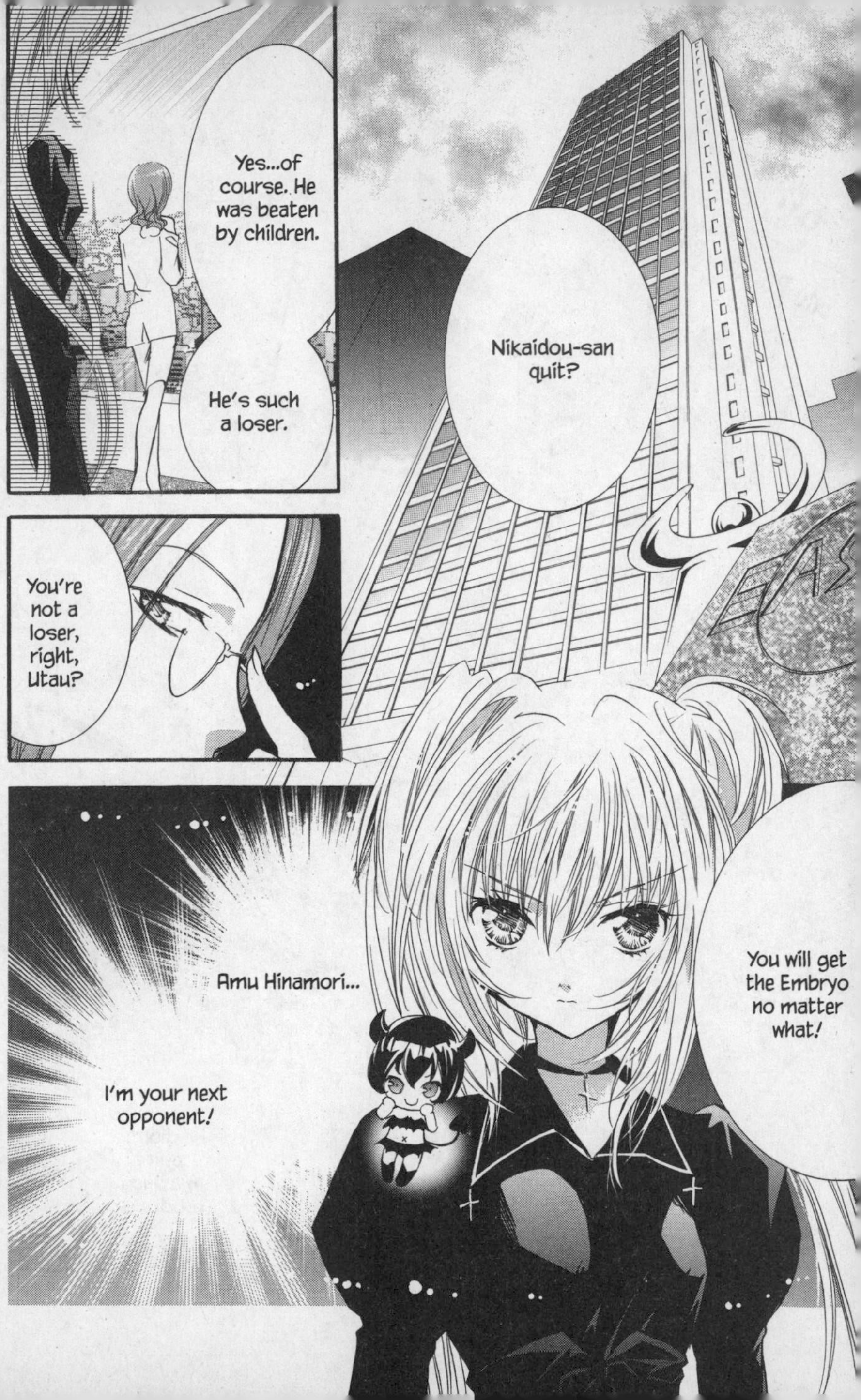

Nikaidou-san quit?
Yes...of course. He was beaten by children.
He's such a loser.
You're not a loser, right, Utau?
You will get the Embryo no matter what!
Amu Hinamori...
I'm your next opponent!

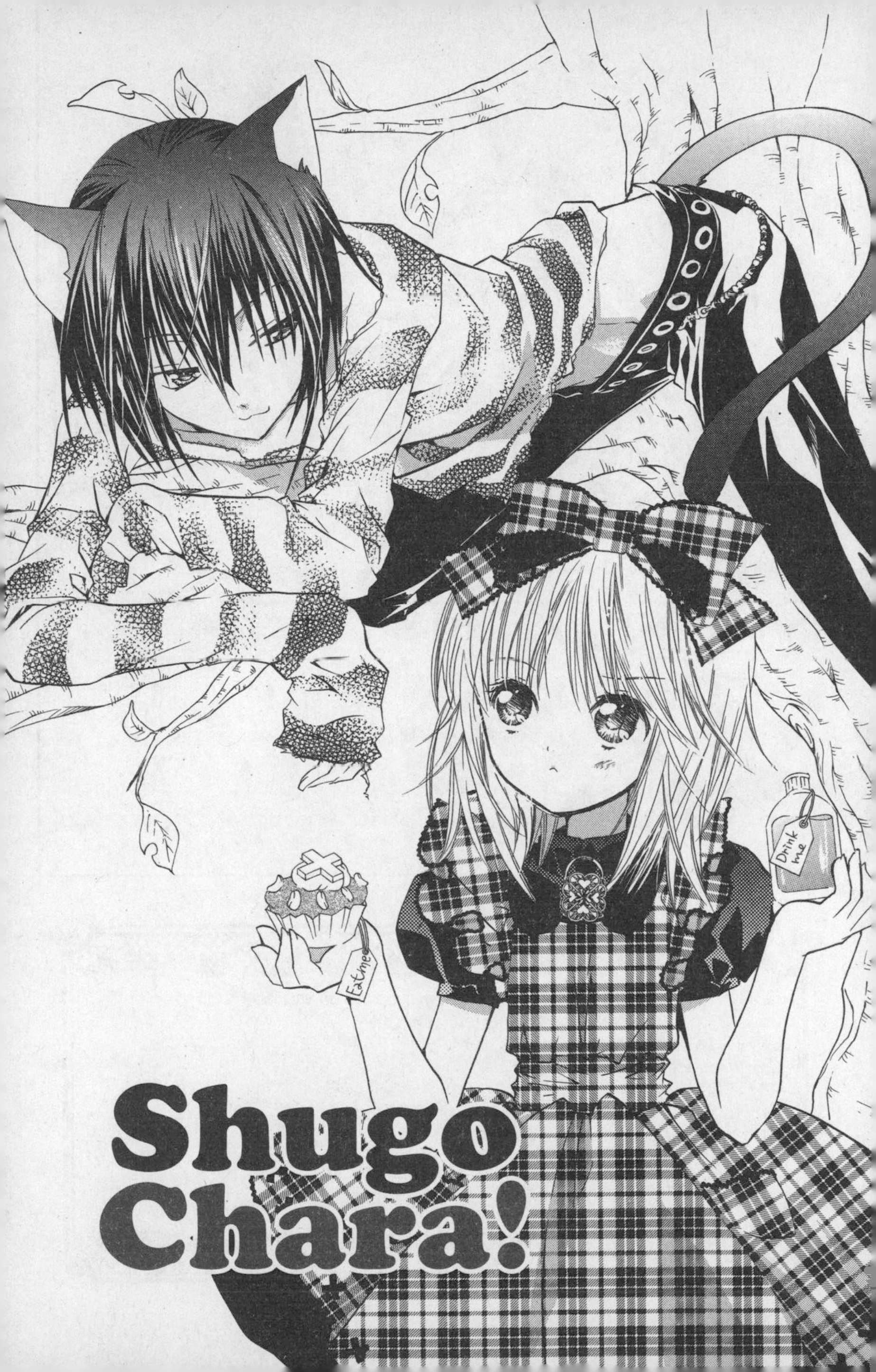
Eat me
Drink me
Shugo Chara!

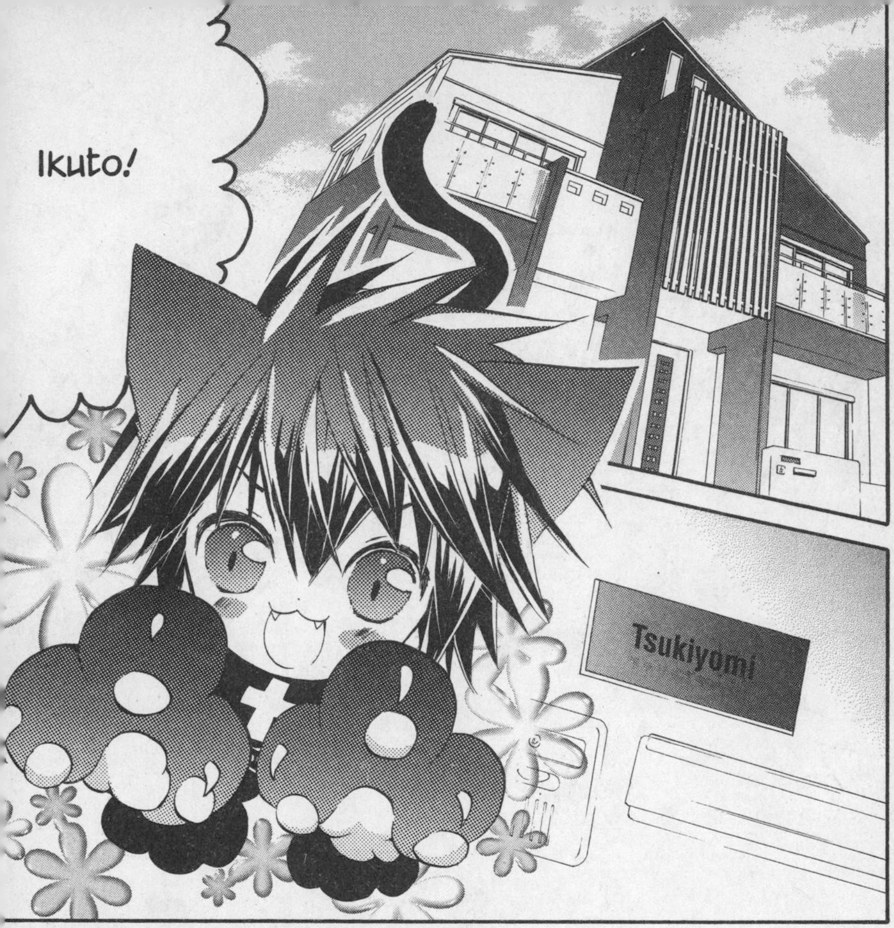
Tsukiyomi
Ikuto!

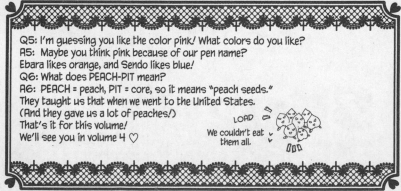

Q5: I'm guessing you like the color pink! What colors do you like?
A5: Maybe you think pink because of our pen name?
Ebara likes orange, and Sendo likes blue!
Q6: What does PEACH-PIT mean?
A6: PEACH = peach, PIT = core, so it means "peach seeds."
They taught us that when we went to the United States.
(And they gave us a lot of peaches!)
That's it for this volume!
We'll see you in volume 4 ♡

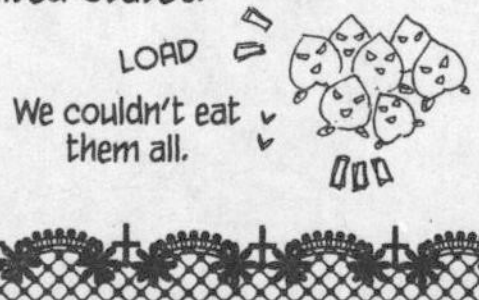
LOAD
We couldn't eat them all.

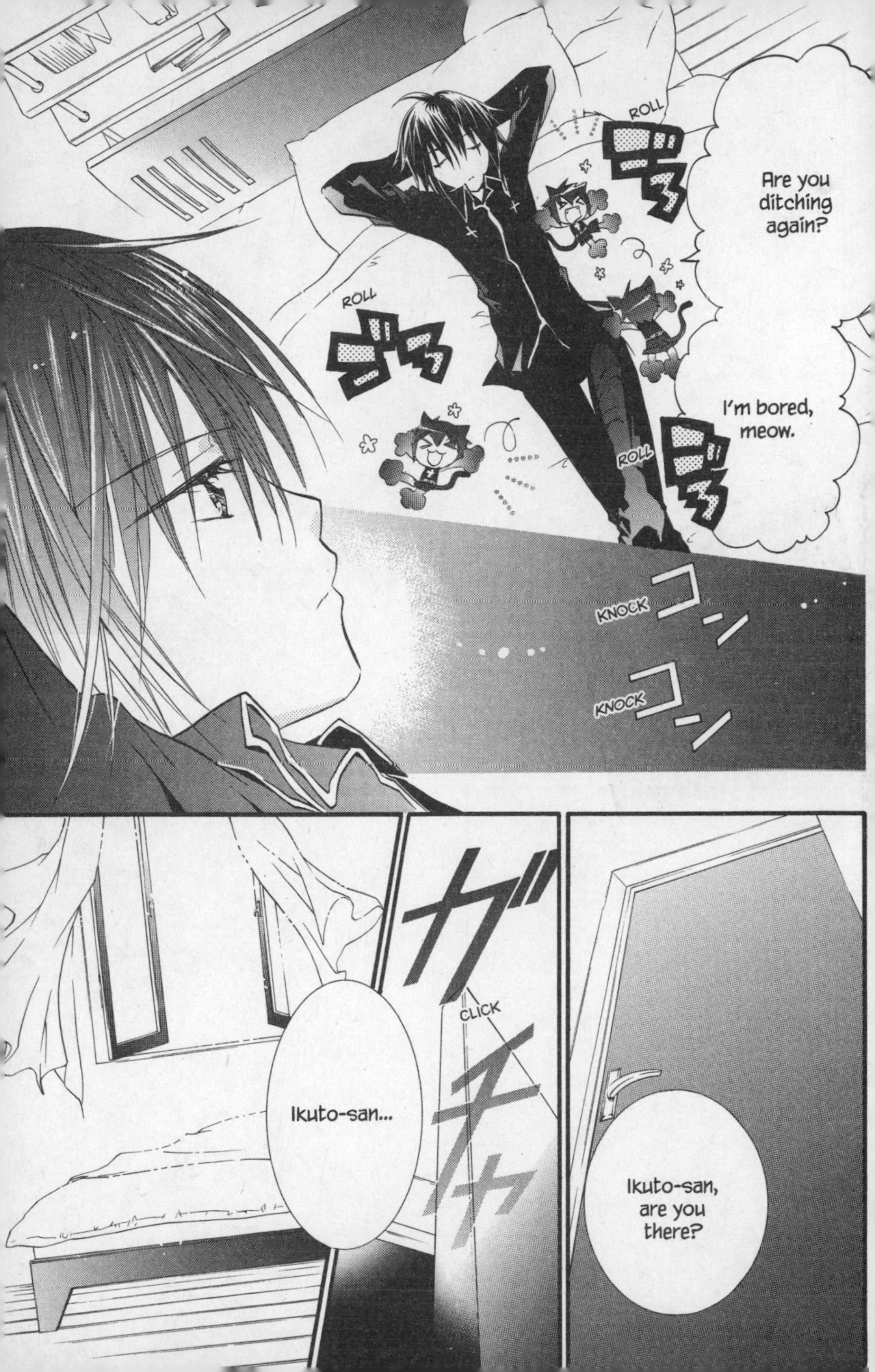
ROLL
Are you ditching again?
I'm bored, meow.
ROLL
ROLL
KNOCK
KNOCK
Ikuto-san, are you there?
CLICK
Ikuto-san...

character profile

Yuu Nikaidou

Birthday: 9/18
Blood Type: A
Sign: Virgo

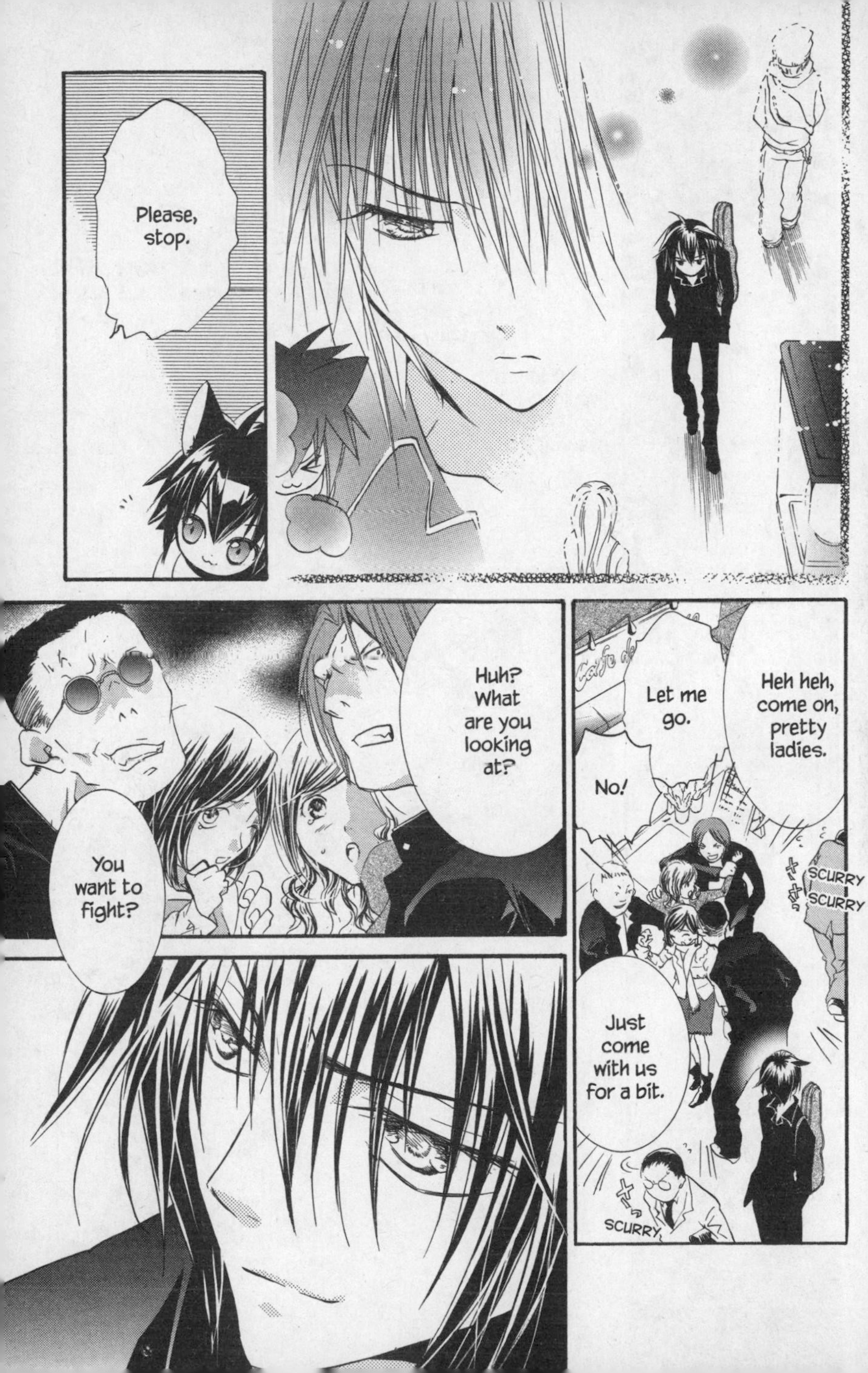
Please, stop.
Heh heh, come on, pretty ladies.
Let me go.
No!
SCURRY
SCURRY
Just come with us for a bit.
SCURRY
Huh? What are you looking at?
You want to fight?

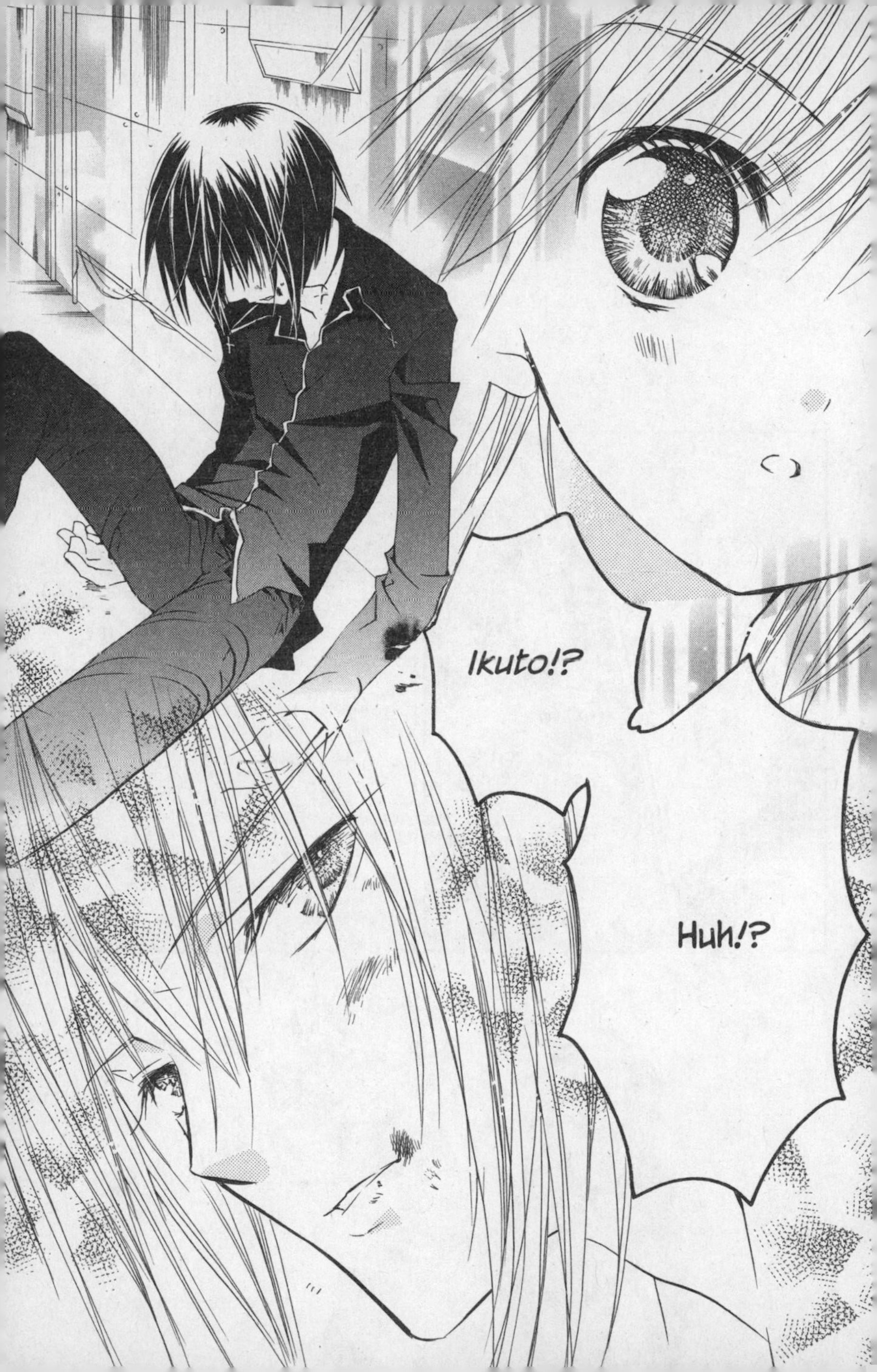
Ikuto!?
Huh!?

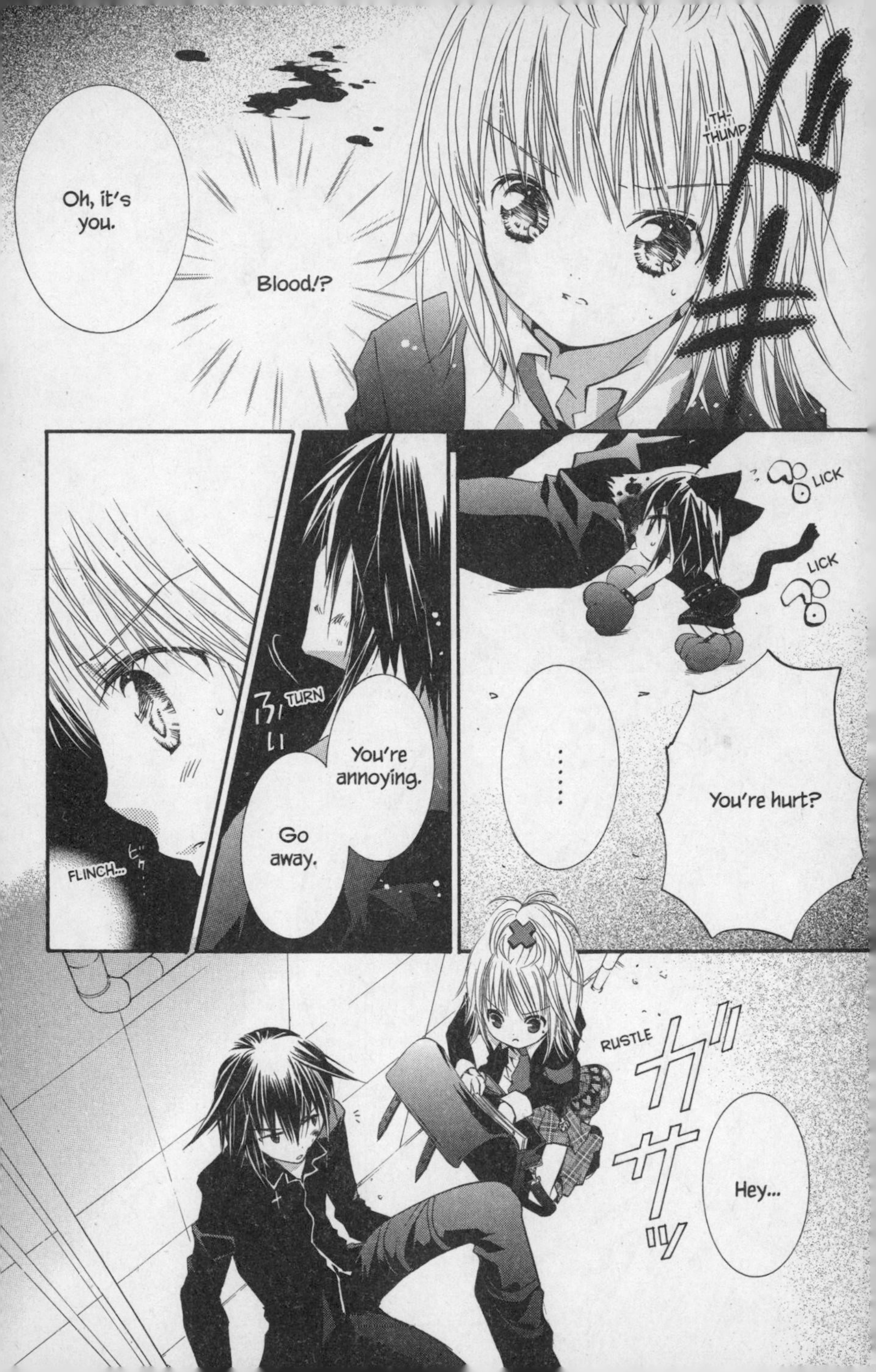
TH-THUMP
Blood!?
Oh, it's you.
LICK
LICK
You're hurt?
......
TURN
You're annoying.
Go away.
FLINCH...
RUSTLE
Hey...

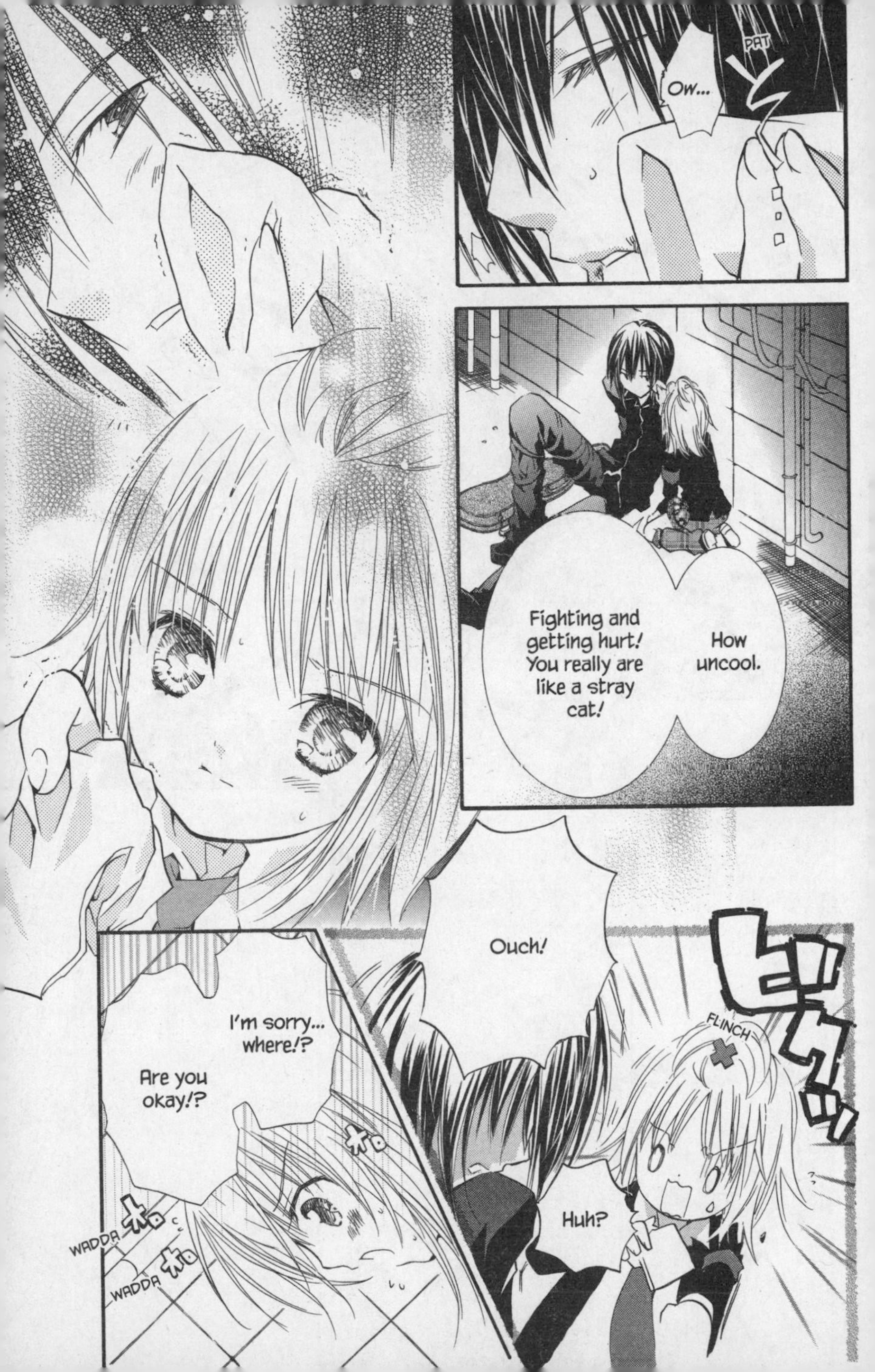
PAT
Ow...
How uncool.
Fighting and getting hurt! You really are like a stray cat!
Ouch!
FLINCH
Huh?
I'm sorry... where!?
Are you okay!?
WADDA
WADDA

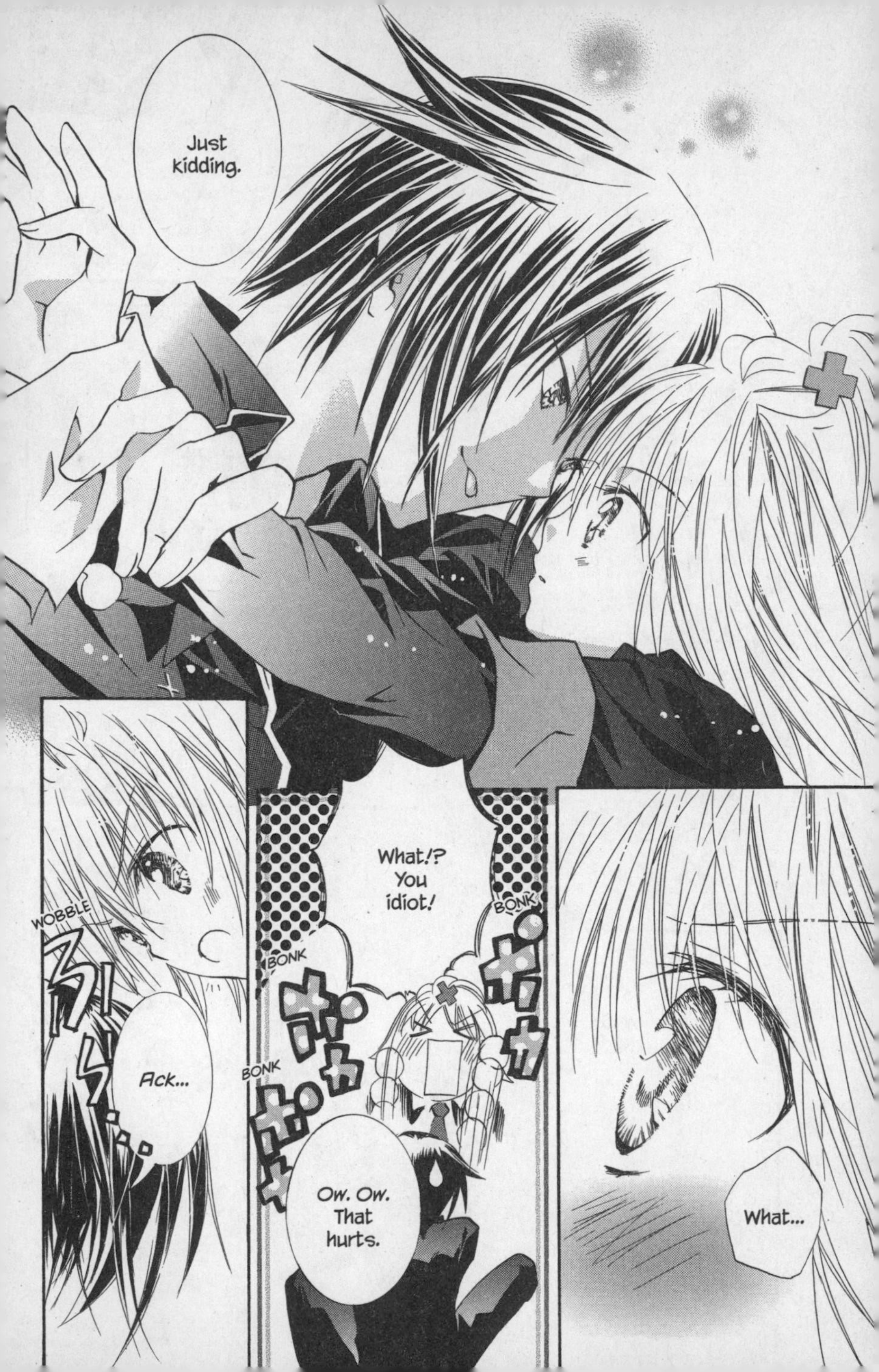
Just kidding.
What...
What!? You idiot!
BONK
BONK
BONK
Ow. Ow. That hurts.
WOBBLE
Ack...

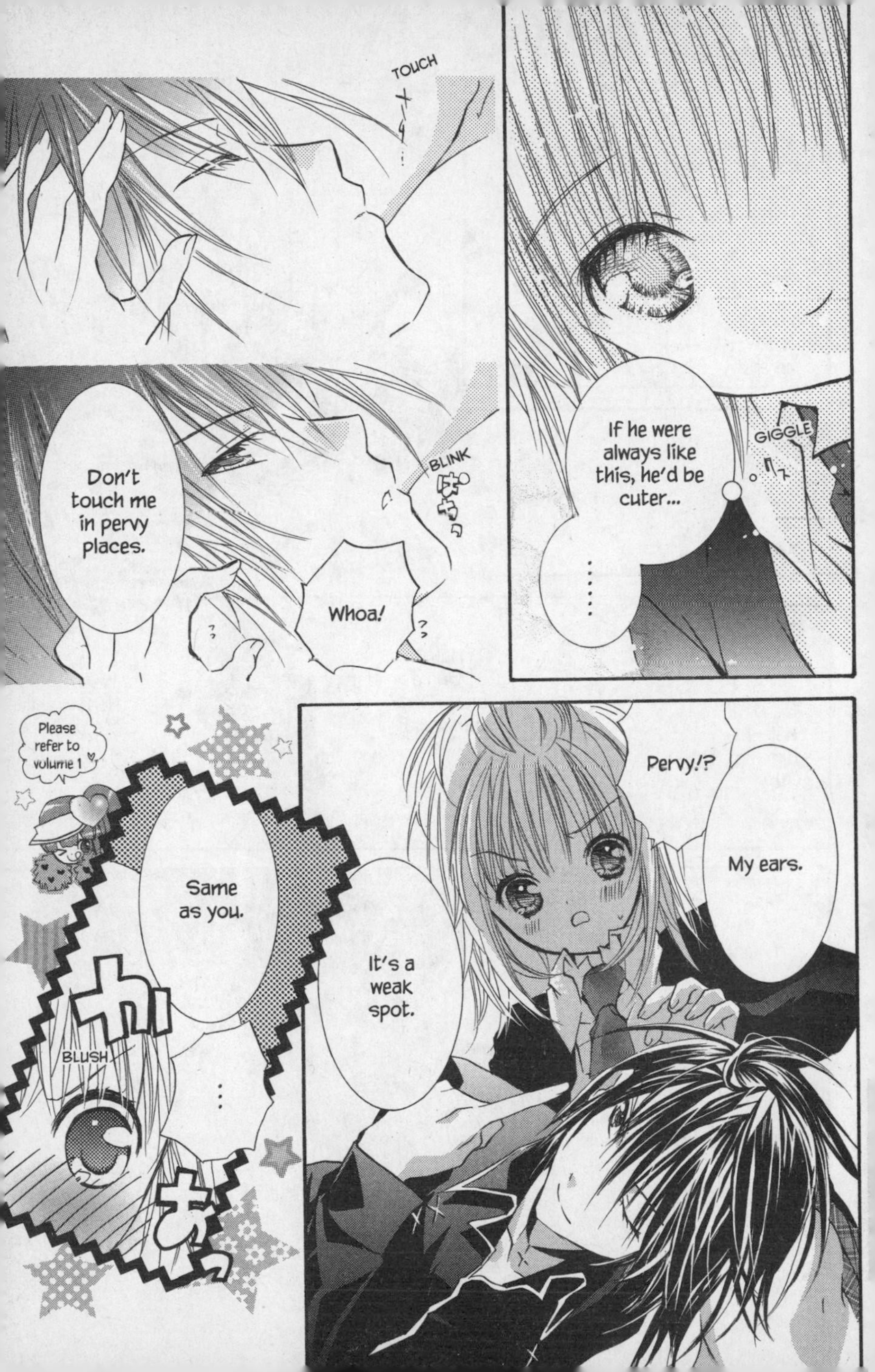
GIGGLE
If he were always like this, he'd be cuter...
......
TOUCH
BLINK
Whoa!
Don't touch me in pervy places.
Pervy!?
My ears.
It's a weak spot.
Same as you.
Please refer to volume 1
BLUSH
...

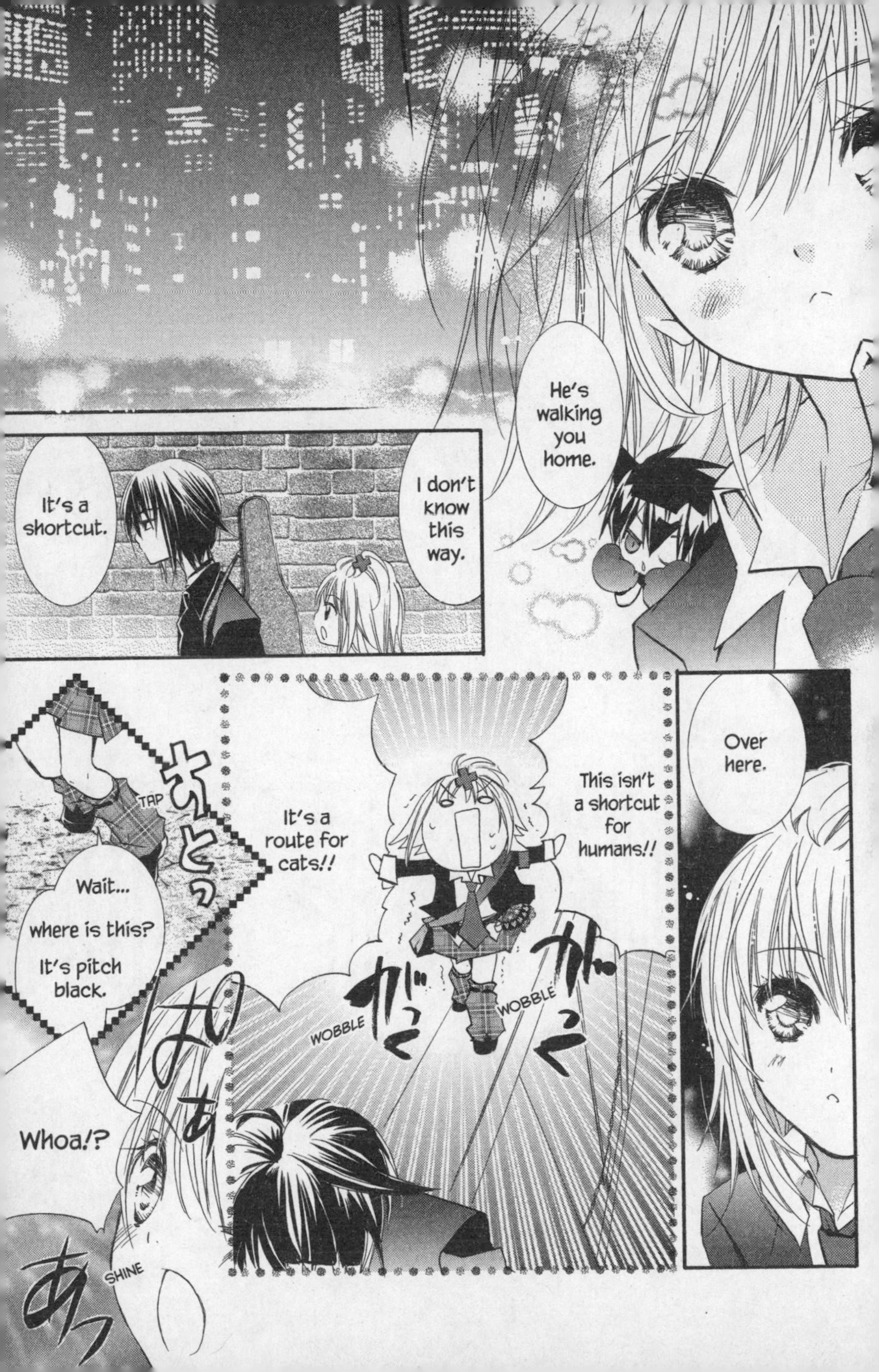
He's walking you home.
I don't know this way.
It's a shortcut.
Over here.
This isn't a shortcut for humans!!
It's a route for cats!!
WOBBLE
WOBBLE
TAP
Wait... where is this?
It's pitch black.
Whoa!?
SHINE

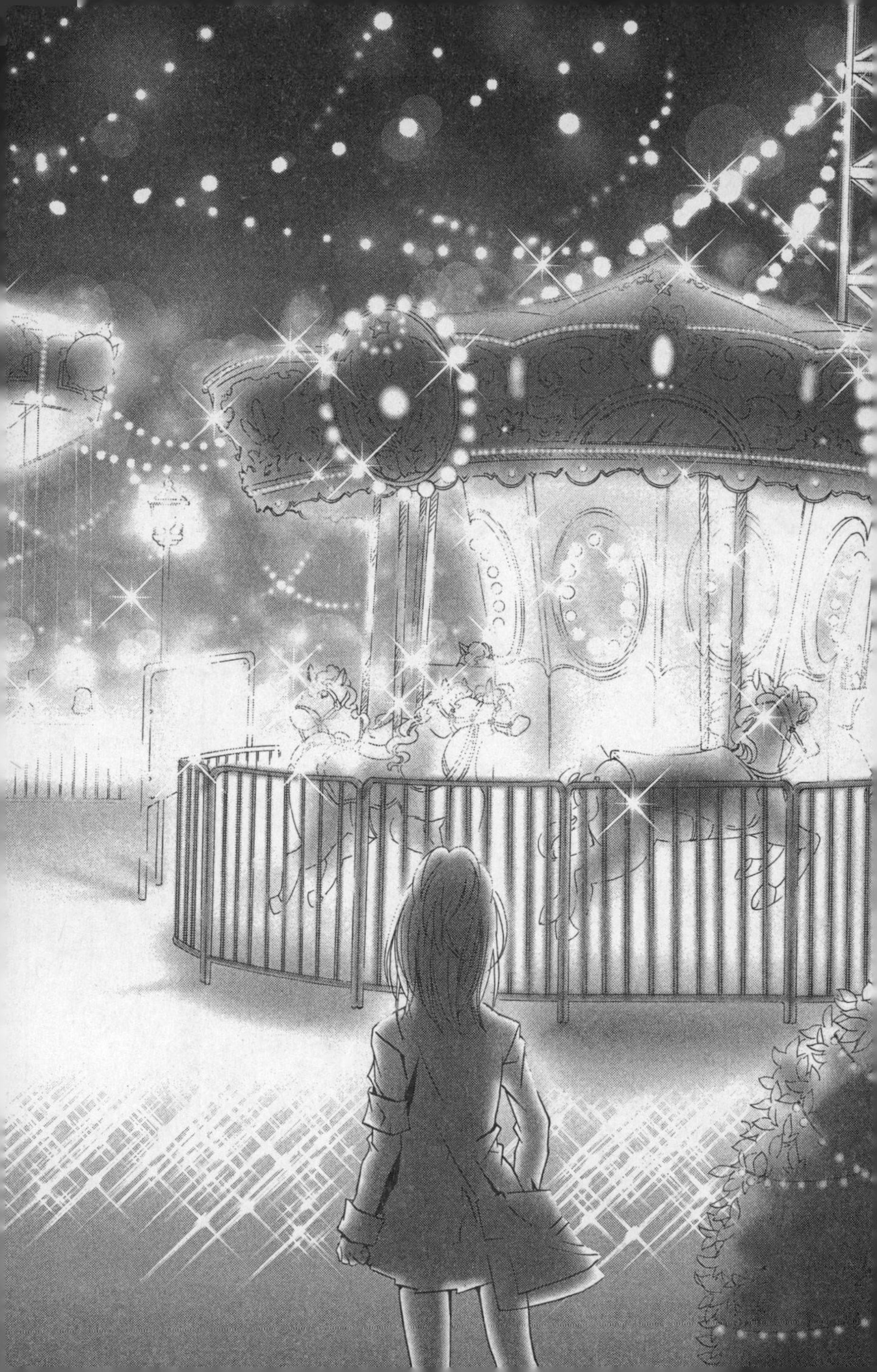

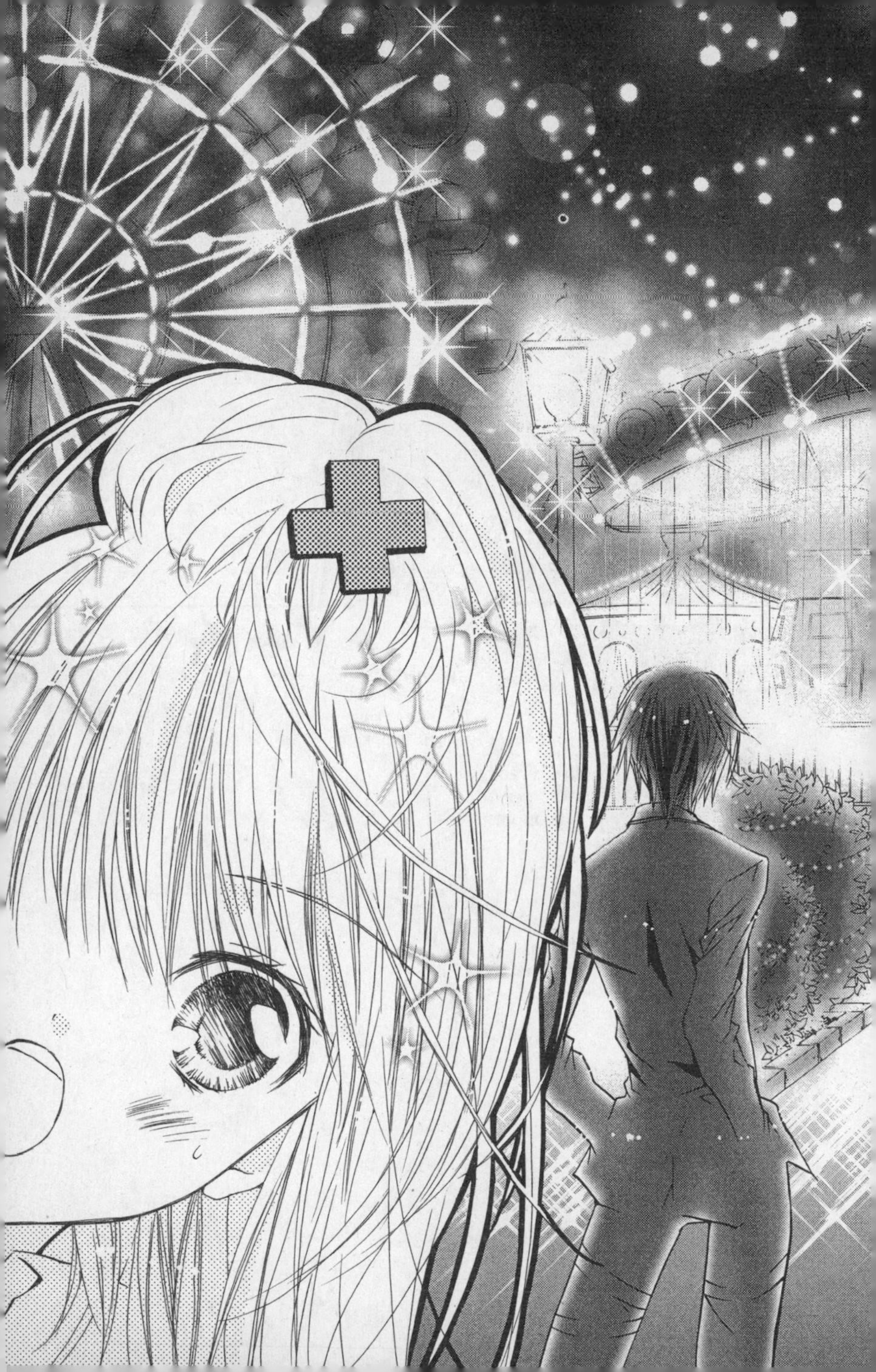

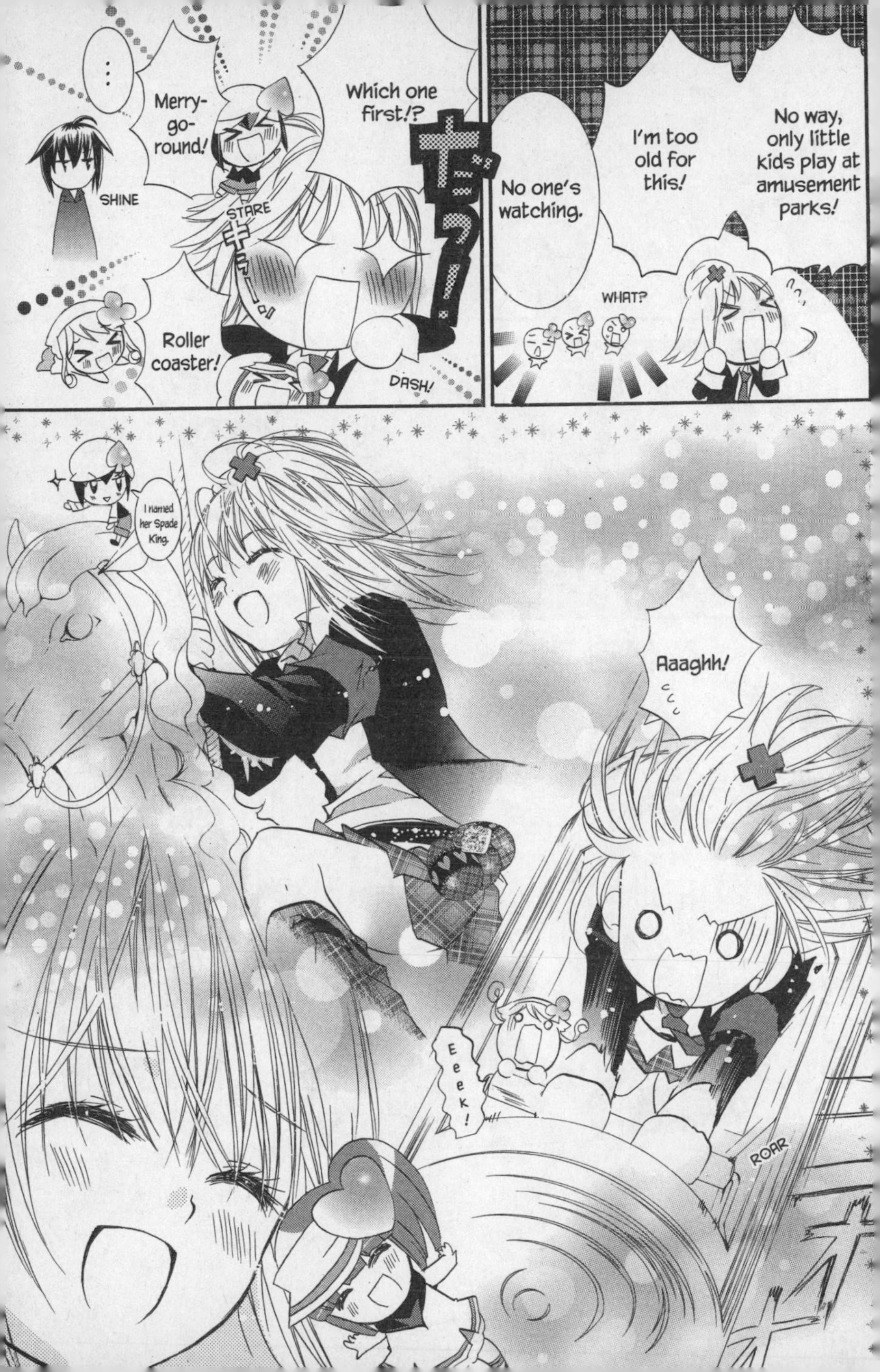
No way, only little kids play at amusement parks!
I'm too old for this!
No one's watching.
WHAT?
Which one first!?
Merry-go-round!
...
STARE
SHINE
DASH!
Roller coaster!
Aaaghh!
ROAR
Eeek!
I named her Spade King.

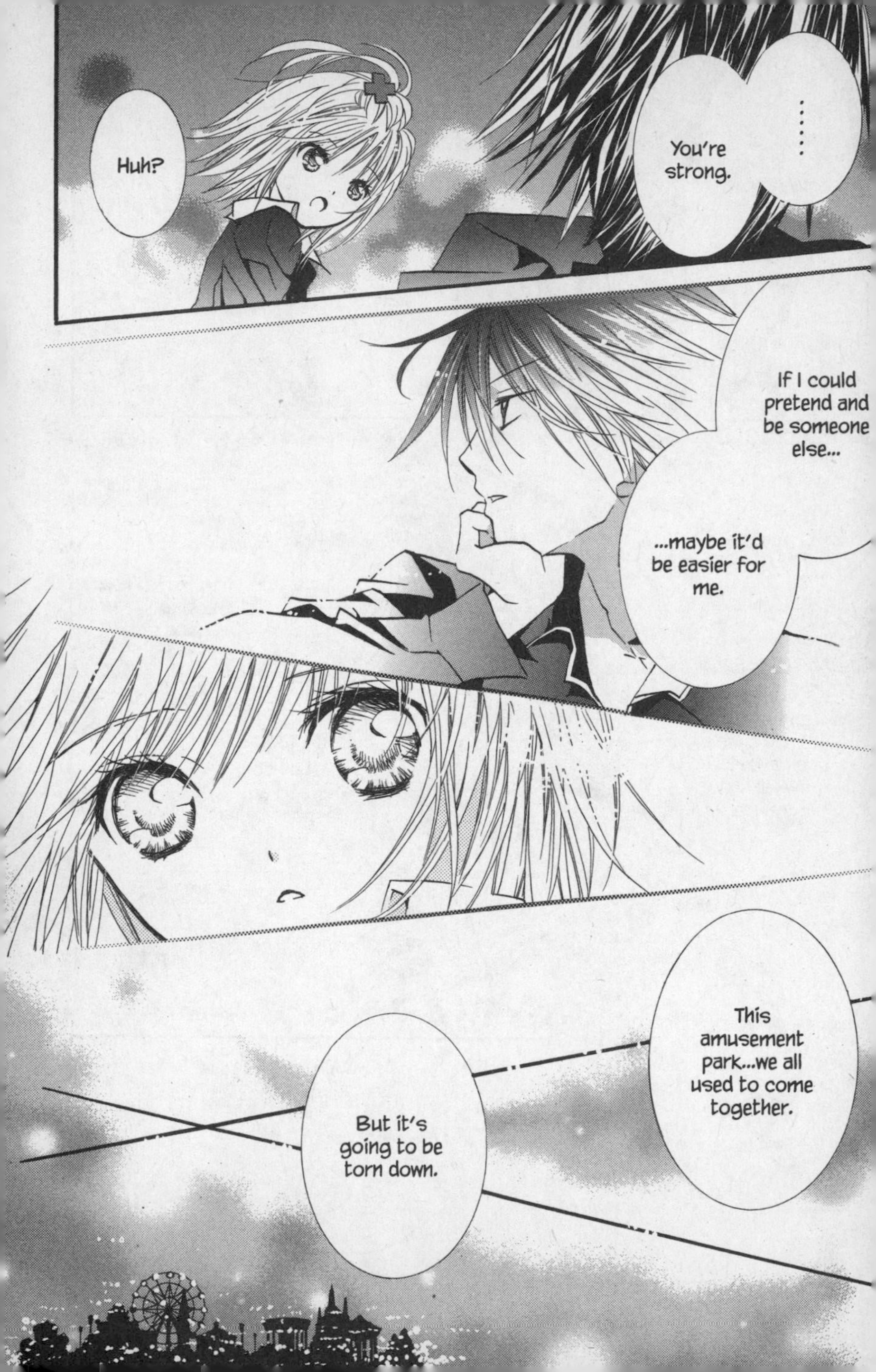
.....
You're strong.
Huh?
If I could pretend and be someone else...
...maybe it'd be easier for me.
This amusement park...we all used to come together.
But it's going to be torn down.

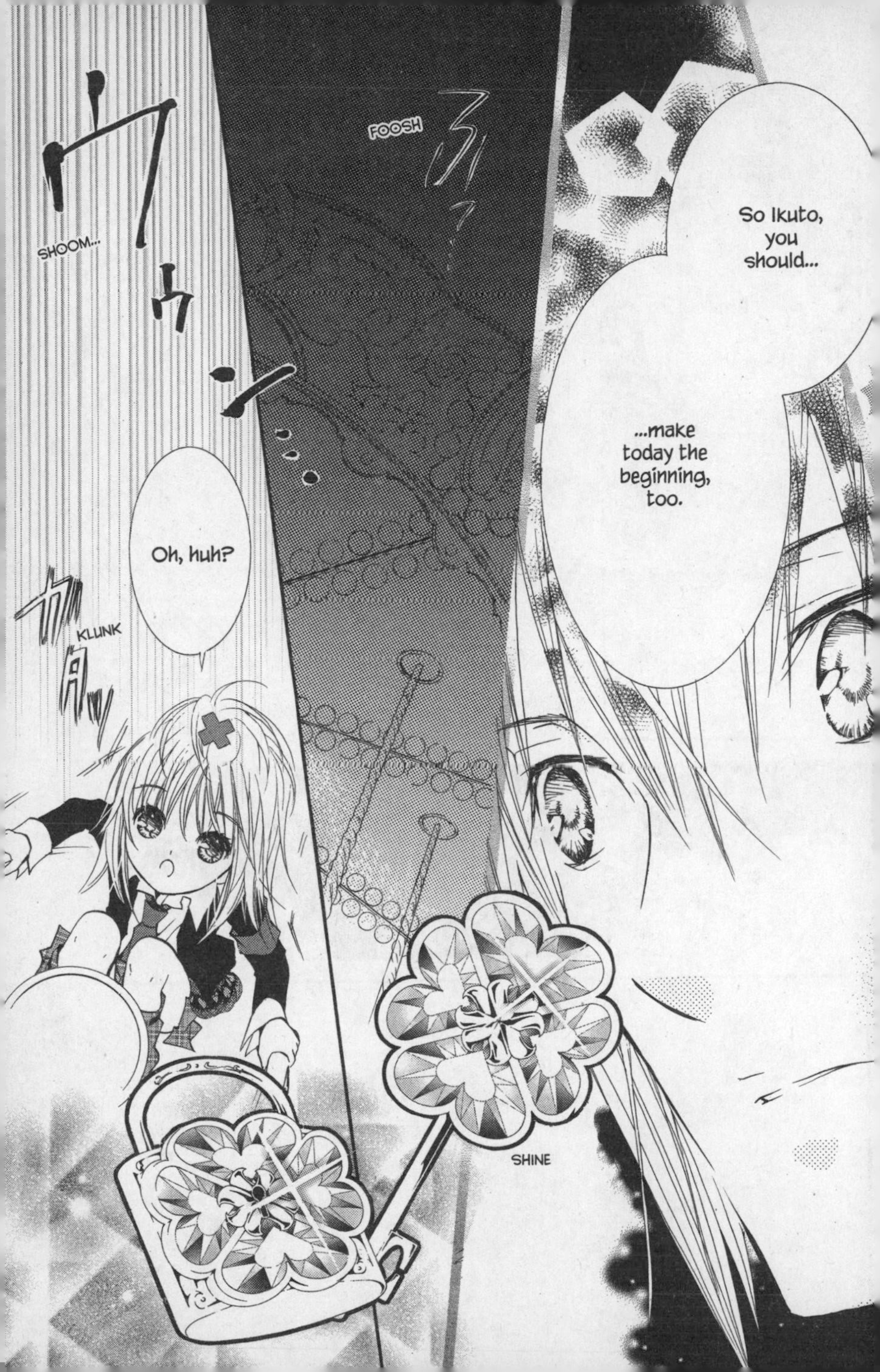
So Ikuto, you should...
...make today the beginning, too.
SHINE
FOOSH
SHOOM...
Oh, huh?
KLUNK

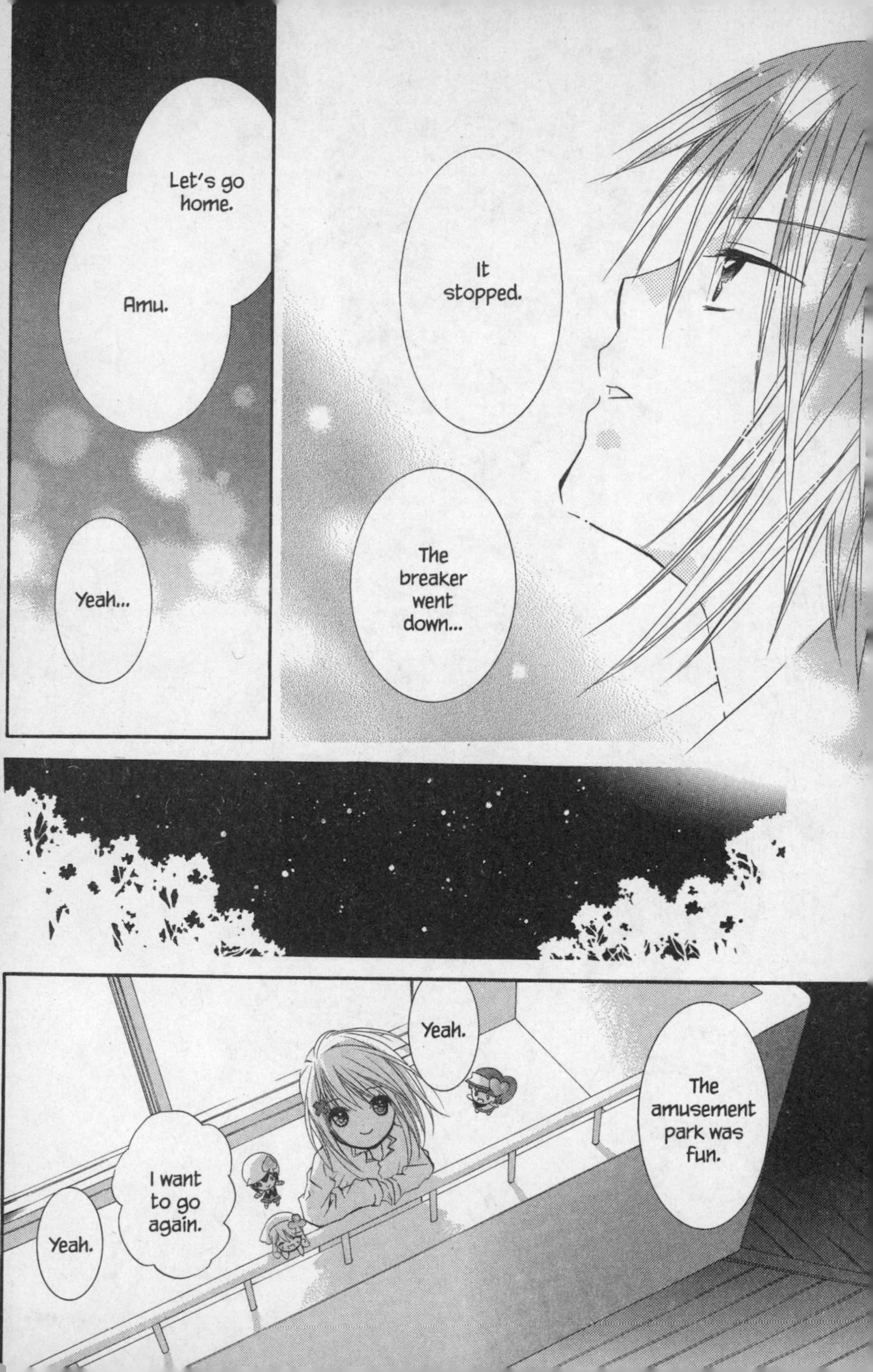
It stopped.
The breaker went down...
Let's go home.
Amu.
Yeah...
The amusement park was fun.
Yeah.
I want to go again.
Yeah.

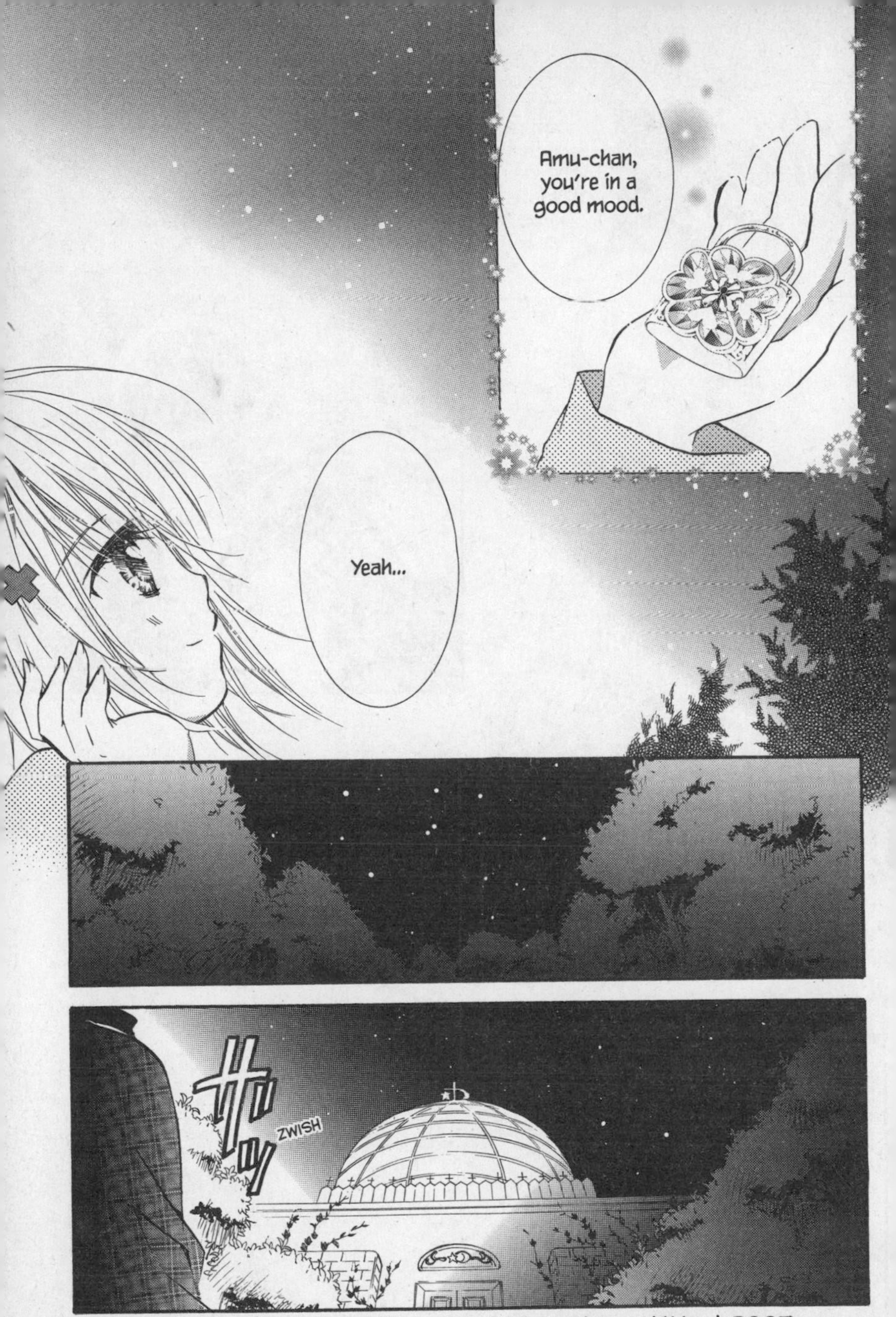
Amu-chan, you're in a good mood.
Yeah...
ZWISH

(Featured in *Nakayoshi* December 2006 - *Nakayoshi* March 2007)

So.

What do you need today?

Yeah.

It's about the movement in the stars.

SIT

And their trajectory...

...is turning the pages in the story.

The Lock and the Key are getting closer.

Huh?

FLIP

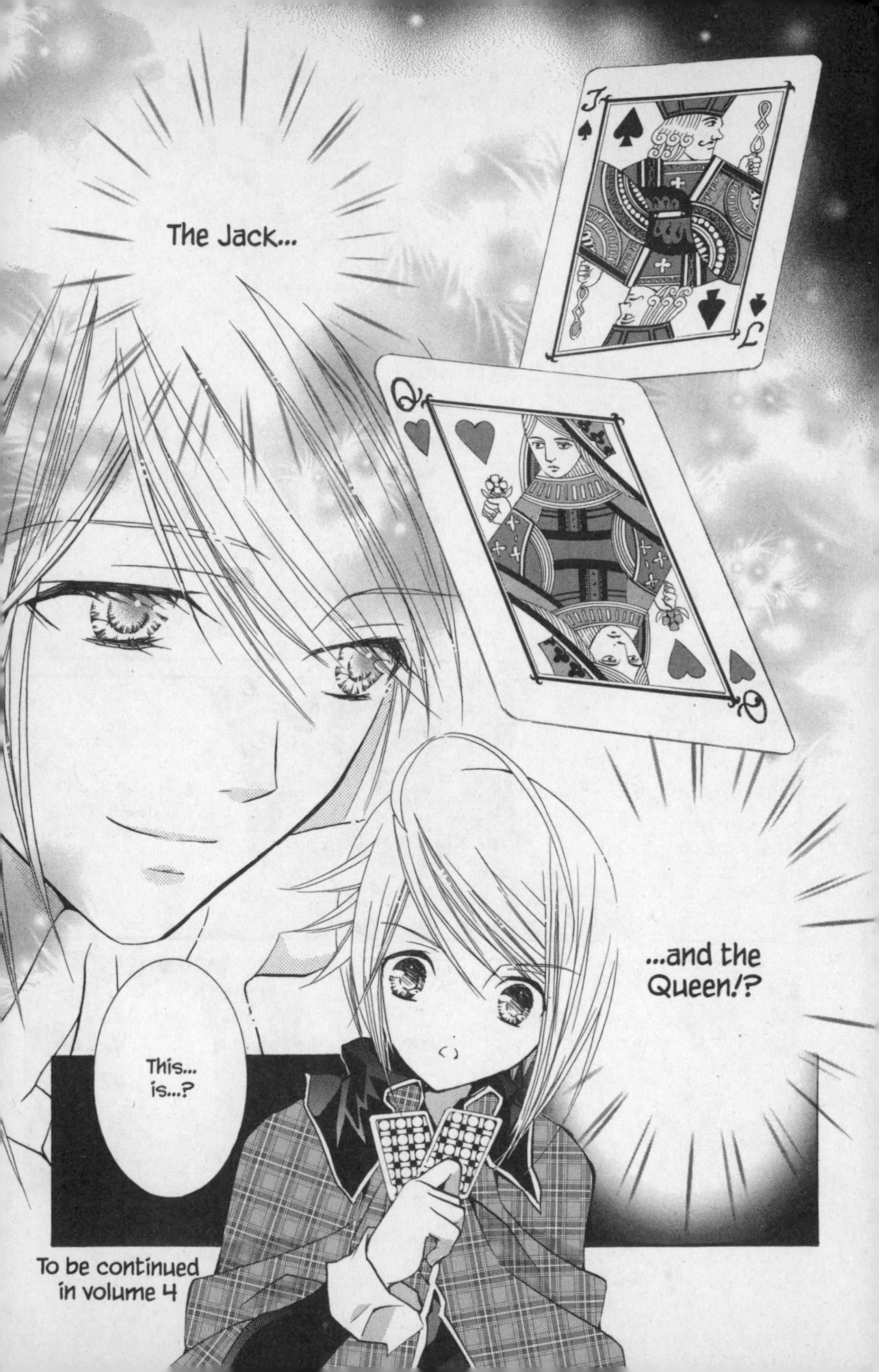
The Jack...
...and the Queen!?
This... is...?
To be continued in volume 4

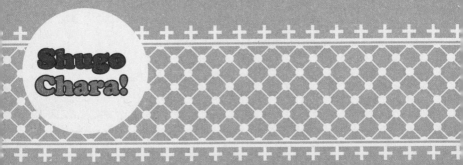

Shugo
Chara!

| Lovely Su | Charismatic Miki |

Lovely Su

You can leave all the girly stuff to me.

Su is always a lovely character.

Charismatic Miki

An artist with fabulous taste...

If I do say so myself.

Miki is always cool as a cucumber.

VROOM

You're in the way.

I love to cook and clean.

Whoa.

SHAKE

Go under the desk!!

Ah, it's an earthquake!

KICK

Take that!

This Egg is taking up space and in the way.

That's my bed!

← Frozen and can't move

↓ Safe haven

Trash Can

VROOM

There's not even dust left in Su's wake.

You were the most freaked out.

Grab the passport and wallet!

TURN

See?

Cool as a cucumber.

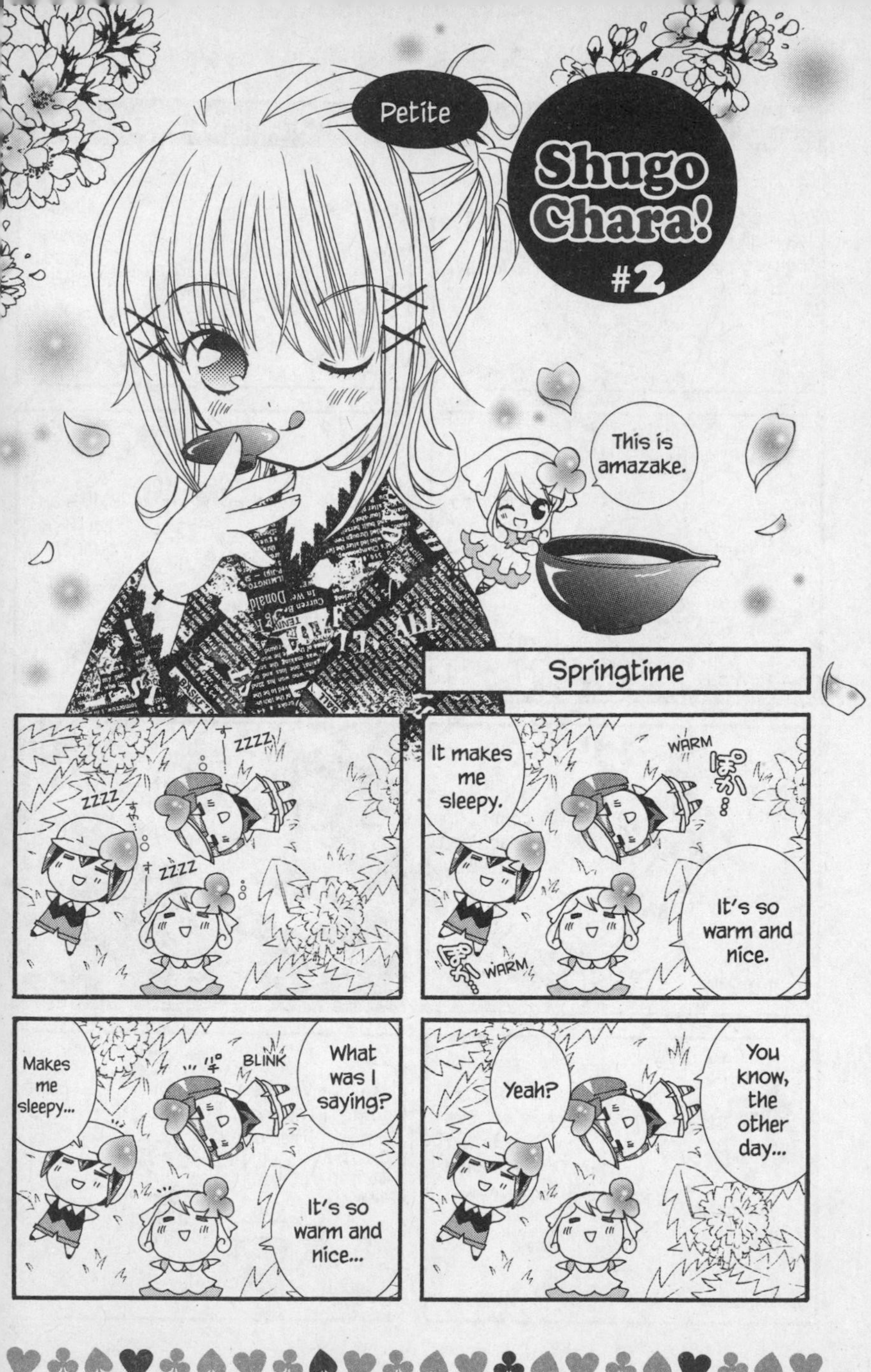

Petite
Shugo Chara!
#2
This is amazake.
Springtime
WARM ぽか…
It makes me sleepy.
It's so warm and nice.
ぽか… WARM
You know, the other day...
Yeah?
BLINK
What was I saying?
Makes me sleepy...
It's so warm and nice...
ZZZZ
ZZZZ
ZZZZ

Spring is About...?

Looking at flowers.
GLOOM
Changing classes...
Entering school!
Being in heat.
Can he say that in this manga?
Because we're cats.

A King's Problem

Spring...
It's a season most unsuitable for world domination.
The peasants become lightheaded and...
...their sense of urgency is gone.
Furthermore...
DRIP
Tadase!! I told you not to open the window!!
BLOW
Sorry...
They both have hay fever.

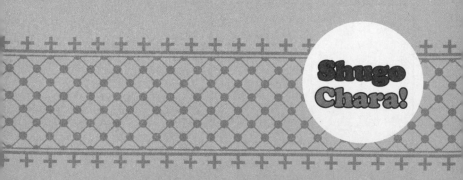

Shugo Chara!

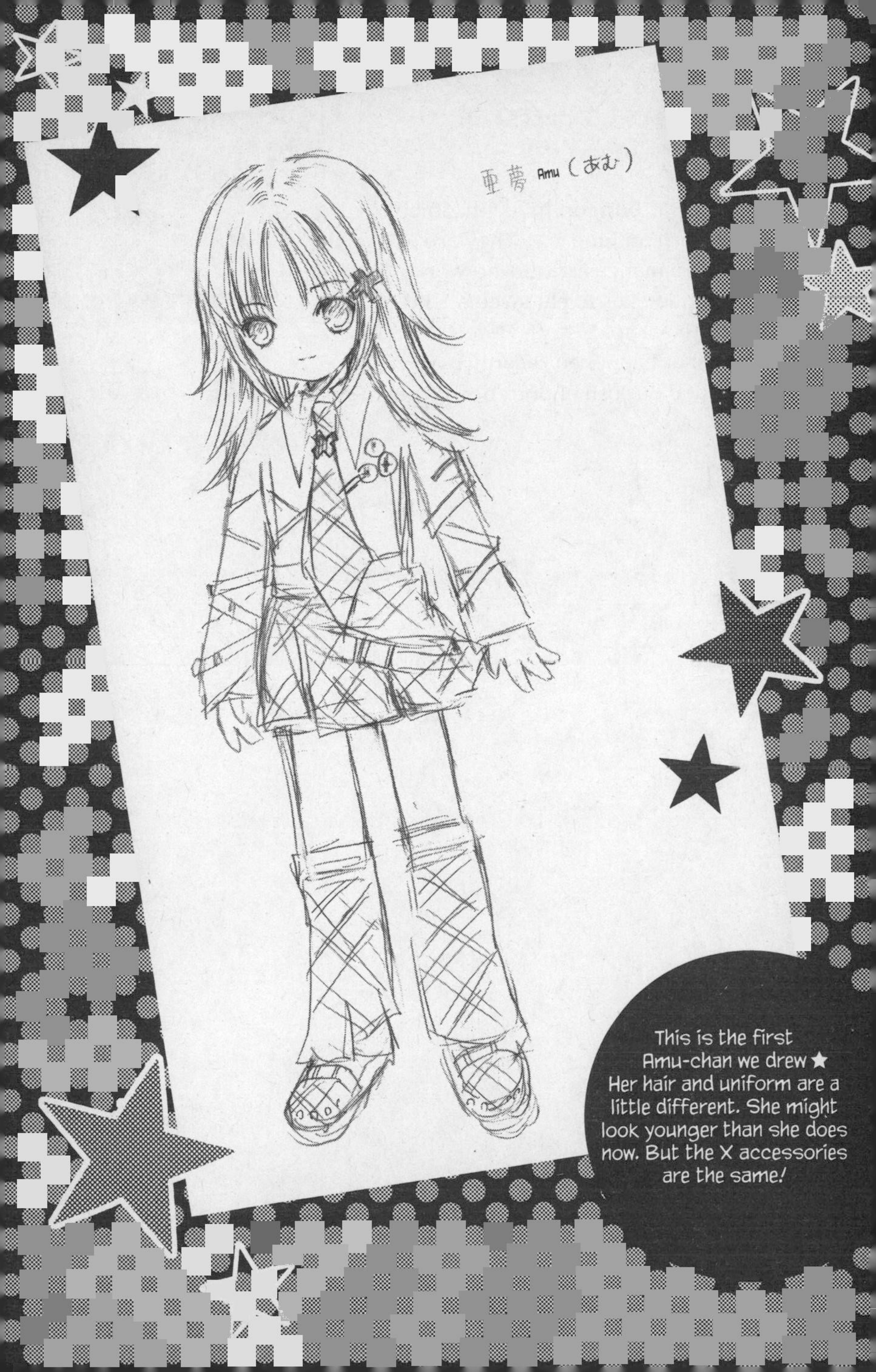
亜夢 Amu (あむ)
This is the first Amu-chan we drew ★ Her hair and uniform are a little different. She might look younger than she does now. But the X accessories are the same!

About the Creators

PEACH-PIT:

Banri Sendo was born on June 7th. Shibuko Ebara was born on June 21st. They are a pair of Gemini manga artists who work together. Sendo likes to eat sweets, and Ebara likes to eat spicy stuff. Here's something that happened recently: We almost flushed our cell phones down the toilet...twice.

Translation Notes

Japanese is a tricky language for most Westerners, and translation is often more art than science. For your edification and reading pleasure, here are notes on some of the places where we could have gone in a different direction in our translation of the work, or where a Japanese cultural reference is used.

Heh heh. You're too late, Himamori-san.

Hima, page 6

This is a pun. *Hima* means "having spare time." *Hima* sounds like "Hina," and Yuu replaces it when he calls Amu by her last name. He started doing this in a previous volume and will continue to call her "Himamori-san" to belittle her. On page 66, he finally calls her by her real name.

Okinawa, page 7

Okinawa is located in the southernmost part of Japan and consists of hundreds of small islands.

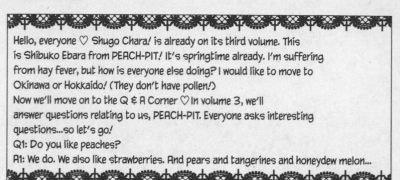

Hello, everyone ♡ Shugo Chara! is already on its third volume. This is Shibuko Ebara from PEACH-PIT! It's springtime already. I'm suffering from hay fever, but how is everyone else doing? I would like to move to Okinawa or Hokkaido! (They don't have pollen!)
Now we'll move on to the Q & A Corner ♡ In volume 3, we'll answer questions relating to us, PEACH-PIT. Everyone asks interesting questions...so let's go!
Q1: Do you like peaches?
A1: We do. We also like strawberries. And pears and tangerines and honeydew melon...

Hokkaido, page 7

Hokkaido is located in the northern part of Japan. It is the second largest island and the biggest prefecture.

TEMARI

Guardian Character of:
Nadeshiko
Special Skill: Naginata
Hates: Mud

Naginata, page 15

A *naginata* is a long-handled sword. It looks like a spear with a short sword at the tip of it. In modern Japan, it is used in women's martial arts.